D1721868

Borg, Daedelow, Johnson (ed.)

From the Basics to the Service

5th RESA Workshop

Borg, Daedelow, Johnson (ed.)

From the Basics to the Service
5th RESA Workshop

DLR e.V.
Kalkhorstweg 53
17235 Neustrelitz

ISBN 978-3-95545-002-1

Bibliographic information of the German National Library

The German National Library registers this publication in the German Nationalbibliography; detailed bibliographic data are available on the Internet at http://dnb.d-nb.de.

ALL RIGHTS RESERVED.
This book contains material protected under International and Federal Copyright Laws and Treaties. Any unauthorized reprint or use of this material is prohibited. No part of this book may be reproduced or transmitted in any form or by any means, electronic or mechanical, including photocopying, recording, or by any information storage and retrieval system without express written permission from the publisher.

Cover picture: with kind permission of the company RapidEye AG
Typesetting and layout: GITO Verlag

Published at GITO Verlag 2013
Printed and bounded in Germany, Berlin 2013

© **GITO mbH Verlag Berlin 2013**

GITO mbH
Verlag für Industrielle Informationstechnik und Organisation
Detmolder Straße 62
10715 Berlin
Tel.: +49.(0)30.41 93 83 64
Fax: +49.(0)30.41 93 83 67
E-Mail: service@gito.de
Internet: www.gito.de

Organiser

DLR e.V.
Kalkhorstweg 53
17235 Neustrelitz

5th RESA Workshop
From the Basics to the Service

Proceedings of the 5th RESA Workshop
resaweb.dlr.de

Neustrelitz, 20. - 21. March 2013
DLR e.V. Neustrelitz

Foreword by the Editors

On March 20-21, 2013 the 5th annual RapidEye Science Archive (RESA) workshop was held in Neustrelitz, Germany. The main topics of the workshop revolved around the identification and development of applications utilizing RapidEye data.

The workshop was organized by the National Ground Segment of the German Remote Data Center (DFD), an institute of the German Aerospace Center (DLR), and was themed "Data for Science: From the Basics to the Service".

The RESA project was created to provide data to the German scientific community in cooperation with the Federal Ministry of Economics and Technology (BMWi), DLR Space Management and RapidEye.

The variety and scope of the technical papers presented during the workshop demonstrate a great scientific interest in RapidEye's data and provided an overview of the methodology used to evaluate the data as well as the value adding possibilities.

Contributions were delivered to the following topics:

- Forest and Agriculture,
- Habitat and Landscape Monitoring,
- Urban Monitoring,
- Hydrology,
- Methods.

This year's paper submissions and proceedings were entirely in English in order to reach a broader audience, which in turn also enhanced the development and structure of the conference proceedings due to a larger number of presenters.

Papers which were accepted by a committee of reviewers are identified as a "Full Reviewed Paper" in the proceedings. Selected short articles are listed as an "Extended Abstract". In addition, we have selected a few additional papers for publication that we found interesting from the numerous entries, and have included them in the section "Non-Refereed Contributions".

The RESA team would like to thank all of the experts who have contributed over the years to the evaluation of the proposals that have been submitted. The success of the project would not possible without their selfless commitment.

We would like to thank all of the RESA workshop participants, especially the authors that submitted their publications. Without you, this edition of the conference proceedings would be insignificant.

In addition, we would like to thank all of the scientists at the Earth Observation Centre of the DLR and the University Würzburg, who have generously taken on the responsibility of assessing submitted contributions. These experts have contributed significantly to the quality of these conference proceedings.

Upon termination of the RESA project in 07/2012 the further funding was supplied by the German Remote Data Center (Institute Director Prof. Dr. Stefan Dech). Since 01/2013 the Director of the DLR Space Research and Technology (Member of the DLR Executive Board Prof. Dr. Hansjörg Dittus) finance the project for a further year. We thank both directors for their generously commitment.

Last but not least, we thank Mrs. Ilka Boldt, who has contributed greatly to the technical implementation of this meeting and Ms. Petra Seiffert from RapidEye, who is responsible for RESA's customer support.

Neustrelitz, Germany March 2013

Erik Borg

Holger Daedelow

Ryan Johnson

Content

Preface (RESA Project)

Full Reviewed Paper

Full Non-Reviewed Paper

Extended Abstracts

RapidEye Science Archive: Remote Sensing Data for the German Scientific Community

Erik Borg[1], Holger Daedelow[1], Marcus Apel[2], Klaus-Dieter Missling[1]

[1] German Aerospace Center (DLR), Earth Observation Center (EOC),
German Remote Sensing Data Center (DFD), Neustrelitz
[2] RapidEye AG, Berlin

E-Mail: erik.borg@dlr.de

RapidEye Science Archive: Remote Sensing Data for the German Scientific Community[1]

Erik Borg, Holger Daedelow, Marcus Apel, Klaus-Dieter Missling

Abstract

The RapidEye Science Archives RESA-project funded by the Bundesministerium für Wirtschaft und Technologie (BMWi - Federal Ministry of Economics and Technology) and provided by the RapidEye and the German Aerospace Center (DLR), Earth Observation Center (EOC) is an essential contribution to a broad scientific environmental applications of RapidEye data and to develop applications, value added products as well as services based on these RapidEye-data. The national project RESA accompanies the GMES initiative (Global monitoring for environment and Security) of the European Union (EU) and the European space agency (ESA) with that.

The uncomplicated and generous appropriation of RapidEye-data by the RESA project innovative services based on satellite and airborne remote sensing can be implemented and combined with terrestrial, maritime and additional data sources. This concerns the cognitive process in operational remote sensing data processing as well as the data providers as e.g. RapidEye.

1. Introduction

Within the last few years the situation of satellite and airborne supported remote sensing has changed fundamentally. The reasons can be explained among others by the following aspects:

- technical and technological developments and factors, such as the increase of the number of earth observation missions (e.g. multiple satellite missions on different or on one orbit), new advanced sensor technologies (e.g. SAR- and hyperspectral sensors of high spatial resolution), new storage media and storage technologies, and new improved data processing (e.g. automated interpretation algorithms and processing chains),

---

[1] This is an updated and translated into English version of the introduction contribution of 4th conference volume "Rapid Eye Science Archive (RESA) – Vom Algorithmus zum Produkt".

- market-oriented aspects
  (e.g. private remote sensing missions, such as QuickBird or RapidEye).

In addition to this the development was politically forced by European Union (EU) and European Space Agency (ESA) having established the program "Global monitoring for environment and Security" (COPERNICUS; erstwhile called GMES), which serves the development of an operative European Earth observation satellite fleet to combine earth observation monitoring with airborne remote sensing supported by terrestrial, maritime in-situ-measuring networks and additional data sources in operative process chains as well as services.

Besides the continuous provisioning of user friendly and reliable earth observation services e.g. to climate protection, for ecological survey, humanitarian assistance or for the reply to security-relevant questions the GMES initiative is aimed at the establishment of a European market for innovative remote sensing based services.

2. The RapidEye-System

The RapidEye system consisting of 5 satellites was launched on August 29th, 2008. The system has switched in the operative phase and provides remote sensing data since February 1st, 2009.

RapidEye is now a leading provider of quality high-resolution satellite imagery. With a constellation of five Earth Observation satellites, RapidEye images up to five million square kilometers of earth every day, and adds over one billion square kilometers of imagery to its archive every year. Every square kilometer imaged by RapidEye can be browsed with its online discovery tool, EyeFind (eyefind.rapideye.com). With an unprecedented combination of wide area repetitive coverage and five meter pixel size multi-spectral imagery, RapidEye is a natural choice for many industries and governments. RapidEye is headquartered in Berlin, Germany and has additional offices in the US and Canada.

The benefits are:

- Regions, states and entire countries can be imaged in a short amount of time
- Cost effective high-resolution data

- Effective for land cover / land use classification applications, change detection, background imagery, mapping, biophysical monitoring, etc.

- Seventy percent (70%) of RapidEye's imagery is taken at 10° off nadir or less

- Over sixty percent (60%) of RapidEye's archive has 10% cloud cover or less

- RapidEye's Red Edge band assists in advanced vegetation discrimination and identification of vegetation health status

- EyeFind is RapidEye's online discovery tool, allowing easy access of the entire RapidEye archive: eyefind.rapideye.com

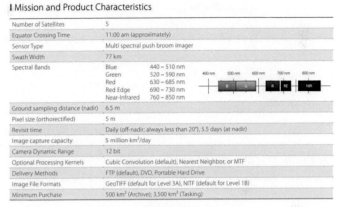

I Mission and Product Characteristics

Number of Satellites	5
Equator Crossing Time	11:00 am (approximately)
Sensor Type	Multi spectral push broom imager
Swath Width	77 km
Spectral Bands	Blue 440 – 510 nm Green 520 – 590 nm Red 630 – 685 nm Red Edge 690 – 730 nm Near-Infrared 760 – 850 nm
Ground sampling distance (nadir)	6.5 m
Pixel size (orthorectified)	5 m
Revisit time	Daily (off-nadir; always less than 20°), 5.5 days (at nadir)
Image capture capacity	5 million km²/day
Camera Dynamic Range	12 bit
Optional Processing Kernels	Cubic Convolution (default), Nearest Neighbor, or MTF
Delivery Methods	FTP (default), DVD, Portable Hard Drive
Image File Formats	GeoTIFF (default for Level 3A), NITF (default for Level 1B)
Minimum Purchase	500 km² (Archive); 3,500 km² (Tasking)

Tab.1:   Mission and Product Characteristics
(http://www.rapideye.com/about/resources.htm)

Depending on the task at hand, two different levels of RapidEye imagery are commercially available:

LEVEL	DESCRIPTION
1B	**RapidEye 1B Basic Product** is radiometric and sensor corrected; and is the least processed of the RapidEye image products. This product is designed for customers who wish to do their own geometric correction and is accompanied by all the needed information for processing the data into a geocorrected form.
3A	**RapidEye 3A Ortho Product** offers the highest level of processing available. Radiometric, sensor and geometric corrections have been applied to the data. The product accuracy depends on the quality of the ground control and DEMs used.

Tab.2:   RapidEye Standard Imagery Processing Level
(http://www.rapideye.com/about/resources.htm)

Additionally, multiple RapidEye satellite images are used to cover a country or region with very minimal cloud cover to generate RapidEye Mosaics™. These images are geometrically aligned and orthorectified to insure that they are precisely located. They are uniformly colour-balanced to ensure a high-quality natural colour image that is produced using the native Red, Green and Blue bands of the RapidEye satellites. The RapidEye Mosaics™ are conveniently formatted into a ready-to-use product, in standard file formats that are Open & GoGIS ready, requiring no further processing.

❙ Off-The-Shelf Mosaic Product Characteristics

Product Components and Format	RapidEye Mosaic product consists of the following file components:
	» Image File: GeoTIFF file that contains image data and geolocation information
	» Metadata File: XML format metadata file
	» Browse Image File: GeoTIFF format
	» Spatial Image Map (SIM) fileset – ESRI shapefile (SHP) format
Image Bands	Natural Color – Red, Green, Blue (RGB)
Image Bit Depth	8-bit
Resolution	5m
Cloud Cover	3% or less
Product Tile Size	Standard tile size is 30 min x 30 min (approx. 55km x 55km at the Equator) < 0.5GB per tile
Horizontal Datum	WGS84
Vertical Projection	UTM

*Tab.3:   Off-The-Shelf Mosaic Product Characteristics
(http://www.rapideye.com/about/resources.htm)*

Features are:

- True natural colour in Red, Green, Blue (RGB) derived from RapidEye's 5 meter resolution satellite imagery,

- Cloud-free imagery whenever possible (always less than 3%),

- The most current high-resolution mosaics available, with narrow acquisition windows,

- Off-the-shelf or custom-made options.

3. The RESA-Project

3.1 Scientific-Data-Pools for Remote Sensing Data

The DLR operates different Scientific Data Pools to guarantee the scientific community a simplified and cost-effective or cost-free access to remote sensing data. Examples of it are the LANDSAT 7/ETM+Scientific Data Pool, the TerraSAR-X Scientific Data Pool (http://sss.terrasar-x.dlr.de/), and the RapidEye Science archive (http://resaweb.dlr.de).

Thus, the recognition is supported that a broader scientific application of remote sensing data benefits not only the community as well as the data provider.

Benefits are (Lievesley, 2009):

- Gain in cognition,

- Promoting of a broader application of remote sensing data,

- Contributions to informed political decisions,

- Support of multiple application and use of data,

- Facilitate of comparative research,

- Increase of the expert user community,

- Feedback on data and data quality,

- Improvement of teaching and ensuring the relevance of official statistics, and

- Feedback to the commercial sector (market enlargement, Saarikivi, 2009).

3.2 Objectives of RESA-Project

Ecological policy needs reliable information about state and development of the environment to be able to recognize undesirable developments on time and react to it after priorities graded adequately (von Gadow, 1995). Therefore, an appropriation of current and full-coverage geo-information becomes required urgently to support decision-making processes in politics, public, and economy.

Against this background, both the European Union (EU) and the European Space Agency (ESA) expect an increasingly national effort for the realization of these objectives.

The national efforts correspondingly are various to comply cost-effectively and innovatively the duties of information to the EU. With respect to this, the RESA project accomplishes essential services in the field of strengthening of the national interests of geo-information industry.

For German science these are the following aspects:

1. preparation and ready provision of the technological infrastructure for the long-term data storage,

2. long-term archiving, distribution, and provision of the RapidEye data,

3. coordination and optimization of the use of the limited data contingent,

4. assessment of project propositions as well as the coordination of data requirements,

5. appropriation of user information by internet portal and annual workshops,

6. monitoring of limitations agreed by contract to exclusively scientific use and compliance to the data use guidelines of the RESA project.

The operative and cost-effective provision of corresponding remote sensing data is the professed business model of the RapidEye. Therefore German Aerospace Center (DLR) and RapidEye have agreed to provide cost free to the German science a data contingent of 29.4 million square kilometer for a time period of seven years. The distribution of the data contingent is operated by the RESA.

During the initial phase of the RESA project, strategic interface projects of national importance to the GMES initiative were in the focus of interest (e.g. DeCOVER-land applications, DeSECURE civil protection, DeMARINE - Ocean applications). During the project, the focus of the project have shifted towards a broad availability of data for users from diverse geo-science topics, to drive the development of RapidEye data processing from the first experience over the first products to first services.

In order to support this process, increasingly educational aspects of the users of RapidEye data were considered by the RESA team. In cooperation with the RapidEye scientific works such as e.g. bachelor's degree, diploma, master's theses, and theses were uncomplicatedly supplied with data.

For this, the initially met restrictions of the contract with the RapidEye were examined. In addition the initially encountered restrictions of contract with the RapidEye concerning the ordered data contingent were reviewed to change the limitations for the benefit of the users, if possible.

3.3 Order System and Order Method of the RESA-Project

The RESA project is supported by the components 1) Science service system, 2) Data information and management system and 3) RapidEye payload ground segment. The science service system offers scientists the opportunity to submit project proposals for the evaluation by independent auditors (see Chapter 3.4).

In the case of a positive evaluation, the service request of the project will transferred by the RESA team to the company RapidEye as an order.

Here archive orders are immediately processed and shipped. Tasking orders (orders for data recording in the future) be merged into the company RapidEye mission planning system. The distribution is controlled by a data server of the RapidEye.

From here, the data are cyclically transmitted and processed through the RESA-ingestion processing system. Then the data is archived in the product library and uploaded into DLR's user interface "Earth Observation on the WEB" (EOWEB). Here, the user has the possibility to search for data of the RESA project and to order these free of charge.

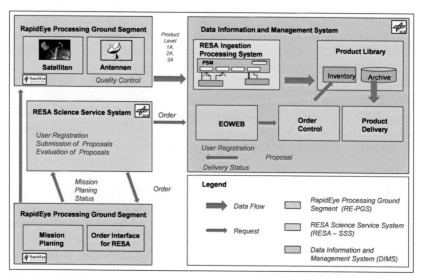

Fig. 1:   Schematic pictogram of the structure the RESA project

3.4 Data Output and Project Submission

Scientists have the ability to prepare proposals on the RESA-portal (resaweb.dlr.de). If the application is fully registered and has the status "submitted", by science service team an assignment is made to an expert.

The status is set to "handed over". These proposals are then examined by experts and evaluated. The expertise passes through different status (see Fig. 2). If the project is being viewed positively by the expert ("evaluated"), a final control is made by the science-service team and the status of the paper is set to "approved".

In this case, the data order is verified and transmitted to the company RapidEye.

However, if the expert formulates requirements and / or suggestions to improve the project proposal, the status of the project proposal is set to "dismissed with modification". Then the proposer has the possibility to improve and consider the suggestions of the expert. Subsequently, a renewed valuation takes place.

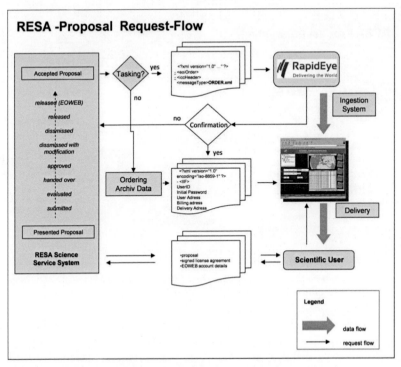

Fig. 2: Schematic pictogram of the request flow of a RESA proposal

If the project proposal be insufficiently substantiated, the proposal is rejected and the status is set "dismissed". In the case of a positive assessment is the request flow of a successful RESA proposal, as described in Chapter 3.2.

3.5 Data Management of the RESA-Project

Essential for the implementation of the RESA project is a reliable and robust infrastructure for data processing. With their help, the accumulating amounts of data from remote sensing missions are received, archived, managed and distributed to users. Accordingly, the data of the RESA project are managed so that the data can be delivered to the scientific community without loss of time and loss of quality. Essential aspects in this context are the long-term archiving of data, as well as providing data for scientific questions about the agreed delivery period.

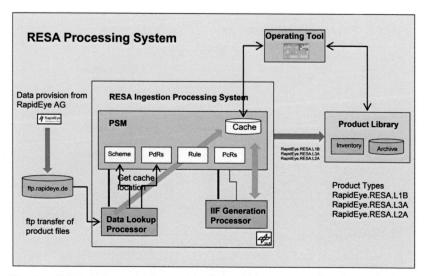

Fig. 3: *Schematic representation of the Data Information and Management System with specific interfaces for the RESA project*

For this task, the German Remote Sensing Data Centre (DFD) operates the Data and Information Management System (DIMS) among other technical infrastructure. A detailed description of the system architecture and the interaction of the components are given by Boettcher et al. (2001) and Kiemle et al. (2005). The system is schematically shown in Fig. 3.

The long-term storage of remote sensing data requires the consideration of:

- aging process of used storage media as well as write and reading devices,

- systems of control mechanisms for early error detection or error correction,

- redundant storage media and write-reader devices to prevent defects and total failures,

- multiple archive copies at different storage locations as well as the systematic and periodic migration of data on different storage technologies and storage media as well as the automatic, systematic error analysis by routine reading.

The long-term archiving of the data is necessary for a data provision to solute scientific questions over the agreed delivery period out of interest.

Long-term archiving of remote sensing data, i.e. the protection of the readability of data over decades, requires more effort than an error free writing to a memory. This includes:

- quality monitoring,
- parallel use of different storage technologies,
- conservation measures, such as refreshing, replication, migration, emulation,
- generation of redundancy information,
- conversion of data formats.

Also backup the interpretation of records will play an important role in the future. At the so-called data curation, records viewed more holistically, and information security, confidentiality, ownership, origin, validity and quality of the data is also stored.

3.6 Data distribution

Since October 2009 the RESA-data are available in the EOWEB. The EOWEB is the data catalogue of the Earth Observation Center (EOC) which allows to visualize the quicklook and metadata of a satellite data set and to deliver stored remote sensing data and / value-added data to interested users. The data from the RapidEye-satellites, the DLR provides by means of the RapidEye Science Archive (RESA).

Scientific institutions and, under certain conditions, geo-informatics firms can apply the RapidEye-data via the furnished website (http://resaweb.dlr.de).

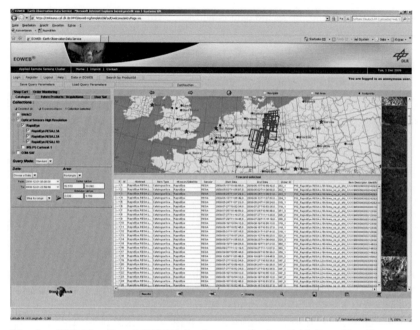

Fig. 4:   DLR-User Portal EOWEB for the research of available RapidEye-data
in the RapidEye-science archive

Independent experts decide for the allocation of a data contingent. In addition to the scientific value added, applicants must demonstrate the exclusively scientific exploitation of the requested data. The data are available for methods and process development, also for those that are to be applied in future products and services in the private and public sector.

3.7 Data Contingent

The functions for long-term storage of RESA-data such as data input, data and process control, archiving, cataloguing, ordering and delivery of the data after scientific assessment are provided by the data and information management system (DIMS). The presently stored data includes currently 4557 GByte.

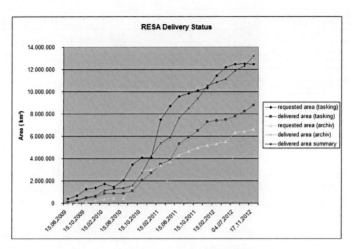

Fig. 5:   Temporal distribution of the data volume of ordered data
           for scientific projects as well as their extradition
           from the direct advance order and from the RapidEye Science archive

The available project data contingent accounts 29.4 million km². This allows
even the submitted project proposals the implementation of scientific objectives
extensive data contingents are provided. Therefore, more than 12,566,792 km²
data in average could be provided to the more than 125 submitted projects. The
geographical distribution of more than 200 test areas can be found in table 2.

The temporal distribution of ordered data volume for scientific projects as well as
their extradition from RapidEye Science Archive, the RapidEye-archive and
direct tasking is represented in figure 5.

The geographical distribution of products (test sites) can be found in the tables
4 and 5.

Number of L1B Products					
	Total	Europe	Africa	Asia	America
2009	276	229	47		
2010	442	263	69	46	64
2011	670	301	79	137	153
2012	236	85	61	90	0

Tab. 4:   Geographical distribution of the test areas, which are supported
           by the RESA project (L1B products)

17

Number of L3A Products					
	Total	Europe	Africa	Asia	America
2009	4008	3761	18	136	93
2010	5385	3505	434	1341	105
2011	6791	5007	101	1566	117
2012	4088	2561	605	896	26

Tab. 5: *Geographical distribution of the test areas, which are supported by the RESA project (L3A-Products)*

The discrepancy between the amount of ordered and supplied data is 1.) in the temporal offset between order and delivery, 2.) the specifics of the RapidEye mission planning system involved in conflicts of interest between different data requests through the same area cannot transpose all jobs, 3.) the duration of the time order, because the shorter the chosen time order is the shorter is the probability of an useful image due to possible cloud cover decreases, and 4.) data are delivered with low cloud cover.

4. Review process

A further component of the RESA project represents the team of renowned scientific experts from various geo-aspects. They guarantee a high scientific standard of the RESA project by these colleagues examining the quality of the submitted project applications in an honorary capacity. After successful evaluation of a scientific proposal the requested data will be delivered. If the requested data already stored in the RapidEye Science Archive (RESA), the applicant access to the data within a few days.

However, if the requested data contingent of an accepted proposal is not stored in the RapidEye Science Archive (RESA), the RESA project generates a data order to RapidEye to provide the desired data contingent.

In this case, the data are searched within the RapidEye archive. These can be found via the Internet platform EyeFind of the RapidEye. If archived data of the RapidEye can be used, the user receives the data generally within a few days until a week. In the case of a tasking order, the data are delivered as soon as the RapidEye satellites were able to record the requested data.

Literature

Boettcher, M.; Reißig, R.; Mikusch, E.; Reck, C. (2001).
Processing Management Tools for Earth Observation Products at
DLR-DFD. In: DASIA 2001 Data Systems in Aerospace, SP-483,
European Space Agency. Data Systems in Aerospace, Nice, 2001.
ISBN 92-9092-773-9.

Borg, E.; Daedelow, H.; Missling, K. D.; Apel, M. (2012).
Das RESA-Projekt: Bereitstellung von RapidEye-Daten für die
Deutsche Wissenschaft.- In: RapidEye Science Archive (RESA) -
Vom Algorithmus zum Produkt.- Hrsg.: Borg, E., Daedelow, H.,
Johnson, R., 4. RESA Workshop, Neustrelitz, 21.-22.03.2012 .-
GITO mbH Verlag, Berlin, ISBN 978-3-942183-61-1.- S. 3-16.

Daedelow, H. (2009).
Prozedur der Datenbereitstellung, 1. RESA-Workshop "RapidEye
Science Archive (RESA)-Daten für die Wissenschaft" am 18.03.2009 -
S. 8. http://resaweb.dlr.de/fileadmin/resa/documents/
20090318_NZ_RESA-Workshop_Daedelow.pdf

Gadow von, A. (1995).
Satellitenfernerkundung für die Umweltpolitik.-
In: Umwelt und Fernerkundung: Was leisten integrierte GEO-Daten für
die Entwicklung und Umsetzung von Umweltstrategien, BACKHAUS, R.;
GRUNWALD, A. (Hrsg.).- Heidelberg, Wichmann-Verlag.- S. 13-25.

Kiemle, S.; Bilinski, C.; Buckl, B.; Dietrich, D.; Kröger, S.; Mikusch, E.;
Reck, C.; Schmid, F.; Schroeder-Lanz, A.-K.; Wolfmüller M. (2005).
Data information and management system for the DFD multi-mission
earth observation data, in Proc. Conf. Ensuring Long-Term Preserv.
Adding Value Sci.Tech. Data PV, Edinburgh, U.K., 2005,
pp. 21.1–23.11.
http://www.ukoln.ac.uk/events/pv-2005/pv-2005-final-papers/019.pdf

Lievesley, D. (2009).
Keynote speech - Information is Power: Overcoming Obstacles
to Data Sharing, Third INSPIRE Conference Rotterdam,
the Netherlands, 15-19 June 2009.

Saarikivi, P. (2009).

Keynote speech-ROADIDEA: Ingredients for Innovative Transport Services, Third INSPIRE Conference Rotterdam, the Netherlands, 15-19 June 2009.

Weichelt, H. (2010).

RESA RapidEye Science Archive Data and Request Workflow - The RapidEye System Status and Overview - 2. RESA-Workshop "RapidEye Science Archive (RESA) - Erste Erfahrungen" am 25.03.2010 - S. 41.
http://resaweb.dlr.de/fileadmin/resa/documents/ws_2010/RESA_ HANNAH HILTONworkshop_neustrelitz_250310_weichelt.pdf.

Forest tree species identification using phenological stages and RapidEye data: a case study in the forest of Freising (Project ID: 317)

Alata Elatawneh[1], Adelheid Rappl[2], Nataliia Rehush[3],
Thomas Schneider[1], Thomas Knoke[1]

[1] Institut of Forest Management, Technische Universität München (TUM)
[2] Bayerische Landesanstalt für Wald und Forstwirtschaft (LWF)
[3] Ukrainian National Forestry University (UNFU)

E-Mail: alataaa@tum.de

Forest tree species identification using phenological stages and RapidEye data: a case study in the forest of Freising

Alata Elatawneh, Adelheid Rappl, Nataliia Rehush,
Thomas Schneider, Thomas Knoke

Tree species identification is a very important part of forest management and planning. In the last three decades, many studies have investigated methods of species identification using multispectral, multiseasonal and multitemporal data. In this study we analyzed multiseasonal and multitemporal RapidEye images from twenty dates for the purpose of tree species classification. The main objective of this work was to investigate the effect of the number of datasets analyzed on the accuracy of the results. Two additional aims were pursued: first, we investigated the influence of the RedEdge band on classification accuracy. Second, we investigated the influence of the Normalized Differenced Vegetation Index (NDVI) and angle indices specifically developed for this study. The Spectral Angle Mapper (SAM) classifier and cross-validation procedures were used for this purpose. The best overall accuracy achieved when separating seven tree species (three deciduous and four coniferous) was about 86%. Increasing the number of analyzed scenes clearly improved the accuracy. Using the RedEdge bands improved the overall accuracy by 1% to 4%, while using the indices additionally enhanced the overall accuracy by 2% to 4%. Interestingly, satisfactory accuracy of about 84% was achieved by using only seven of the 20 scenes we acquired and tested.

1. Introduction

Forest management which takes into consideration both economic and sustainability aspects requires constant inventory of forest conditions (Stoffels et al. 2012). Management planning and statistics assortment at the enterprise level, as well as fulfillment of reporting duties at the national and international levels should be based on these inventories. Every ten years there is an update of the national forest inventory in Germany, as well as for the Bavarian state-owned forests. Typically, a regular sampling grid is established and used in data collection for the creation of inventory databases containing various forest stand data, such as detailed species composition, age information, timber volume and other management-relevant features. However, such terrestrial inventories are cost-intensive and time-consuming.

In recent decades, multispectral remotely sensed data have emerged as an attractive resource to complement and optimize forest inventories (Holmgren/ Thuresson 1998, Vohland et al. 2007). Remote sensing-based inventory has focused on 1) forest (timber) type discrimination and 2) estimation of biophysical and biochemical properties (Boyd/Danson 2005, Holmgren/Thuresson 1998). It is of great value to use such parameters as inputs for forest prognosis models, which offer an alternative solution to terrestrial inventories for forest management planning for the next 10 to 20 year period. Especially single-tree competition approaches like SILVA, which is used for management of the Bavarian State Forests (Pretzsch et al. 2002), take advantage of tree species information.

Still, tree species identification is a challenging task for the remote sensing community. Under mid-European conditions, tree species discrimination on the basis of high resolution (5m -30m) multi- to hyperspectral data has failed using mono-temporal approaches. However, the effectiveness of these classifications for species identification can be enhanced using multiseasonal and multitemporal data. By multiseasonal data, we refer to multiple datasets from the same year but from different growing seasons (phenological stages), while multitemporal data refers to datasets from different years but from similar growing seasons. The classification of multiseasonal data sets allows the detection of seasonal changes in the spectral responses of different forest tree species types which result from phenological activity (Boyd/Danson 2005).

Since the early 1980s, many studies have utilized multitemporal and multiseasonal multispectral data in order to enhance tree species classification results. Data obtained from sensors such as Landsat (Dorren et al. 2003; Franco-Lopez et al. 2001; Mickelson et al. 1998; Reese et al. 2002; Schriever/Congalton 1995; Townsend/Walsh 2001; Walsh 1980; Wolter 1995) SPOT (Davranche et al. 2010) and ASTER (Stoffels et al. 2012) has all been used for this purpose. However, previous studies using high spatial resolution data (5 m - 30 m) have generally not focused on the effect of the temporal resolution on the classification accuracy, due perhaps to the limited number of scenes available. The data from the upcoming RapidEye satellite constellation which has very high temporal resolution, is potentially ideal for the testing and use of phenological monitoring (Stoffels et al. 2012).

In this study, our main objective is to evaluate the effect of an increase in the number of scenes analyzed on the tree species classification accuracy using the

RapidEye time series data. In addition, this paper has two specific subgoals: first, the evaluation of the Red Edge band influence on the result accuracy, and second, the evaluation of the influence of several derived indices on this accuracy.

2. Study Area and Materials

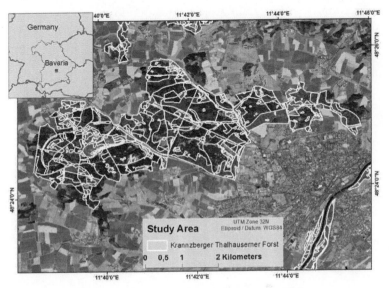

Figure 1: Freising forest study area in Bavaria, Germany.

2.1 Study Area

The study area, Kranzberger and Thalhausener Forests, in Freising (2178.9 ha), is located in the southern part of Bavaria near the city of Freising (Figure 1). It lies within the growth zone of the Bavarian Tertiary Hills, which has high growth potential for several different tree species. The annual mean temperature is 7.5°C, and the annual mean precipitation rate is 800 mm, with its maximum in summer time. The Bavarian State Forestry agency is responsible for forest management in the study area. Spruce is the dominant tree species, covering 60% of the area, with the remaining 40% made up of a mix other species (Table 1). The forest is managed with two different strategies. The first is an old strategy that maintains pure even-age stands. The second strategy maintains mixed stands with different age classes, managed with the aim of increasing the stability of the forest.

2.2 Data set

Field observation

The field observation data used in this study to train and validate the tree species classification were collected in the field during the years 2010 and 2011. The tree species positions were recorded using hand-held GPS units, or located using digital aerial images (20 cm spatial resolution) from the year 2009. However, many observations were not representative and therefore were not taken into consideration. This is due to the invisibility of the tree crowns which don't reach the overstory – a problem that has also been reported in previous studies (Key et al. 2001; Waser et al. 2011). In the end, 546 training sample points were considered for this study (Table 1).

Scientific name	Common name	Symbol	# of samples
Picea abies (L.)	Norway Spruce	Fi	212
Pseudotsuga menziesii (M.F.)	Douglas Fir	Do	32
Pinus sylvestris (L.)	Scots Pine	Ki	34
Larix decidua (MILL.) Larix kaempferi	European Larch Japanese Larch	La	41
Fagus sylvatica	Beech	Bu	153
Quercus petraea (Mattuschka)	Oak	Ei	38
Acer pseudoplatanus	Maple	Ba	36

Table 1: Tree species samples in the study area.

RapidEye images

A total of 20 RapidEye images of Level 3A were provided by RESA, covering a period of 3 years - from May 2009 to November 2011. The images delivered were at-sensor radiometrically and geometrically corrected. However, the geometric correction was not precise enough for the intended multi-seasonal image analysis. Therefore, enhancement of the geometric correction was carried out.

ID	Date time and sensor	ID	Date time and sensor
1	2009-05-20T110408_RE4	11	2011-06-04T110442_RE1
2	2009-07-27T105426_RE1	12	2011-06-28T110849_RE1
3	2010-04-22T105818_RE3	13	2011-07-10T111720_RE3
4	2010-06-08T110621_RE2	14	2011-07-16T110430_RE5
5	2010-07-21T110853_RE2	15	2011-08-23T112009_RE4
6	2010-08-15T111131_RE3	16	2011-09-03T111442_RE1
7	2010-10-10T110933_RE2	17	2011-09-25T111227_RE4
8	2011-03-22T110819_RE3	18	2011-10-06T110644_RE1
9	2011-04-07T110454_RE5	19	2011-10-22T112135_RE2
10	2011-05-06T111258_RE5	20	2011-11-04T111457_RE1

Table 2:   The RapidEye images used in this study.

3. Methods

3.1 Data preprocessing

For many of the RapidEye images, the geometric correction was improved by performing shifts in both directions (easting and northing) if necessary. This was an essential step for the multitemporal image analysis. Then, atmospheric correction was carried out for all images, using ATCOR 3, implemented in the PCI Geomatica 10.3 environment. This process requires a digital elevation model (DEM) in order to consider the topographical effects on the spectral reflectance during the correction process and thus, eliminate errors due to the topography. For this purpose, a DEM of 5 meter spatial resolution was ordered from the Bavarian State Office for Survey and Geoinformation (LVG).

3.2 Image analysis

Typically, the assumption is that individuals of the same tree species have similar reflectances at the same phenological stage. However, it is often the case that the illumination among individuals of the same tree species is different, due to shadow effects from the surroundings and topographical effects (even after the topographic correction). The Spectral Angle Mapper (SAM) (Kruse et al. 1993) was chosen to perform the classification because it is highly insensitive to illumination effects, as it uses only the direction of the vector, and not its length (Eckert/Kneubühler 2004, Elatawneh et al. 2012a). Additionally, to further minimize these effects; when choosing our training samples we followed procedures used by Korpela et al. (2011), to interpret Leica ADS40 very high resolution (VHR) data, and by Immitzer et al. (2012), to analyze WorldView-2 data. These authors selected solely sunlit crown areas for picking the spectra of tree species to be used as training samples for classification. In our case, only the brightest pixels belonged to collective homogeneous training areas, and thus belonged to a pure group of tree species were selected as samples.

From our observations of the reflectance of individual tree species, we noticed that the reflectance is often similar in many bands, but not in all of them. Therefore, angle indices (Figure 2) could be expected to emphasize the differences among tree species, as they represent the reflectance ratios between individual bands. Similarly, Khanna et.al. (2007) reported that the wavelength relationship between multispectral bands may have similar importance as the reflectance value of individual bands.

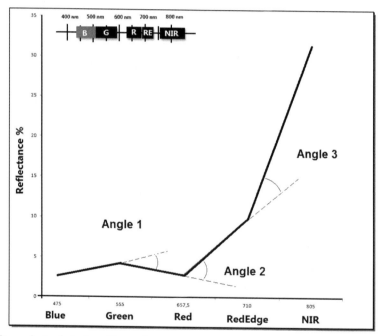

Figure 2: Angle indices illustration.

As these indices exploit the difference in the slopes of the vectors, they are expected to be less affected by illumination variations, and thus able to improve the classification accuracy. They are calculated as explained in the following equations:

$$\text{Angle } 1 = 2\,\frac{(\rho\,Red - \rho\,Green)}{\lambda\,Red - \lambda\,Green} - \frac{(\rho\,Green - \rho\,Blue)}{\lambda\,Green - \lambda\,Blue} \quad\ldots\ldots\ldots\ldots equation\ 1$$

$$\text{Angle } 2 = \frac{(\rho\,RedEdge - \rho\,Red)}{\lambda\,RedEdge - \lambda\,Red} - 2\,\frac{(\rho\,Red - \rho\,Green)}{\lambda\,Red - \lambda\,Green} \quad\ldots\ldots\ldots\ldots equation\ 2$$

$$\text{Angle } 3 = \frac{(\rho\,NIR - \rho\,RedEdge)}{\lambda\,NIR - \lambda\,RedEdge} - 0.5\,\frac{(\rho\,RedEdge - \rho\,Red)}{\lambda\,RedEdge - \lambda\,Red} \quad\ldots\ldots\ldots equation\ 3$$

Where, ρ = reflectance and λ = band central wavelength. All indices were then enhanced by duplicating their values as seen in the equations. In addition, the NDVI was also calculated and used in the classification.

$$NDVI = \frac{\rho\,NIR - \rho\,Red}{\rho\,NIR + \rho\,Red} \quad\ldots\ldots\ldots\ldots equation\ 4$$

3.3 K -fold cross-validation

The K-fold cross-validation technique (Geisser 1975, Stone 1974) is a strategy that partitions data randomly into a number of K subsets. The technique uses each subset in turn as a training set for a model classification and the remaining data as a validation set. Then, the process is repeated K times, and the K results are either averaged or combined to produce one final result. The advantage of using this strategy is that all datasets are used for both training and validation. For this study a 10-fold cross-validation strategy was used to carry out the classification.

3.4 Image combination selection and classification

To investigate the effect of an increase in the number of images used on the classification accuracy, 20 image combinations were selected. The first step was to evaluate the classification result accuracy for each of 20 images, using only the original bands (without the addition of angle indices or the NDVI). The classification and evaluation were carried out for each dataset using the cross-validation strategy described above and the Spectral Angle Mapper (SAM) classifier.

Once the accuracies derived from individual scenes were evaluated, the twenty image combinations were established as follows: The first classification included only the scene which achieved the best individual accuracy, the second used the two scenes with the best and second best accuracy etc, up to the twentieth combination (table 3). Then, each image combination was classified, and the result was evaluated again using the cross-validation strategy.

To investigate the influence of the RedEdge band on the classification, the same procedure and image combinations were implemented, this time excluding the RedEdge band. Then, the same procedure was implemented once again, this time, however, including the angle indices and NDVI as additional bands to evaluate the influence they might have on the accuracy.

4. Results

The general trends, as seen in Table 3 and Figure 3, illustrate that with the increase of the number of datasets used, the overall accuracy also increased. This was the expected result. However, this trend followed an inverse exponential function (IEF). In other words, the result improved dramatically at the beginning but showed only a slight increase at the end. One important point can be revealed that a satisfactory classification accuracy of about 84%, which was achieved by using only a subset of the images obtained - only seven scenes were sufficient.

The results of the band combination selections show that the scenes from the spring or early phenological stage in April, May and June delivered, in general, better accuracy than the scenes from the autumn. This is explained by the low solar angle during autumn, which results in a decrease in radiometric quality of these images. Kan and Weber (1978) and Shen et.al. (1985) also indicated that Landsat images acquired early in the growing season are better able to separate forest tree species. However, in our analysis, scenes from the summer (for example, the first-, fifth-, and sixth-best images) were among the least affected by the atmospheric attenuation. And thus the quality of those images was the best of all scenes. However, this study was not meant to investigate the effect of the quality of the images on the achieved accuracy. Therefore, this point will not be further discussed in this paper.

Regarding the effect of the RedEdge band on the accuracy, Figure 3 shows clearly that using the RedEdge band slightly improved the accuracy – an average of about 1%. However, it is notable that the RedEdge band did not improve the results when using the combination of the best 2, 3 or 4 image dates, but for combinations of 5 or more images, the increase in accuracy when this band was included was clear.

While the results show that the indices developed for this study improved the accuracy, the effect of the individual indices on the accuracy was not evaluated. On the one hand, the average improvement in the accuracy was about 4% when using combinations of the first, second, third and fourth best images in conjunction with the indices. However, the rate of improvement was slightly decreased - to 2% - when the indices were used in combination with all twenty images. Using different, more or even fewer indices could further improve the accuracy, but for this study only the NDVI and the indices developed for this investigation have been considered.

# of images	ID of the images used (see Table 2)	Overall Accuracy %		
		All bands	4 bands without RE	All bands + Indices
1	14	67.07	63.92	72.81
2	14,3	73.71	73.02	77.25
3	14,3,11	77.61	77.29	80.12
4	14,3,11,9	78.71	78.75	81.44
5	14,3,11,9,13	79.43	78.57	82.40
6	14,3,11,9,13,2	81.26	78.90	83.19
7	14,3,11,9,13,2,8	82.60	82.01	84.03
8	14,3,11,9,13,2,8,1	81.91	81.12	84.19
9	14,3,11,9,13,2,8,1,12	82.38	81.03	84.62
10	14,3,11,9,13,2,8,1,12,4	83.25	81.97	85.14
11	14,3,11,9,13,2,8,1,12,4,11	83.03	82.17	85.10
12	14,3,11,9,13,2,8,1,12,4,11,20	83.92	83.46	85.88
13	14,3,11,9,13,2,8,1,12,4,11,20,19	83.74	82.68	85.94
14	14,3,11,9,13,2,8,1,12,4,11,20,19,10	83.54	82.36	85.55
15	14,3,11,9,13,2,8,1,12,4,11,20,19,10,6	83.60	82.32	85.49
16	14,3,11,9,13,2,8,1,12,4,11,20,19,10,6,7	83.70	82.84	86.06
17	14,3,11,9,13,2,8,1,12,4,11,20,19,10,6,7,17	84.43	83.37	86.35*
18	14,3,11,9,13,2,8,1,12,4,11,20,19,10,6,7,17,15	84.21	83.11	86.20
19	14,3,11,9,13,2,8,1,12,4,11,20,19,10,6,7,17,15,18	84.41*	83.46*	86.30
20	14,3,11,9,13,2,8,1,12,4,11,20,19,10,6,7,17,15,18,16	84.29	83.27	86.32

Table 3: Overall classification accuracy for image combinations from different dates (* highest accuracy)

In analyzing the results of the overall accuracies, we noticed that there was often a decrease in the accuracy with an increase in the amount of data analyzed; this is known as "Hughes Phenomenon" (Hughes 1968). It explains why the use of all twenty images, in addition to the indices, achieved a lower overall accuracy than when using only the combination of seventeen of the scenes.

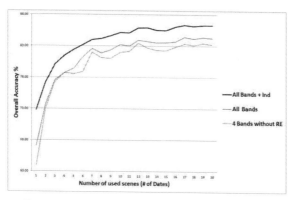

Figure 3: overall accuracy for date combinations (see also Table 3).

The confusion matrix of the best result - achieved from the combination of seventeen images and the indices - is shown in Table 4. The producer accuracy for the individual classes ranges from about 64% to 94%. The highest accuracy - 94.52% - was achieved for the spruce class, whereas most other classes (those for Douglas fir, pine, beech and maple) achieved producer accuracies ranging between 82% and 86%. The two lowest accuracy values were 64% for larch and 74% for oak. The highest amount of confusion with the larch class was between it and the pine and oak classes. This is however, not surprising, as similarity in the reflectance of larch was noted with these two classes in most of the phenological stages.

Class	Reference data								
	Spruce	Douglas	Pine	Larch	Oak	Beech	Maple	Sum	User Acc. %
Spruce	**1899**	9	0	0	0	0	0	1908	99.53
Douglas	46	**229**	0	0	0	19	0	294	77.89
Pine	2	12	**1033**	53	37	18	15	1170	88.29
Larch	3	1	56	**223**	17	37	12	349	63.90
Oak	20	2	55	41	**203**	2	19	342	59.36
Beech	28	9	16	7	3	**450**	0	513	87.72
Maple	11	3	76	22	16	4	**206**	338	60.95
Sum	2009	265	1236	346	276	530	252	**4914**	
Prod. Acc. %	94.52	86.42	83.58	64.45	73.55	84.91	81.75	Overall Acc. %	**86.35**

Table 4: Confusion matrix of the classification using the best 17 dates (all bands + Indices)

Discussion

This study used multiple sets of multiseasonal RapidEye data (twenty datasets from 2009, 2010 and 2011) to classify seven tree species (four coniferous and three deciduous) in a typical mid-European forest area. The main purpose of this analysis was to evaluate the effects of an increase in the number of datasets included in a classification on the accuracy of the classification. The results show that as the number of datasets used increased, the accuracy also increased. However, satisfactory classification accuracy was achieved using less than the full number of images acquired and tested (seven images).

The effect of using the RedEdge band and various derived indices was also evaluated in this work. The results show that using the RedEdge band slightly improved the accuracy by a range of 1% to 4%, while using the indices additionally improved the accuracy from 2% to more than 4% (see table 3). However, it is possible that not all indices have had an equal effect on the improvement of the accuracy. Further research could focus on the effects of the use of individual indices on the classification accuracy.

The best overall accuracy of about 86% (kappa 0.82) was achieved, using a combination of the best 17 images in addition to their indices and including their RedEdge bands. Key et.al. (2001) achieved the highest overall accuracy of 76% (kappa 0.51) using only five of a potential nine aerial photographs. Also Hill et.al. (2010) achieved the highest overall accuracy of 83.8% (kappa 0.79) using only three of a potential five Airborne Thematic Mapper (ATM) images. Though both studies used airborne sensors with much higher resolution (0.36 m and 2 m respectively) than the data used here, the results are still similar.

It is interesting to present results of the following studies, which used Landsat and ASTER images, though none has evaluated the increased number of the datasets on the tree species accuracy. This is perhaps due to the limited number of images available, or due to their focus on the best achieved result. Thus, Schriever & Congalton (1995) classified seven different forest types in Ireland using Landsat TM data with an accuracy that ranged from (62%) in September to (74%) in October. Moreover, Mickelson et al. (1998) used a time-series of three Landsat TM images and achieved a classification accuracy of 79%, separating 21 forest type classes in USA. Also in the USA, Townsend & Walsh (2001) demonstrated a surprisingly high overall accuracy of about 90% for 20 forest cover types by using eight Landsat images. While Stoffels et al. (2012) distinguished five main forest types in Germany with an accuracy of 87% using five ASTER images.

There are some interesting points which were not investigated here, for example, determining the best scenes (single and multiseasonal) for separating individual tree species classes using as few scenes as possible. Or computing the classification success at the end of each year (2009, 2010 and 2011) to be implemented for an operational annual update in the frame of the remote sensing based inventory and monitoring system for the forest-wood chain in Bavaria was not investigated. As well as, using the multiseasonal approach to update these databases on an annual basis, through the integration of additional information from other sensor types, e.g. height information (Elatawneh et al. 2012b) was also not investigated here.

Acknowledgments

The presented research work is funded by the Federal Ministry of Economics and Technology under number 50EE0919 within the program "synergistic use of RapidEye and TerraSAR-X data for applications" of the Space Agency of the German Aerospace Centre (DLR). Our thanks go to RESA of the DLR for the provision of RapidEye data and especially for the excellent support.

Literature

Boyd D, Danson F. 2005.
Satellite Remote Sensing of forest resources: three decades of research
development. prog phys geogr 29 (1):1-26.

Davranche A, Lefebvre G, Poulin B. 2010.
Wetland monitoring using classification trees and SPOT-5 seasonal
time series. Remote Sensing of Environment 114 (3):552-62.

Dorren LKA, Maier B, Seijmonsbergen AC. 2003.
Improved Landsat-based forest mapping in steep mountainous terrain
using object-based classification. Forest Ecology and Management
183 (1-3):31-46.

Eckert S, Kneubühler M, eds. 2004.
Application of hyperion data to agricultural land classification
and vegetation properties estimation in Switzerland.

Elatawneh A, Kalaitzidis C, Petropoulos GP, Schneider T. 2012a.
Evaluation of diverse classification approaches for land use/
cover mapping in a Mediterranean region utilizing Hyperion data.
International Journal of Digital Earth. International Journal of Digital
Earth: 1-23.

Elatawneh A, Tian J, Schneider T, Reinartz P. 2012b.
Welche Auflösung wird für Aussagen auf Betriebsebene benötigt?
Erkennen von Strukturveränderungen in heterogener Waldgebiete.
AFZ – Der Wald (67):17-19.

Franco-Lopez H, Ek AR, Bauer ME. 2001.
Estimation and mapping of forest stand density, volume, and cover
type using the k-nearest neighbors method. Remote Sensing of
Environment 77 (3):251-74.

Geisser S. 1975.
The Predictive Sample Reuse Method with Applications. Journal
of the American Statistical Association 70 (350).

Hill RA, Wilson AK, George M, Hinsley SA. 2010.
Mapping tree species in temperate deciduous woodland using
time-series multi-spectral data. Applied Vegetation Science
13 (1):86-99.

Holmgren P, Thuresson T. 1998.
  Satellite Remote Sensing for forestry planning A review. Scandinavian
  Journal of Forest Research 13 (1-4):90-110.

Hughes G. 1968.
  On the mean accuracy of statistical pattern recognizers. Information
  Theory, IEEE Transactions on 14 (1):55-63.

Immitzer M, Atzberger C, Koukal T. 2012.
  Tree Species Classification with Random Forest Using Very High
  Spatial Resolution 8-Band WorldView-2 Satellite Data. Remote
  Sensing 4 (9):2661-93.

Kan EP, Weber FP, eds. 1978.
  The Ten-Ecosystem Study: Landsat ADP mapping of forest and
  rangeland in the United States. 12th International Symposium
  on Remote Sensing of Environment. Ann Arbor, Michigan.
  Pp. 1809-1825.

Key T, Warner TA, McGraw JB, Fajvan MA. 2001.
  A Comparison of Multispectral and Multitemporal Information
  in High Spatial Resolution Imagery for Classification of Individual
  Tree Species in a Temperate Hardwood Forest. Remote Sensing
  of Environment 75 (1):100-12.

Khanna S, Palacios-Orueta A, Whiting ML, Ustin SL, Riaño D, Litago J.
2007.
  Development of angle indexes for soil moisture estimation,
  dry matter detection and land-cover discrimination. Remote Sensing
  of Environment 109 (2):154-65.

Korpela I, Heikkinen V, Honkavaara E, Rohrbach F, Tokola T. 2011.
  Variation and directional anisotropy of reflectance at the crown scale
  Implications for tree species classification in digital aerial images.
  Remote Sensing of Environment 115 (8):2062-74.

Kruse FA, Lefkoff AB, Dietz JB. 1993.
  Expert system-based mineral mapping in northern death valley,
  California/Nevada, using the Airborne Visible/Infrared Imaging
  Spectrometer (AVIRIS). Airbone Imaging Spectrometry.
  Remote Sensing of Environment 44 (2-3):309-36.

Mickelson Jr. J, Civco D, Silander Jr. J. 1998.
Delineating forest canopy species in the northeastern United States using multi-temporal TM imagery. Photogrammetric Engineering & Remote Sensing 64 (9):891-904.

Pretzsch H, Biber P, Ďurský J. 2002.
The single tree-based stand simulator SILVA: construction, application and evaluation. National and Regional Climate Change Impact Assessments in the Forestry Sector. Forest Ecology and Management 162 (1):3-21.

Reese HM, Lillesand TM, Nagel DE, Stewart JS, Goldmann RA, et al. 2002.
Statewide land cover derived from multiseasonal Landsat TM data: A retrospective of the WISCLAND project. Remote Sensing of Environment 82 (2-3):224-7.

Schriever J, Congalton R. 1995.
Evaluating Seasonal Variability as an Aid to Cover-Type Mapping from Landsat Thematic Mapper Data in the Northwest. Photogrammetric Engineering & Remote Sensing 61 (3):321-27.

Shen SS, Badhwar GD, Carnes JG. 1996.
Separability of Boreal Forest Species in the Lake Jennette Area, Minnesota Separability of Boreal Forest Species in the Lake Jennette Area, Minnesota. Photogrammetric Engineering & Remote Sensing 51 (11):1775-83.

Stoffels J, Mader S, Hill J, Werner W, Ontrup G. 2012.
Satellite-based stand-wise forest cover type mapping using a spatially adaptive classification approach. Eur J Forest Res 131 (4):1071-89.

Stone M. 1974.
Cross-Validatory Choice and Assessment of Statistical Predictions. Journal of the Royal Statistical Society. Series B (Methodological) 36 (2):111-47.

Townsend P, Walsh S. 2001.
Remote Sensing of forested wetlands: application of multitemporal and multispectral satellite imagery to determine plant community composition and structure in southeastern USA. Plant Ecology 157 (2):129-49.

Vohland M, Stoffels J, Hau C, Schüler G 2007.
Remote Sensing techniques for forest parameter assessment:
multispectral classification and linear spectral mixture analysis.
Silva Fennica 41 (3):441-56.

Walsh SJ. 1980.
Coniferous tree species mapping using LANDSAT data. Remote
Sensing of Environment 9 (1):11-26.

Waser LT, Ginzler C, Kuechler M, Baltsavias E, Hurni L. 2011.
Semi-automatic classification of tree species in different forest
ecosystems by spectral and geometric variables derived from Airborne
Digital Sensor (ADS40) and RC30 data. Remote Sensing
of Environment 115 (1):76-85.

Wolter P, Mladenoff D.J., Host G.E., Crow T.R. 1995.
Improved forest classification in the northern Lake States using
multi-temporal Landsat imagery. Photogrammetric
Engineering & Remote Sensing 61 (9):1129-43.

Assessing the required temporal frequency of optical EO acquisitions for the modelling of winter wheat yield in Northern Germany (Project ID: 345)

Tobias B. Hank[1], Toni Frank[1], Heike Bach[2], Katharina Spannraft[2], Wolfram Mauser[1]

[1] Dept. of Geography, Ludwig-Maximilians-Universität, Munich, Germany
[2] VISTA Remote Sensing in Geosciences GmbH, Munich, Germany

E-Mail: tobias.hank@lmu.de

Assessing the required temporal frequency of optical EO acquisitions for the modelling of winter wheat yield in Northern Germany

Tobias B. Hank, Toni Frank, Heike Bach, Katharina Spannraft, Wolfram Mauser

Information on land surface heterogeneity, derived from satellite-based Earth Observation (EO) systems, may successfully contribute to agricultural management decisions. Time series of observations of plant growth status can be assimilated into models of agricultural production, thus increasing the spatial accuracy of model results. In order to guarantee for an adequate frequency of observations available for assimilation, the model systems should be capable of using multisensoral data. However, due to the known limitations of optical EO systems, even the number of multisensoral observations during the active growth period generally is rather small. This study therefore aims to assess the impact of observation frequency on the modelling of winter wheat yield. An exhaustive data set was available, consisting of RapidEye and Landsat TM images acquired during the growing seasons of 2010 and 2011 over a test site in Northern Germany. The data was used for a spatially explicit field-scale simulation of winter wheat yield by deriving plant physiological properties with help of the reflectance model SLC and assimilating these into the land surface process model PROMET. By gradually degrading the number of included observations and comparing the modelled yield to spatial yield measurements, the impact of observation frequency was assessed. The results indicate that the most reliable match between modelled and measured data can be obtained by using the maximum number of available observations (2010: 5; 2011: 7). The average accuracy was significantly reduced, when less than four observations per season were used.

1. Introduction

1.1 Temporal requirements of agricultural applications of EO data

The continuing growth of the world population currently leads to a tightened competition between food, energy and environmental demands (Tilman et al. 2009). From the necessity of satisfying the need for food and energy of an increasing number of people, based on the yield that is generated on the bioproductive land surface of the planet, results the requirement of increased agricultural production (Tilman et al. 2002). Due to climatic, pedogenetic or ecological limitations, further expansion of farmland is rarely feasible. An increase of agricultural production therefore has to be achieved by gaining higher amounts of yield from the already existing agricultural acreage, i.e. by reasonably increasing the efficiency of agricultural production (Mauser et al. 2012). Smart farming practices, such as site specific seeding, fertilization or plant protection, as well as advanced computer aided farm management systems may significantly contribute to this increase of efficiency (McBratney et al. 2005). Improved management thereby is highly dependent on reliable information. Especially for site specific management of agricultural sites, information on crop status during the different development stages of the growth period is relevant. Site specific approaches are based on the awareness of heterogeneities of growth conditions and their distribution in space. Therefore, only measuring techniques able to deliver spatially explicit data can be applied for the generation of the required information. Remote sensing represents the only technological solution able to provide continuous information on spatial land surface heterogeneities and, if advanced retrieval strategies are applied, also on the status of specific plant physiological variables. In farming practice, spatially explicit information on crop status is required one or two days in advance of the actual execution of the management measure in order to allow for the generation of efficient application maps. The temporal availability of information therefore is very critical. Different restrictions associated with optical remote sensing (e.g. weather conditions, number of available sensors etc.) regularly lead to the fact that only few observations of a specific target can be acquired during a single growth period. The dates of these few acquisitions rarely coincide with the date the decision makers actually are needing information for. Growth processes are highly influenced by dynamic variables on the land surface, such as weather conditions, human or animal interference, occurrence of pests and diseases etc. Plant development therefore cannot be considered to be a linear process. Simple interpolation between satellite observations over longer spans of time consequently is not sensible. Advanced information systems have been developed that are able to overcome these temporal constraints by assimilating the EO data into process-based models of agricultural production (Hank et al. 2012a). With each EO scene that is assimilated into the model system, the EO based information gradually is enriched within the model, leading to improved model results (Hank et al. 2012b). Applying these advanced combined model systems, the desired information, e.g. the current distribution of aboveground biomass, can be provided on an hourly basis, mostly independent from the time of the satellite data acquisition. Using meteorological data from the weather forecast, the simulation may even be expanded several days into the future, thus providing spatially explicit information on crop status on time for the exact moment that is required for the planning of a certain management measure (Hank/Bach 2011). Nonetheless, also the combined model approach is dependent on satellite observations, although the absolute date of the acquisition may be of less significance, compared to conventional information systems that are solely relying on satellite observations, without combining them with process models. The general necessity to acquire high quality earth observation in order to produce high quality information products for smart farming leads to two research questions: 1. How many EO scenes actually are required for the generation of a reasonably accurate information product? 2. Are there preferred periods during a growing season, where EO acquisitions may contribute more information to the final result as during other periods? This study consequently investigates the impact of satellite observation frequency on assimilation-based simulations of winter wheat yield. Thereby, also the question of preferable acquisition dates for winter wheat yield modelling in Northern Germany is addressed.

1.2 The combined EO supported process model PROMET/SLC

Remote sensing as a stand-alone technique is limited with respect to the derivation of information products with practical farming relevance. To overcome this limitation, an approach is proposed that combines information on the spatial heterogeneity of the land surface from EO data sources with information on the dynamics of temporal development of non-linear land surface processes from a physically based model. For the land surface simulation component, the model PROMET (Process of Radiation, Mass and Energy Transfer; Mauser/Bach 2009) is used, while the optical remote sensing part of the combined model system (Fig. 1) is represented by the complex canopy reflectance model SLC (Soil-Leaf-Canopy; Verhoef/Bach 2007; Verhoef/Bach 2012). SLC is used to derive spatially explicit maps of photosynthetically active leaf area from EO data, so that green LAI may be used as exchange variable between the land surface model and the satellite observation. Major management events, such as harvest, are derived from hyperfrequent X-band SAR time series and are made available to the land surface model on field level (Fig. 1).

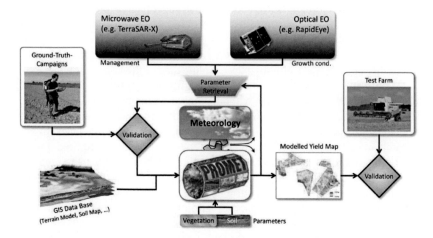

Figure 1: EO data sources, parameters and components of the combined assimilation system, including different levels of validation options.

With the help of this integrated EO/model system, it is possible to simulate a variety of land surface variables at an hourly time step, among them being highly sophisticated outputs such as e.g. agricultural yield. Yield is a variable that is very sensitive to growth conditions, mostly because all growth influencing factors, such as the duration of the single phenological stages, the water and nutrient supply, the occurrence of pests and diseases or unexpected natural hazards such as wind break or hail damage, more or less are aggregated within the final product. A correct simulation of yield therefore implies the correct representation also of other growth influencing variables in the model. Due to this interconnectedness of the variable yield and also due to the fact that yield more or less is the only biophysical variable that can be spatially measured without destroying the crop during the active growth phase, it was decided to use yield as the benchmark variable for the analyses of this study.

2. Materials and Methods

2.1 Test area Saxony-Anhalt

The combined assimilation approach is applied to a test site in Saxony-Anhalt, North-Eastern Germany, thus choosing one of the most intensively cultivated areas of Germany for the experiment. Winter wheat fields of two large farms in the vicinity of Blankenburg, east of the Harz mid range mountains, were modelled for the growing seasons of the years 2010 and 2011. While for 2010 more than 280 hectares of wheat were modelled, the test site was tilled with more than 560 hectares of wheat in 2011. The area is generally characterized through relatively large acreages, fertile soils (mostly chernozems) and low annual precipitation sums (approx. 600 mm) combined with a continentally dominated climate. The required spatial parameters for the model setup could mostly be derived from publicly available data sources or from own observations respectively, while the meteorological driver variables were commercially acquired from the European Weather Consult (EWC) measuring network (Table 1).

Data set	Data source	Year	Resolution
Soil Map	FAO / HWSD	2009	30 arcsec
DTM	NASA / SRTM	2008	90 m
Land use map	field observation	2010/2011	field-based
Mask	FMIS	2010/2011	20 m
Meteorology	EWC	2009 - 2011	10 stations

Table 1: Basic parameters used for the setup of the PROMET model.

The geometric features of the modelled fields could be derived from the Farm Management Information Systems (FMIS) of the test farms. The spatial resolution of the simulation should represent a compromise between the characteristics of the available sensors, the computational efficiency and the requirements for information density on field level. All spatial input data sets thus were resampled to a common resolution of 20 x 20 meters.

2.2 Time series of EO data and model setup

The applied assimilation concept allows for the integration of multisensoral data. Accordingly, combinations of RapidEye and Landsat 5 TM images were used. The images from both sensors were equally resampled to a resolution of 20 x 20 meters. Five scenes could be obtained for the season of 2010, while even seven acquisitions were available for 2011 (Table 2).

Date 2010	May 21	June 16	June 29	July 8	July 20
Sensor	RE	RE	TM	TM	RE
AZA [°]	10.33	6.96	Nadir	Nadir	-12.04
GSD [m]	5	5	30	30	5

Date 2011	Mar 3	Apr 2	Apr 18	May 5	Jun 2	Jun 29	Jul 27
Sensor	RE	RE	RE	RE	RE	RE	TM
AZA [°]	-19.55	3.60	6.73	6.99	0.34	-6.18	Nadir
GSD [m]	5	5	5	5	5	5	30

Table 2: Earth Observation data available for assimilation into the PROMET model (AZA = Acquisition Zenith Angle, GSD = Ground Sampling Distance, RE = RapidEye, TM = Landsat 5 TM).

In order to investigate the influence of the assimilation of single observation dates on the final result, repeated model runs were performed for both growing seasons, while the absolute number of observations that were included in the assimilation chain was gradually varied. For each number of observations that were taken into account, the possible combinations of the available acquisition dates were iteratively tested. This data mining approach is comparable to a study by Murakami et al. (2001), who investigated the discrimination of favourable scene combinations for agricultural land cover classification. The five satellite observations from 2010 resulted in up to 32 different combinations of the available observation dates. Based on the seven observation dates available for 2011, even 128 combinations could be investigated (Table 3).

Scenes available 2010:	0	1	2	3	4	5		Total
No. of Combinations:	1	5	10	10	5	1		32
Scenes available 2011:	0	1	2	3	4	5	6	7	Total
No. of Combinations:	1	7	21	35	35	21	7	1	128

Table 3: Potential combinations of available EO acquisitions for 2010 & 2011.

The iterative model runs for both seasons were designed to calculate yield maps for the respective harvest days of the individual fields (around the middle of August). To account for the intensive computational demands, the task was distributed to a 27-node cluster computer located at the Department of Geography of the LMU Munich. The model outputs generated from each possible combination of included observation dates were individually compared to the validation data set through direct regression between the modelled results and the measured yield map (see 2.3). Accounting for different aspects of model accuracy, two statistical indicators were calculated for each combination. While the coefficient of determination (R^2) indicates the agreement of spatial patterns, the Root-Mean-Square-Error (RMSE) represents the matching of absolute values between modelled and measured yield. The statistical results were grouped into categories of available observations (6 for 2010 and 8 for 2011, see Table 3) and averaged. The comparison of averaged results was preferred to the ranking of absolute values in order to give a general indication of the change in confidence and stability of the model results with increasing temporal frequency of assimilated EO scenes.

2.3 Preprocessing of validation data

For the validation of the model outputs, spatially explicit yield maps could be used that were supplied by the managers of the test sites. Being collected during the actual harvesting process by a GPS supported combine harvester of the Type Claas Lexion 600, the yield maps allow for a spatial analysis of absolute wheat yield. The yield maps obtained with this method nonetheless suffer from some serious uncertainties, which partly can be reduced through a sensible calibration (Blackmore 1999). The raw data provided by the combine harvester consists of data points that are spatially referenced, but do not have a defined spatial extent. They were converted into a spatially continuous validation raster through inverse distance interpolation (30 neighbours, weighting parameter = 0.5). Measurement outliers lower than 0.5 or higher than 18 t ha^{-1} were excluded. Although the yield maps indicate the spatial distribution of harvested yield, the absolute values recorded by the combine harvester may incorporate a strong bias. The yield map thus was calibrated with the absolute weights of the harvest mass of the respective fields. With the help of field-based moisture content measurements, the yield values of each field finally were standardized to a dry matter content of 86 %, which is the ideal percentage of dry matter aspired for wheat harvest and which is also assumed in the outputs of the PROMET model. After these corrective steps, the yield map was considered to represent a reliable spatial validation raster data set.

3. Results and Discussion

3.1 Results for the assessment of required temporal frequency

The results obtained for the season of 2010 show that the accuracy of the modelled winter wheat yield increases with respect to spatial patterns (increasing R^2) as well as with respect to the simulation of absolute yield values (decreasing RMSE), when a higher number of EO data sets are included in the simulation process (Fig. 2).

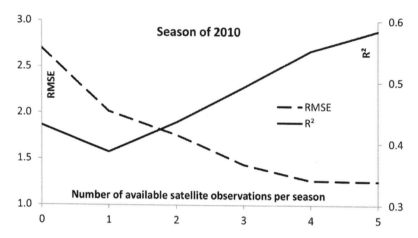

Figure 2: Statistical error indices derived from the comparison of modelled and measured yield of winter wheat on >280 hectares on a test site in Saxony-Anhalt (Germany) for the season of 2010 in dependence of the absolute number of satellite observations that were included in the assimilation chain.

It was found that the RMSE decreased significantly, when up to four observation dates were included. The inclusion of a fifth scene did not result in a further improvement. The agreement of spatial patterns, indicated through the R^2 value, nonetheless shows a definite increase with every observation that was added to the assimilation chain of the season 2010, with only one exception. Surprisingly the model returned a slightly higher R^2 value without EO support compared to the average achieved when only one observation date was used. This is due to the fact that the variety specific parameterization of the PROMET model for the year 2010 returned two clusters of data points (one relatively high, one relatively low). The resulting correlation only indicates an agreement of field averages and should not be statistically misinterpreted as positive correlation of in-field heterogeneities. The bold decline of RMSE with the inclusion of a single observation date nonetheless clearly indicates the positive effect of the additionally assimilated information on the model results. Also for 2011, a general increase of the regarded accuracy measures can be observed with an increasing number of EO scenes involved (Fig. 3). However, the increase of accuracy is not linear, so that with an increasing number of observation dates included, effects of saturation can be observed. While the gain in accuracy is strong, when up to four scenes are successively added to the assimilation chain, including more than four scenes only led to a moderate but nonetheless positive increase of model accuracy. This saturation trend was equally observed for 2010 and 2011.

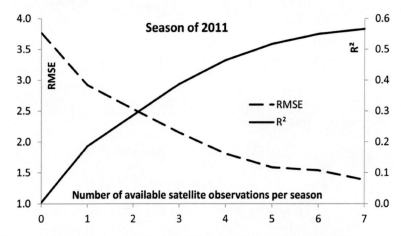

Figure 3: Statistical error indices derived from the comparison of modelled and measured yield of winter wheat on >560 hectares on a test site in Saxony-Anhalt (Germany) for the season of 2011 in dependence of the absolute number of satellite observations that were included in the assimilation chain.

The gradual increase of agreement between model outputs and spatial validation measurement is visualized in Fig. 4. It can be observed in Fig. 4a that without EO information the model results represent optimal growth conditions and thus overestimate yield. The spatial patterns are determined through the rough resolution of the static spatial input data sets (DTM, soil map etc.). By adding more and more observation dates to the assimilation chain, these drawbacks are gradually resolved. For both seasons, the best results could be achieved by using the maximum number of available observations (Fig. 4f; Table 4).

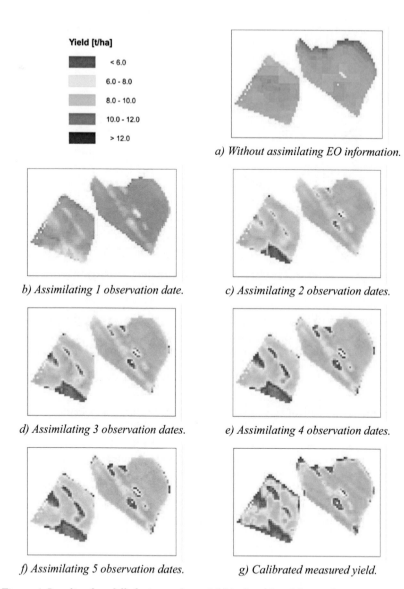

Yield [t/ha]

- ▣ < 6.0
- ▢ 6.0 - 8.0
- ▨ 8.0 - 10.0
- ▦ 10.0 - 12.0
- ▰ > 12.0

a) Without assimilating EO information.

b) Assimilating 1 observation date.

c) Assimilating 2 observation dates.

d) Assimilating 3 observation dates.

e) Assimilating 4 observation dates.

f) Assimilating 5 observation dates.

g) Calibrated measured yield.

Figure 4: Results of modelled winter wheat yield (a-f) achieved for a subset of the test area (approx. 70 ha) for the season of 2010 in comparison to the calibrated measured yield map (g).

	R²	RMSE	A
Season of 2010:	0.58	1.25 t ha⁻¹	> 280 ha
Season of 2011:	0.57	1.38 t ha⁻¹	> 560 ha

Table 4: Statistical measures achieved for the validation of both seasons (2010 & 2011) under consideration of the respective maximum number of observation dates.

The results achieved for the season of 2011 (Fig. 3) seem to indicate more stable trends compared to the results for 2010 (Fig. 2). This surely is due to the higher number of available EO acquisitions, but may also be caused by the higher homogeneity of the EO data used for 2011 (6 out of seven from the same system, i.e. RapidEye, see Table 2) and may also be due to smoothing effects induced by the larger area that was covered by the 2011 experiment (2010: approx. 280 ha, 2011: approx. 560 ha, see Table 4).

3.2 Results for the assessment of preferable observation dates

In order to analyse the importance of single observation dates as well, the data was mined to find the combination of included satellite observations that resulted in a model output with the best overall results. In order to assess the achieved model accuracy in spatial as well as in absolute terms, the two complementary error indices (R^2 and RMSE) were normalized to the actual data range, thus generating equally dimensionless quality measures. The average of the two normalized error indices was used as overall quality indicator. According to this average indicator, the 20 % best performing combinations of each season were selected (6 out of 32 for 2010 and 26 out of 128 for 2011) and analyzed according to the actual observation dates that had been included for the respective simulations. It could be found for the season of 2010 that among the 20 % best performing combinations, the satellite observations from June 29th and from July 20th were selected most frequently (6 out of 6 times = 100 %), while the early observation from May 21st was least frequently represented among the best performing combinations (Fig. 5). Not only providing a higher number of available scenes, but also showing a more even distribution of observations in the course of the season, the analysis of the results achieved for the season of 2011 returned slightly different findings (Fig. 5) that nonetheless mostly confirm the results achieved for 2010. From the 20 % best performing combinations of available observation dates for 2011 (26 out of 128), the RapidEye observation from the 2nd of June was selected most frequently (26 out of 26 = 100 %).

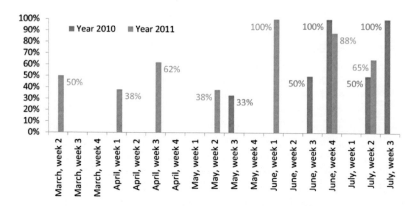

Figure 5: Frequency of selection of the EO dates that were available for the season of 2010 and 2011 among the 20 % of possible combinations (6 out of 32 for 2010 and 26 out of 128 for 2011) that performed best in comparison to the validation data.

Unfortunately, for 2010 no observation exists close to that date, so that the dominating importance of this observation cannot be confirmed. In accordance to the results found for 2010, the satellite observation from June 29th, which fortunately was available for both seasons, was second mostly selected (88 %). Additionally confirming the results achieved for 2010, the observation during May was significantly less often selected also for 2011, while the observation from the middle of July for both seasons seems to contribute average significant information, being selected 3 out of 6 times (50 %) for 2010 and 17 out of 26 times (65 %) for 2011. This may be due to the fact that satellite observations during late July may capture spatial patterns that distinctly appear during the ripening phase of the crop. Very late observations additionally may be of increased importance, when unforeseen damages are affecting yield even at late development stages. The results for 2011 also indicate that very early observations from March or April may also contribute significant information. This may confirm the assumption that the variable yield indeed incorporates a memory of growth influencing events that have occurred during the whole growing season. Interpreting the results, it has to be taken into account that, due to climatic differences, phenological development was approximately one week earlier during May 2011 compared to May 2010, while during the rest of the growth period the development was rather parallel between the two seasons. A sensor-related preference of observations could not be detected in the results.

Summary and Conclusion

The presented study underlines the necessity of careful selection of acquisition dates for agricultural EO applications. It was found that a general increase of model accuracy can be observed, when more observation dates are included in the calculation process. However, the gain of accuracy contributed by adding more observation dates decreased, when more than four scenes were included in the assimilation chain. The importance of single observation dates is very hard to assess, mostly because it is not the absolute date that is determining the information content contributed to the model through an EO data set, but more the phenological stage that is covered by the observation. Phenological progress occurs with a temporal dynamic of weeks rather than months. Even more frequent satellite observations as they were available for this study, accompanied by highly frequent phenological field sampling, therefore are required in order to properly assess favourable acquisitions. The results of both seasons nonetheless showed that observations from end of June contributed most information, while observations from the middle of May seemed to have the least positive impact on the results. The findings initially only apply to the PROMET model. It may be a major future challenge to confirm these results by combining different growth models and assimilation techniques within model ensembles. Taking the difficulties of obtaining multi-seasonal optical remote sensing acquisition series into account, a more precise assessment of the information content of single observation dates will still require a lot of effort. Some highly frequent systems are about to be launched in the near future that allow for agricultural applications, such as ESA Sentinel-2. These systems will complement the existing data sources, e.g. RapidEye, so that the problems mentioned above may successfully be approached in the upcoming years.

Acknowledgements

The authors would like to thank the agricultural holdings of Mr. Klamroth and Mr. Münchhoff for the supply of validation data. RapidEye data was provided via the RapidEye Science Archive (RESA) operated by the German Aerospace Centre (DLR) Neustrelitz, Germany. TerraSAR-X data was provided via DLR Oberpfaffenhofen, Germany. The research shown here mostly was done in the frame of the Project 'RapidSAR - Integrative use of RapidEye and TerraSAR-X through data assimilation into models of agricultural production (grant code numbers 50 EE 0920/22), supported by the Space Agency of DLR through funding by the German Federal Ministry of Economics and Technology (BMWi).

References

Blackmore, S., 1999.
Remedial Correction of Yield Map Data. *Precision Agriculture*, 1 (1), pp. 53-66.

Hank, T., Bach, H., 2011.
Satellitengestützte Ertragsmodellierung - Realistische Vorhersagen. *Neue Landwirtschaft - Das Fachmagazin für den Agrarmanager,* 11/2011, pp. 57-61, Deutscher Landwirtschaftsverlag GmbHS.

Hank, T., Bach, H., Spannraft, K., Friese, M., Frank, T., Mauser, W., 2012a. Prozessbasierte Modellierung der Wachstumsheterogenität landwirtschaftlicher Bestände durch Assimilation von Erdbeobachtungsdaten. In: Borg, E., Daedelow, H., Johnson, R. (Eds.): *RapidEye Science Archive - Vom Algorithmus zum Produkt.* ISBN: 978-3-942183-61-1, pp. 219-238, GITO Berlin.

Hank, T., Bach, H., Spannraft, K., Friese, M., Frank, T., Mauser, W., 2012b. Improving the process-based simulation of growth heterogeneities in agricultural stands through assimilation of earth observation data. Proceedings of the International Geoscience and Remote sensing Symposium 2012, Munich, *IEEE Xplore*, pp. 1006-1009.

McBratney, A., Whelan, B., Ancev, T., Bouma, J. 2005.
Future Directions of Precision Agriculture. *Precision Agriculture*, 6 (1), pp. 7-23.

Mauser, W., Bach, H., Hank, T., Zabel, F., Putzenlechner, B., 2012.
How spectroscopy from space will support world agriculture. Proceedings of the International Geoscience and Remote sensing Symposium 2012, Munich, *IEEE Xplore*, pp. 7321-7324.

Mauser, W., Bach, H., 2009.
PROMET – Large scale distributed hydrological modelling to study the impact of climate change on the water flows of mountain watersheds. *Journal of Hydrology*, 376, pp. 362-377.

Murakami, T., Ogawa, S., Ishitsuka, N., Kumagai, K., Saito, G., 2001.
Crop discrimination with multitemporal SPOT/HRV data in the Saga Plains, Japan. *International Journal of Remote Sensing*, 22 (7), pp. 1335-1348.

Tilman, D., Cassman, K.G., Matson, P.A., Naylor, R., Polasky, S., 2002.
Agricultural sustainability and intensive production practices. *Nature*,
418, pp. 671-677.

Tilman, D., Socolow, R., Foley, J.A., Hill, J., Larson, E., Lynd, L., Pacala, S.,
Reilly, J., Searchinger, T., Somerville, C., Williams, R., 2009.
Beneficial Biofuels – The Food, Energy, and Environment Trilemma.
Science, 325 (5938), pp. 270-271.

Verhoef, W., Bach, H., 2007.
Coupled soil-leaf-canopy and atmosphere radiative transfer modeling
to simulate hyperspectral multi-angular surface reflectance and TOA
radiance data. *Remote Sensing of Environment*, 109, pp. 166-182.

Verhoef, W., Bach, H., 2012.
Simulation of Sentinel-3 images by four stream surface atmosphere
radiative transfer modeling in the optical and thermal domains.
Remote Sensing of Environment, 120, pp. 197-207.

Improving agricultural land use mapping in West Africa using multi-temporal Landsat and RapidEye data (Project ID: 493)

Gerald Forkuor[1], Christopher Conrad[1], Tobias Landmann[2], Michael Thiel[1], Evence Zoungrana[3]

[1] Department of Remote Sensing, Universität Würzburg, Am Hubland, 97074, Würzburg
[2] International Center of Insect Physiology and Ecology, Nairobi, Kenya
[3] West African Science Service Center on Climate Change and Adapted Land Use, Ouagadougou, Burkina Faso

E-Mail: gerald.forkuor@uni-wuerzburg.de

Improving agricultural land use mapping in West Africa using multi-temporal Landsat and RapidEye data

Gerald Forkuor, Christopher Conrad, Tobias Landmann,
Michael Thiel, Evence Zoungrana

1. Introduction

Rapid population growth has triggered expansion in croplands in West Africa, resulting in high deforestation rates.

At the same time, climate models predict higher temperatures and increased rainfall variability which will affect agricultural production and increase food insecurity (Conway 2009). In order to reduce these, it is essential to improve agricultural land use mapping, here defined as the spatial distribution of crops. Such information can, for instance, improve the forecasting of crop production and yields through crop models (Bastiaanssen / Ali 2003), which subsequently can feed into formulating an adaptation and mitigation policy for the region.

Mapping agricultural land use in West Africa has been challenging. The size of croplands vis-à-vis the spatial resolution of commonly available satellite images (Turner / Congalton 1998) poses a mapping constraint. Landsat, the most widely used data for land use and land cover (LULC) mapping (Roy et al. 2010) is unable to capture the typical smallholder farms (< 1 ha) due to spatial resolution limitations. Sub-canopy cultivation also leads to a highly heterogeneous landscape.

Poor temporal sequence of available satellite data also poses challenges. Successful crop classifications require multi-temporal observations during the cropping season, because key phenological stages enable the differentiation between spectrally similar crops. But in West Africa, images of key phenological periods in the cropping season are mostly unavailable for analysis due to nearly permanent cloud cover limiting optical sensors (e.g. Landsat) to obtain useful data.

Previous studies on agricultural land use mapping in West Africa have focused on national to regional scales using moderate to low resolution satellite imagery such as MODIS or AVHRR (Groten 1993, Vintrou et al. 2012). Although these studies are relevant for regional crop area assessments, they are of little use at local scales where fundamental changes take place. However, local scale studies using medium resolution multi-temporal data (SPOT-XS) were also unable to provide information on the spatial distribution of crop types (e.g. cereals, legumes, etc.) due to heterogeneity of the landscape and a high variation in field sizes (Marsh et al. 1992, Turner / Congalton 1998). To overcome the limitations of these studies, and improve the detection of crops in West Africa, high resolution imagery acquired during the cropping season is required.

The following investigations address the integrative use of satellite data from RapidEye (RE) and Landsat to improve agricultural land use mapping in West Africa. RE data and multi-temporal Landsat data recorded during the cropping season were combined and explored to improve the detection of crops. The main objectives were (1) to ascertain whether the integrative use of data with varied spatial and temporal resolution allows for the mapping of agricultural land use classes (e.g. cereals, legumes, etc.) and (2) determine the important months, during the cropping season, for which availability of satellite data is essential for improved agricultural land use mapping.

2. Study area

The study area is located at the border of Ghana and Burkina Faso. It forms part of the West African Science Service Center on Climate Change and Adapted Land Use (WASCAL) focal catchments (Figure 1). Agriculture, i.e. cultivation of crops and livestock rearing is the main occupation of the inhabitants of these catchments. Official statistics for two districts in Ghana (Bongo and Kassena Nankana) which overlap the catchments indicate that agriculture employs about two-thirds of the inhabitants (GSS 2005). The combined population of these two districts as of the year 2000 was 227,376 (GSS 2005) with an average population density of 108 inhabitants per/km^2.

Agriculture in the area is mainly rainfed and dominated by smallholders. The main cropping season spans from May to October, in accordance with the uni-modal rainfall distribution the area experiences. The main crops cultivated are: millet, sorghum, maize, groundnuts and rice. Dry season cultivation is done on a limited scale from November to March. The major cropping system is intercropping, where farmers plant multiple crops on a piece of land to reduce risk of crop failure.

3. Data and Methods

3.1 Satellite and reference data

Landsat data: Landsat Thematic Mapper (TM) data acquired on 3rd June, 6th August, 23rd September and 25th October 2009 were obtained from the United States Geological Survey's (USGS) Global Visualization Viewer (GLOVIS). The data were radiometrically corrected by converting the raw Digital Numbers (DN) to at-sensor-reflectance. Normalized Difference Vegetation Index (NDVI) was computed for each of the four images. The Near Infrared band (NIR) and the NDVI of each of the four images were combined and used in subsequent analysis. For purposes of combining this data with the RapidEye data, it was resampled from 30m to 5m using the nearest neighbor approach.

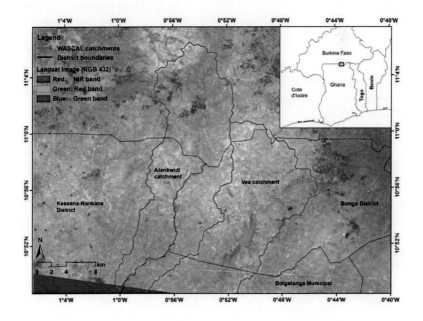

Figure 1: Map of the study area.

RapidEye data: A RapidEye image of 25th November 2009 was obtained from the RapidEye Science Team. A total of 10 Ground Control Points (GCPs) were used to geometrically correct the data. A Root Mean Square Error (RMSE) of

61

0.8 pixels was obtained. Spectral analysis was conducted on the original five spectral bands (blue, green, red, rededge, NIR) to produce twenty-four additional indices (Schuster et al. 2012). A preliminary classification using only RE data revealed that six, out of the twenty-four indices, were the most important based on the variable importance measure of the random forest algorithm. These six indices are: difference between NIR and rededge, NIR and red, NIR and green and ratio of NIR and green, and NIR and rededge. An NDVI calculated based on NIR and the rededge band was also included.

Reference data: Reference data for classification was collected in a field survey conducted between May and July 2012. Pre-selected sample points were captured using a handheld GPS. Around each point, a minimum area of 900m^2 (i.e. 30x30m) was defined and surveyed. The Land Cover Classification System (LCCS) protocol developed by the Food and Agricultural Organization (FAO) was modified and used in the survey. The main modification was made in the "cultivated terrestrial area and managed land" section. For each cultivated field surveyed, information gathered included: (1) the number and type of crops cultivated, (2) the date each crop was planted and the anticipated harvest date and (3) crops the farmer has been cultivating on the plot for the past ten years (i.e. from 2002 to date). Thus, from the survey results, it was possible to determine which crops were cultivated on each surveyed plot in 2009. It is worth noting that for most surveyed plots, farmers have been planting the same crops for the past 10 years.

3.2 Classification algorithm

The Random Forest classification algorithm (Breiman 2001) was used for classification because it allows the integration of a large set of variables (predictors/bands). The algorithm generates large sets of classification trees, each tree trained on a bootstrapped sample (randomly selected) of the original training samples. These large set of trees help in reducing generalization error and increases classification accuracy (Gislason et al. 2006). At each tree node, a user-defined number of variables are randomly selected from the total number of variables from which the best is chosen to split the node (Liaw / Wiener 2002). This approach reduces the computational load of the algorithm (Gislason et al. 2006) and is robust against overfitting (Breiman 2001). Each generated tree in the forest cast a unit vote for the most popular class. Output of the classification is determined by a majority vote of the trees.

Random forest allows for an estimation of a classification error rate using the training samples that are omitted from the bootstrapped samples used in creating the forest (i.e. out-of-bag, OOB). To estimate the error rate, the trees grown with the bootstrap samples are used to predict the OOB data which is aggregated and compared to the actual labels. The OOB estimate of error rate is an accurate measure of classification error provided enough trees are grown (Liaw / Wiener 2002).

Random forest algorithm optionally provides additional information on the relative importance of the predictor variables used in the classification (Liaw / Wiener 2002). An increase or decrease in prediction error when OOB data for a variable is permuted is a measure of its importance. In this study, the mean decrease gini (MDG), which has been noted to be more stable than the mean decrease accuracy (Calle / Urrea 2010) was used.

3.3 Generating training samples

Training samples were generated for ten land use and land cover types, based on analysis of the collected field data. Table 1 provides information about the classes, their description and the number of samples generated for each. All pixels that fell in, or overlapped, a training site (i.e. the boundaries of a surveyed field) were used as training samples. Due to the resampling of Landsat to 5m, each of the resulting thirty-six 5m pixels within an original 30m Landsat pixel would have the same value. Thus, to avoid generating duplicate samples from the Landsat data, only one pixel/value (and the corresponding RE pixel/value) was selected as training sample.

Class	Description	No. of Samples
Cereals	Intercropping: millet/sorghum/maize/beans	119
Legumes	Groundnuts and/or bambara beans	79
Rice	Regularly flooded	61
Grassland	Natural and semi-natural	53
Closed Forest	Crown density > 70% and height >5m	38
Mixed Vegetation	Open woodland, shrubs and grassland	21
Urban Areas	Buildings, hamlets, rock outcrops	69
Bare Areas	Red soil with no vegetation	56
Sparse woodland	Crown density < 10-20%	53
Water	Small reservoirs artificially constructed	76

Table 1: Land use and land cover classes mapped and their description.

3.4 Experimental design

The main objective of the study was to (1) ascertain whether the combined use of RapidEye and Landsat improves agricultural land use mapping and (2) determine important month(s) within the cropping season for which availability of satellite data is essential for improved agricultural land use mapping. In order to achieve these objectives, nine separate random forest classifications were conducted with different combinations of satellite data and the resulting accuracies compared. For each experiment, 1000 trees were generated, while the number of variables tried at each split was set to default (i.e. sqrt (total number of variables)). The option to calculate variable importance was set to true in all cases. Specifically, the following experiments were conducted:

a) **RapidEye only (5m)**: only RE data (i.e. eleven bands comprising five original bands and six indices) were used in the classification.

b) **Landsat only (30m)**: only Landsat data (i.e. eight bands comprising NIR and NDVI for each of the four acquisitions) were used in the classification.

c) **RapidEye and Landsat (5m)**: all RE and Landsat data (i.e. nineteen bands comprising eleven RE and eight Landsat) were used in the classification.

d) **Experiments (d)-(g) (5m)**: Using the nineteen band stack in (c) above, the monthly Landsat data were eliminated one after the other and the remainder used in the classification.

h) **RapidEye plus Landsat of August and October (5m)**: Landsat data of June and September were removed and the remainder used in the classification.

i) **RapidEye plus Landsat of June and August (5m)**: Landsat data of September and October were removed and the remainder used in the classification.

Experiments (a) to (c) were conducted to answer objective 1, while (d) to (i) were for objective 2. The rational for (d) to (g) was to access the impact of each of the four Landsat acquisitions on classification accuracy. (i) and (h) were to access how the unavailability of late season imagery (September and October) and early/late season imagery (June and September) can affect classification accuracy respectively.

4. Results and discussion

4.1 Accuracy assessment

Figure 2 shows the overall classification error (i.e. OOB error estimate) and the minimum and maximum class errors for all experiments conducted, while Tables 2-4 provides the confusion matrices of the first three experiments (a-c).

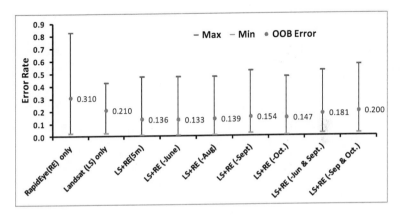

Figure 2: Overall classification error and min. and max class errors of the different experiments (RE refers to RapidEye, LS refers to Landsat).

For these three experiments, the best result was obtained when Landsat and RE were combined, while the worse result was when only the November 2009 RE image was used. The low accuracies achieved by simply using RE is coherent as the cropping season ends in October (harvesting of Maize and Sorghum begins in September), thus, by November, some farmlands could be weedy with grass. This could be the reason for the high confusion between the crop type classes and grassland when only the November RE image is used. Also, identification of "cereals" and "legumes" on already harvested plots is impossible irrespective of any pixel resolution. This could be the reason why about 40% of legumes pixels are misclassified as cereals. But a comparison of the confusion matrixes showed the value of including this time step (i.e. RE) for discerning natural land cover types from crop types. The poor showing of the RapidEye only classification confirms results of previous studies that have indicated the limitations of the use of mono-temporal data for crop classification (Conrad et al. 2010).

OOB Error Rate = 0.306; Kappa = 0.65											
		Classified									
	Class	Cereal	Legu.	Rice	Grass	Forest	Mixed	Urban	Bare	Woodland	Water	Error
Groundtruth	Cereal	83	19	4	10		2				1	0.30
	Legu.	33	34	2	7			1	2			0.57
	Rice	9	1	41	6			4				0.33
	Grass	27	7	1	9	1	5			3		0.83
	Forest				1	31	4			2		0.18
	Mixed	4		1	6	3	6			1		0.71
	Urban			6				62	1			0.10
	Bare		5						51			0.09
	Woodla				2	5	3			43		0.19
	Water			1						1	74	0.03

Table 2: Classification accuracy – the use of November RE data only - (experiment a).

OOB Error Rate = 0.214; Kappa = 0.76											
		Classified									
	Class	Cereal	Legu.	Rice	Grass	Forest	Mixed	Urban	Bare	Woodland	Water	Error
Groundtruth	Cereal	101	7		5		2	1	2	1		0.15
	Legu.	20	51			2	1	1	3	1		0.35
	Rice	6	3	48		1	1			2		0.21
	Grass	10	2		39				2			0.26
	Forest		3			35						0.08
	Mixed	2		1	4	2	12					0.43
	Urban	8			1			58	2			0.16
	Bare	7	3		3			1	42			0.25
	Woodla	16	2	2		2				31		0.42
	Water			2							74	0.03

Table 3: Classification accuracy – the use of June, August, September and October Landsat data only - (experiment b).

OOB Error Rate = 0.136; Kappa = 0.84											
		Classified									
	Class	Cereal	Legu.	Rice	Grass	Forest	Mixed	Urban	Bare	Woodland	Water	Error
Groundtruth	Cereal	105	7	1	5		1					0.12
	Legu.	19	58		1				1			0.27
	Rice	7	4	49				1				0.20
	Grass	7	2	1	41					2		0.23
	Forest					35	1			2		0.08
	Mixed	2			5	3	11					0.48
	Urban	2						66	1			0.04
	Bare	1	3	1					51			0.09
	Woodla	2			1	1				49		0.08
	Water			1							75	0.01

Table 4: Classification accuracy – the combined use of RE and Landsat data - (experiment c).

The use of the multi-temporal Landsat imagery improved the overall accuracy and reduced the class errors as compared to the RapidEye only. For example the class error for the "legumes" and "grassland" classes decreased from 0.57 and 0.83 to 0.35 and 0.26 respectively. This improvement can be attributed to the fine temporal sequence of the Landsat data, which spans almost the whole cropping season (except July). This notwithstanding, Figure 3 reveals that although the multi-temporal Landsat data improved the separation of the agricultural classes, its spatial resolution does hamper an explicit delineation of the land use and land cover classes mapped. The high level of confusion between the woodland class (which include single trees) and the cereal class (error of 0.42 - Table 3) is a further indication of the spatial limitation of Landsat to differentiate between trees on a farm plot and the crops on the farm. Additionally, the relatively high error rate (16%) of the "urban" class may be attributed to Landsat's spatial resolution, which in most cases will be bigger than the hamlets around which plots are cultivated (note that the main confusion is with the cereal class).

Table 4 indicates that, combination of the Landsat and RapidEye produced the best results and achieved a better separability between the crop classes and grassland. Overall classification error reduced from 0.214 in the case of Landsat only to 0.136 when the two datasets are used. Figure 3 shows that the inclusion of the RapidEye data improved the explicit delineation of land use and land cover units as compared to Landsat only. For instance, the error rates of the woodland and urban classes reduced from 0.42 and 0.16 (Landsat only) to 0.08 and 0.04 (Landsat + RapidEye) respectively. This improvement by RE is mainly due to its spatial resolution, which is sufficient to adequately capture certain cover classes (e.g. woodland and urban) that Landsat was unable to adequately distinguish, leading to better separability and less confusion. Thus, the multi-temporal information contained in the Landsat series, and the high spatial resolution of the RapidEye data, contributed to the overall improvement in the results of experiment (c) in terms of crop type separability and explicit delineation of land use and land cover units.

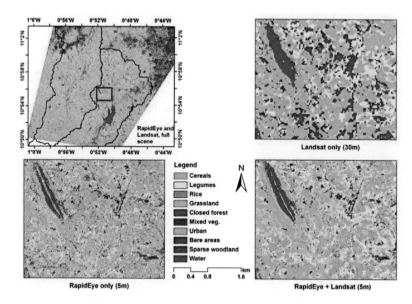

Figure 3: Snapshots of results obtained for experiments (a) to (c).

4.2 Variable importance

The variable importance measures were analyzed for experiments (c) to (i), since (a) and (b), as discussed above, did not achieve optimal results. For each experiment, the first six most important variables were extracted. Figure 4 shows the results. It shows that the June and August images are rarely important, especially compared to the September image which showed up to be the most important in all experiments in which it was included (c, d, e, g). The red, red edge and ratio of NIR and green bands of RapidEye were also important in all experiments (RapidEye was included in all analysis).

Comparing this to Figure 2, it is evident that unavailability of images acquired during early stages and peak of the cropping season (June, August) may not appreciably affect the accuracy of the results as the exclusion of these images causes only a change of 0.003 in overall classification error. With the peak of cropping season falling in July/August, and at a time that all vegetation are likely at maximum phenology, an August image, for example, may be unable to adequately achieve separability between crop and non-crop areas as well as between different crops.

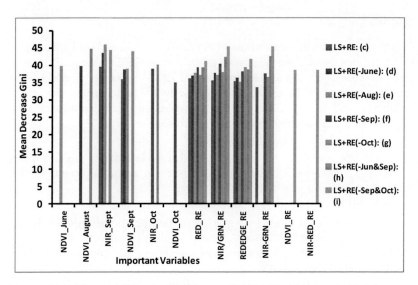

Figure 4: Variable importance for experiments (c) to (i). Variables on the X-axis are a compilation of the first six most important variables in each experiment. The number of bars indicates the number of times a particular variable came within the first six most important variables of an experiment.

On the other hand, images acquired close to the end of the cropping season (possibly the start of senescence onwards, i.e. September and October) are important for crop mapping in the study area. Exclusion of the September or October images causes a relatively significant change (0.02 and 0.01 respectively) to the overall classification error. Worse still is when both September and October are excluded; this produces a change in overall error rate of 0.06. Although most farmers harvest early millet (which is mostly intercropped with sorghum or late millet) in mid to late July, the bulk of harvesting starts from mid-September (e.g. of sorghum/guinea corn and maize) and could continue till late October. Legumes (e.g. groundnuts), which are normally planted a bit later (i.e. after millet, maize, sorghum, etc.), are harvested between late October and mid-November, depending on the variety planted. These differences in harvest dates may have contributed to the achievement of a better separation using the September and October images. Although a strict comparison between sensors was impossible due to data availability, results of the analysis conducted with Landsat data (i.e. optimal acquisition months/periods) indicate that, in general, optical data (irrespective of sensor) acquired in late season may be more useful in crop mapping than early season images.

5. Conclusion

This study explored the possibilities of improving agricultural land use mapping in West Africa through the integration of multi-temporal Landsat and RapidEye data. We conclude that the combined use of Landsat and RE produces better results compared to the use of either of the two. The inclusion of one high resolution RE time step resulted in a better separability between woodland and cropland as well as a better recognition of cropland structure.

The study also revealed that images acquired at the later stages of the cropping season (e.g. September, October) are more useful in separating crop types than those recorded during the early or peak stages.

Results obtained in this study are important for the operationalization of land use and land cover mapping in West Africa. Availability of multi-temporal RE acquired during the cropping season is expected to further improve agricultural land use mapping in the region.

6. Acknowledgements

This research was conducted within the framework of WASCAL with financial assistance from the German Federal Ministry of Education and Research (BMBF). Authors are grateful to the German Aerospace Center (DLR) and the RESA Science Team for providing RapidEye satellite images for RESA project number 493.

References

Bastiaanssen, W.G.M., Ali, S., 2003.
A new crop yield forecasting model based on satellite measurements applied across the Indus Basin, Pakistan. Agriculture, Ecosystems and Environment, 94: 321-340.

Breiman, L., 2001.
Random forests. Machine Learning, 45(1):5-32.

Calle, M.L., Urrea, V., 2010.
Letter to the Editor: Stability of Random Forest importance measures. Briefing in Bioinformatics, 12(1): 86-89.

Conrad C., Fritsch S., Zeidler J., Rücker G., Dech S.
Per-Field Irrigated Crop Classification in Arid Central Asia Using SPOT and ASTER Data. *Remote Sensing*. 2010; 2(4):1035-1056.

Conway, G., 2009.
The science of climate change in Africa: Impacts and adaptation. Grantham Institute for Climate Change, Discussion paper No. 1, London: Grantham Institute for Climate Change.

Gislason, P.O., Benediktsson, J.A., Sveinsson, J.R., 2006.
Random forests for land cover classification. Pattern Recognition Letters, 27:294-300.

Groten, S.M.E., 1993.
NDVI crop monitoring and early yield assessment of Burkina Faso. International Journal of Remote Sensing, 14:1495-1515.

GSS (Ghana Statistical Service), 2005.
2000 population and housing census: analysis of district data and implications for planning. Accra: GSS.

Liaw, A., Wiener, M., 2002.
Classification and regression by random Forest. R News, 2(3): 18-22.

Marsh, S. E., Walsh, J. L., Lee, C. T., Beck, L. R., Hutchinson, C. F., 1992.
Comparison of multitemporal NOAA-AVHRR and SPOT-XS satellite data for mapping land cover dynamics in the west African Sahel. International Journal of Remote Sensing, 13: 2997- 3016.

Roy, D.P., Ju, J., Mbow, C., Frost, P., Loveland, T., 2010.
Accessing free Landsat data via the Internet: Africa's challenge.
Remote Sensing Letters, 1: 111-117.

Schuster, C., Förster, M., Kleinschmit, B., 2012.
Testing the red edge channel for improving land-use classifications
based on high-resolution multi-spectral satellite data. *International
Journal of Remote Sensing*, 33(17): 5583-5599.

Turner, M.D. and Congalton, R.G., 1998.
Classification of multi-temporal SPOT-XS satellite data for mapping
rice fields on a West African floodplain. International Journal
of Remote Sensing, 19(1): 21-41.

Vintrou, E., Desbrosse, A., Begue, A., Traore, S. Baron, C., Lo Seen, D., 2012.
Crop area mapping in West Africa using landscape stratification
of MODIS time series and comparison with existing global land
products. International Journal of Applied Earth Observation
and Geoinformation, 14:83-93.

Mapping habitat diversity from multi-temporal RapidEye and RADARSAT-2 data in Brandenburg, Germany (Project ID: 451)

Stefan Erasmi[1], Guido Riembauer[1], Catrin Westphal[2]

[1] Georg-August-Universität Göttingen,
Inst. of Geography, Cartography, GIS & Remote Sensing Sect.,
37077 Göttingen, Germany
[2] Georg-August-Universität Göttingen,
Department for Crop Sciences, Agroecology,
37077 Göttingen, Germany

E-Mail: serasmi@uni-goettingen.de

Mapping habitat diversity from multi-temporal RapidEye and RADARSAT-2 data in Brandenburg, Germany

Stefan Erasmi, Guido Riembauer, Catrin Westphal

Land use and habitat type mapping from remote sensing provides key parameters for the analysis of ecosystem services and their interference with the landscape at different scales. An important issue in this context is the appropriate choice of sensors and acquisition windows throughout the growing period as well as the meaningful definition of thematic classes with regard to functional habitat types on the one hand and sensor resolution on the other. A combined approach based on high resolution RapidEye and polarimetric RADARSAT-2 multi-temporal intra-annual data for the year 2011 has been tested for the optimal combination of optical and SAR acquisitions in habitat type mapping. Semi-natural habitats could successfully be mapped together with the most relevant land use types. Best results were achieved by using a combination of RapidEye acquisitions at an early stage of the growing period together with a RADARSAT-2 image of mid-July. The results confirm the general capability of multi-temporal RapidEye data for habtitat mapping and underline the synergistic potential of combined optical / SAR data analysis in land use studies.

1. Introduction

Human-dominated landscapes are characterised by complex mosaics of agricultural, seminatural and natural habitats. Several studies have shown that landscape heterogeneity affects species diversity and ecosystem functions, such as pollination or biocontrol (Thies et al. 2003, Westphal et al. 2006, Tscharntke et al. 2012). Remote sensing based mapping and monitoring concepts are a prerequisite for any study that aims to account for spatial scales and environmental heterogeneity as an indicator for biological diversity. The implementation of remote sensing data in spatial statistical workflows is a standard task in many ecological studies (e.g. Gillespie et al. 2008, Perovic et al. 2010). Recent studies have shown the large capabilities of advanced optical satellite sensors like e.g. RapidEye for enhanced land cover type mapping (Schuster et al. 2012, Förster et al. 2011) and with special regard to conservation and landscape heterogeneity (Franke et al. 2012, Walz/Hou 2011). Also, the synergistic potential of optical and SAR data with regard to mapping measures of landscape structural heterogeneity has been subject to latest empirical studies (e.g. Bindel et al. 2012, Riedel et al. 2011). Landscape heterogeneity in the context of biodiversity research is mainly determined by the heterogeneity of more natural cover types (e.g. semi-natural habitats) but also by the heterogeneity of production land cover types which are mainly represented by arable fields and the annual crops grown in these fields (Fahrig et al. 2011). In many cases, these classes are neither well represented in remote sensing based land cover maps nor in official data of the regional authorities. Further to this, they are highly dynamic at a yearly to perennial base.

In this context, the present study investigated the potential of RapidEye data together with SAR-satellite data from RADARSAT-2 in order to map crop type and landscape heterogeneity within the framework of a biodiversity project in the federal state of Brandenburg, Germany (Schorfheide-Chorin). The study addresses two main research questions: (1) What is the optimal combination of acquisition dates and spectral parameters from optical satellite data for the detection of crop type and semi-natural habitats? (2) How can fully polarimetric SAR data contribute to an enhanced detection of habitat types that fulfil a specific function for certain species or species groups? In our case study, the selection of land use and habitat types complies with the ecosystem service of pollinating insects.

2. Data and methods

2.1 Study area and field data

The study area is located in the vicinity of the UNESCO-biosphere reserve "Schorfheide-Chorin" in Eastern Germany, about 50 kilometres North of Berlin. It is characterized by sander areas and moraines which are representative for the glacially formed lowlands of North-eastern Germany. The cultural landscape is dominated by intensive agricultural production fields (cropland and grassland) that are flanked by many small to large lakes, fens and mires. Besides intensive agriculture, there are considerable areas of extensive cultivation and semi-natural habitats.

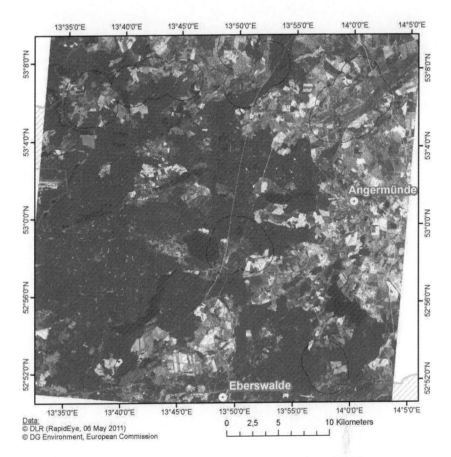

Figure 1: Study area „Schorfheide-Chorin" with outline of the UNESCO biosphere reserve (dashed) and outline of the 5 land use clusters under investigation (black).

Land use type and seminatural habitats were mapped in a field campaign in 2009 in 5 different land use clusters comprising more than 3000 polygons and covering a total area of 22891 ha. An overview of the study area is given in Fig. 1. A more detailed description is available from BEO (2011). Additionally, information on crop type as well as productive grassland was available for the investigation period (2011) from the agricultural ministry of the federal state of Brandenburg (MIL 2013). These two data sources were merged to a comprehensive ground truth data set for our investigation. The time span of two years between the data sources is not assumed to be critical, because we only used those semi-natural habitat types from the field survey that were assumed to be stable throughout the past few years. Further geometric-topological processing sieved out all polygons < 100 m^2 and all polygons < 500 m^2 with a perimeter-area-ratio of < 0.5 in order to account for the spatial resolution limitations of the satellite data. The resulting two-level classification system includes 6 general land use types (GLUT) at the first level and 18 habitat subtypes at the second level that are representative for the relevant habitat types and subtypes within the scope of the investigation (see tab. 1).

GLUT_ID	GLUT_Name	Subtpye_ID	Subtype_Name
		11	Clover
1	Grassland	12	Grassland (int.)
		13	Meadows
		20	Grassland (ext.)
2	Seminatural habitats	23	Wetland
		22	Fallow
4	Water	40	Water
		61	Hedges
6	Bushland	62	Alleys
		63	Trees outside forest
		64	Scrupland
7	Urban	70	Urban
		81	Winter wheat
		82	Summer grain
8	Cropland	83	Corn (maize)
		84	Legumes
		85	Rapeseed
		86	Other

Table 1: Two-level classification system for the study area "Schorfheide-Chorin".

2.2 Satellite data

In total, six RapidEye level 1B and four RADARSAT-2 scenes (fine beam Quad polarization) were successfully acquired during the growing season 2011. The processing of the RapidEye data included rigorous orthorectification after Toutin (2004), co-registration, atmospheric correction (ATCOR) and calculation of the Normalized Difference Vegetation Index (NDVI). All processing was done using PCI Geomatica 10.3 software. The output is a data set of six spectral parameters (blue, green, red, rededge, NIR, NDVI) at 5 m spatial resolution for each acquisition (t1 to t6, see fig. 2). However, for analysis, only for parameters were used (green, rededge, NIR, NDVI) to minimized redundancy in the input variables.

RADARSAT-2 single look complex (SLC) data were filtered using the SCL Gaussian DE MAP Filter (Nezry/Yakam Simen 1999). Filtering was followed by a "Pauli coherent decomposition" of the fully polarimetric SLC data set in terms of elementary scattering mechanisms (Cloude/Pottier 1996). Geometric and radiometric calibration (sigmaθ, dB) together with mosaicking of a pair of two adjacent scenes resulted in a dataset of seven polarimetric layers (HH, HV, VH, VV, Pauli1, Pauli2, Pauli3) at 15 m spatial resolution for each acquisition period (t1, t2, see fig. 2). All SAR processing was done using ENVI/SarScape4.4 software. Figure 2 illustrates the distribution of the data acquisitions for both sensors along the growing period from April to mid of July. Due to weather constraints, no optical acquisitions were possible after 29th June 2011. The availability of RADARSAT-2 data was limited by the provider.

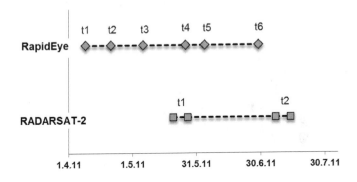

Figure 2: Overview of acquisitions for RapidEye and RADARSAT-2 data.

2.3 Classification workflow

The classification concept builds on the object (or patch) as the smallest entity. This means that each set of parameters from the optical and SAR data is examined at the patch-level (polygons) of the existing ground truth base map. This ensures that every single object in the ground truth data base is assigned a single land use type and within-field heterogeneity or mis- assignments are minimized. In the present study, spatial statistics (mean, range, standard deviation) were calculated at the patch level for each spectral and polarimetric parameter using standard GIS software (ArcGIS10.0). The outcome was a database of 114 independent variables that built the input for the classifier. The variables were grouped by date of acquisition and were systematically evaluated using different combinations of acquisitions in a classification and regression tree (CART) algorithm (Breiman et al. 1984). Overall, 27 combinations were tested (Table 2). Training data were selected from the ground truth data set using a random split-sample validation approach with 30 % training and 70 % validation samples. Accuracy of the classification result was accounted for by calculating the overall accuracy assessment (OAA) as well as producer's accuracy (PA) and Kappa's coefficient. Additionally, in order to evaluate the best predictors, a normalized importance factor (NI) was computed based on the importance of each independent variable for the regression tree weighted over the number of classification attempts where the variable was used:

$$NI_p = \sum_{i=1}^{n} \left(\frac{I_{p,i}}{n}\right), \qquad \text{with}$$

NI_p = normalized Importance of independent variable / parameter p
$I_{p,i}$ = importance of parameter p in classification i
n = number of classifications with parameter p as independent variable

RapidEye (RE) acquisitions	No. of RE observations	RADARSAT-2 (RS) acquisitions	No. of RS observations	CART-ID
t1	1			1
t2	1			2
t3	1			3
t4	1			4
t5	1			5
t6	1			6
t1+t3	2			7
t3+t5	2			8
t1+t2	2			9
t2+t3	2			10
t1+t5	2			11
t1+t2+t3	3			12
t1+t3+t5	3			13
t1+t3+t5+t6	4			14
all	6			15
		t1	1	16
		t2	1	17
		t1+t2	2	18
t1+t3	2	t1	1	19
t1+t3	2	t2	1	20
t1+t3	2	t1+t2	2	21
t3+t5	2	t1	1	22
t3+t5	2	t2	1	23
t3+t5	2	t1+t2	2	24
t1+t3+t5+t6	4	**t1**	1	25
t1+t3+t5+t6	4	t2	1	26
t1+t3+t5+t6	4	t1+t2	2	27

Table 2:   Summary of classification runs for different combinations of RapidEye and RADARSAT-2 observations (see figure 2 for details on acquisition dates)

3. Results

Based on the input dataset a subset of 27 meaningful combinations of acquisition data and sensors was made in order to reduce the data amount for classification. Meaningful refers to the selection of data acquisitions where special emphasis was on the inclusion of the most relevant growth and management stages in crop / grassland production (e.g. mowing in grassland, flowering of rapeseed). The classification results at the level of the general land use types yielded considerable variation in OAA and PA (Fig. 3). OAA ranges between 70 and 88 %

and shows strong variation for the RapidEye classifications depending on data acquisitions. Highest OAA (85.39 %) for RapidEye data was achieved using a combination of four dates (CART-ID 14, see table 2) covering the entire observation period from 09th April to 29th June in nearly equal time steps (compare fig. 2). Single date classifications performed best for the earliest acquisition (CART-ID 1: 9th April, OAA 80.21 %) and worst for CART-ID 4 (26th May, OAA 70.17 %). Highest OAA for RADARSAT-2 data was reached with CART-ID 17 (7th/14th July, OAA 83.05 %). Overall, the best classification results was attained with a combination of four RapidEye dates and both RADARSAT-2 acquisitions (CART-ID 27, OAA 88.17 %, Kappa 0.82). Class accuracy (PA) highly differs between the land use types with highest accuracy for grassland and lowest for semi-natural habitats in all classification attempts. Highest PA for semi-natural habitats is accomplished with two RapidEye dates (CART-ID 11, PA 72.31 %), but overall, the results are weak for this class with a mean PA for all combinations of 50.16 %.

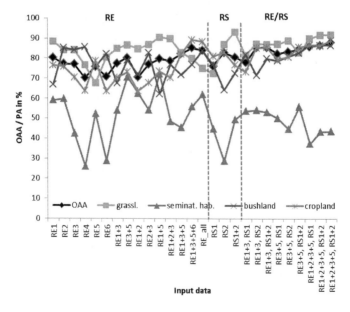

Figure 3: Overall accuracy (OAA) and producer's accuracy (PA) for selected combinations of data acquisition and sensor (RE = RapidEye / RS = RADARSAT-2) for the classification of general land use types (GLUT).

At the level of the habitat subtypes the best OAA again was reached with CART-ID 27 (OAA 71.28, Kappa 0.66) but, in general, the results are poor compared to the GLUT classifications. Moreover, all classifications completely failed in four and up to seven subtypes with a PA of 0 %. This is why an adjusted classification scheme was developed for the remaining classification attempts as a compromise of spectral and thematic information in the dataset. The results for the aggregated habitat subtypes are summarized in figure 4. For reasons of readability, only most relevant data combinations are included. Highest OAA was observed for CART-ID 20 (OAA 84.01 %, Kappa 0.80) which comprises a combination of two early RapidEye scenes with the second RARDARSAT-2 acquisition. In general, combined RapidEye-/RADARSAT-2 classifications maximized the OAA compared to single sensor attempts. The class accuracy shows high variation with highest PA for grassland as well as rapeseed and lowest for other crops which comprises a collection of all remaining crop types that were considered of minor importance for this study. Due to the failure of the detailed classification of habitat subtypes, the class semi-natural habitats was aggregated again to the top level of general land use types. However, the PA of this class significantly increased up to 78.87 % with a mean PA for all combinations of 57.15 %.

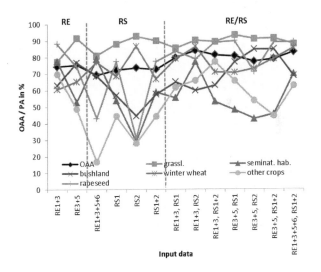

Figure 4: Overall accuracy (OAA) and producer's accuracy (PA) for selected combinations of data acquisition and sensor (RE = RapidEye / RS = RADARSAT-2) for the classification of habitat subtypes.

The second part of analysis focused on the importance of input parameters for the decision tree classifier and the classification result. The CART algorithm computes a measure of importance within the regression tree for every single independent variable. The normalized importance factor (NI) that has been developed in this study summarizes the importance of any independent variable over all classification runs. The values of NI for the best 15 variables are summarized in figure 5. RADARSAT-2 data feature the highest relative importance for all CART runs. Here, the HV-cross-polarized acquisition of 20/27th May was ranked highest with a value of 1.0, meaning that this variable owns the highest information content in any classification combination that included this variable. Overall, the May acquisition of RADARSAT-2 contains the three most important independent variables for the CART. RapidEye data proofed to be important throughout the growing period whereas the image of 6th May gains the highest cumulated importance regarding all spectral parameters.

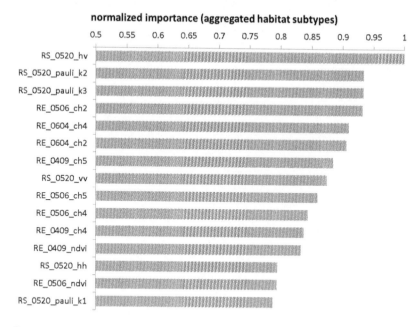

Figure 5: Normalized importance factor of spectral and polarimetric parameters for all classifications of aggregated habitat subtypes. A value of 1.0 means that the parameter shows highest relative importance (100 %) in all CART runs.

The results of the classification at the level of the GLUT proof the general ability of RapidEye data for mapping and monitoring land use type in a heterogeneous agricultural landscape. The quality of mapping considerably increases with the availability of multiple datasets for the growing period. However, high accuracy could be obtained with single and double date observations, where acquisitions at an early stage during the growing season yielded highest accuracy assessments.

The detection of (semi-natural) habitat subtypes for pollinating insects was limited by the spectral, temporal and spatial resolution (minimum mapping unit) of the underlying dataset. In the present case, additional optical acquisitions during the summer time were hampered by weather constraints. Fortunately, the RapidEye time series could be complemented and extended by RADARSAT-2 data. Here, it could be demonstrated, that high resolution polarimetric SAR data provide a considerable potential for synergistic optical / SAR habitat type mapping. Our results show an increase in OAA as well as in PA for all relevant classes when the RapidEye time series were complemented by RADARSAT-2 data. Furthermore, it was revealed that the best classification is not a result of the number of available acquisitions but of the careful choice of appropriate dates within the growing season. Here, the best of all results was obtained by using a combination of only two optical scenes, early during the growing season (9th April and 6th May), complemented by a polarimetric SAR image mosaic later in the growing period (7/14th July, see figure 6).

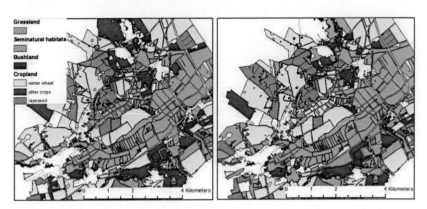

Figure 6: Comparison of ground truth data set (left) and classification result of CART-ID 20 (right).

Acknowledgements

We thank the German Aerospace Center (DLR) and RapidEye AG for the kind provision of the RapidEye data from the RapidEye Science Archive (RESA) within the project RESA-451. We further thank the Canadian Space Agency (CSA) and MacDonald, Dettwiler and Associates Ltd. for the kind provision of the RADARSAT-2 data within the project SOAR-5040.

References

BEO (2011).
Biodiversity Exploratories - Exploratories for large-scale
and long-term functional biodiversity research.
URL: http://www.biodiversity-exploratories.de/
(last access: 12 January 2013).

Bindel, Marcus; Hese, Sören; Berger, Christian; Schmullius, Christiane;
Bostater, Jr. Charles R.; Neale, Christopher M. U. et al. (2012).
Evaluation of red-edge spectral information for biotope mapping using
RapidEye: SPIE (Proc. SPIE 8174, Remote Sensing for Agriculture,
Ecosystems, and Hydrology XIII, 81740X (October 07, 2011)).

Breiman, Leo; Friedman, Jerome H.; Olshen, Richard A.; Stone, Charles J.
(1984).
Classification and regression trees. Belmont, California:
Wadsworth Publishing Company.

Cloude, SR; Pottier, E. (1996).
A review of target decomposition theorems in radar polarimetry. In:
IEEE TRANSACTIONS ON GEOSCIENCE AND REMOTE SENSING
34 (2), S. 498-518.

Förster, M.; Schuster, C.; Sonnenschein, R.; Bahls, A.; Kleinschmit, B. (2011).
Möglichkeiten der Erfassung von Landbedeckung und Vegetations-
gesellschaften mittels RapidEye-Daten. In: Erik Borg (Hg.): RapidEye
Science Archive - erste Ergebnisse. Tagungsband ; Neustrelitz,
23. - 24. März 2011, Orangerie Neustrelitz. Berlin: Gito, S. 3-17.

Franke, J.; Keuck, V.; Siegert, F. (2012).
Assessment of grassland use intensity by remote sensing to support
conservation schemes. In: *JOURNAL FOR NATURE CONSERVATION*
20 (3), S. 125-134.

Gillespie, T. W.; Foody, G. M.; Rocchini, D.; Giorgi, A. P.; Saatchi, S. (2008).
Measuring and modelling biodiversity from space.
In: *PROGRESS IN PHYSICAL GEOGRAPHY* 32 (2), S. 203-221.

MIL (2013).
Ministerium für Infrastruktur und Landwirtschaft - Ansprechpartner.
URL: http://www.mil.brandenburg.de/cms/detail.php/bb1.c.138832.de
(last access: 12 January 2013).

Nezry, E.; Yakam Simen, F. (1999).
A family of distribution-entropy MAP speckle filters for polarimetric
SAR data, and for single or multi-channel detected and complex SAR
images. In: *Proceedings of the CEOS SAR Workshop* (ESA SP-450).

Perovic, D. J.; Gurr, G. M.; Raman, A.; Nicol, H. I. (2010).
Effect of landscape composition and arrangement on biological control
agents in a simplified agricultural system: A cost-distance approach.
In: *BIOLOGICAL CONTROL* 52 (3), S. 263-270.

Riedel, T.; Elbertzhagen, I.; Menz, G.; Schmullius, C. (2011).
Synergetische Nutzung von hochauflösenden optischen und SAR
Daten zur automatisierten Ableitung von Landbedeckungsprodukten.
In: Erik Borg (Hg.): RapidEye Science Archive - erste Ergebnisse.
Tagungsband ; Neustrelitz, 23. - 24. März 2011, Orangerie Neustrelitz.
Berlin: Gito, S. 165-175.

Schuster, Christian; Förster, Michael; Kleinschmit, Birgit (2012).
Testing the red edge channel for improving land-use classifications
based on high-resolution multi-spectral satellite data. In:
INTERNATIONAL JOURNAL OF REMOTE SENSING 33 (17),
S. 5583-5599.

Thies, C.; Steffan-Dewenter, I.; Tscharntke, T. (2003).
Effects of landscape context on herbivory and parasitism at different
spatial scales. In: *OIKOS* 101 (1), S. 18-25.

Toutin, T. (2004).
Review article: Geometric processing of remote sensing images:
models, algorithms and methods. In: *INTERNATIONAL JOURNAL
OF REMOTE SENSING* 25 (10), S. 1893-1924.

Tscharntke, T.; Tylianakis, J. M.; Rand, T. A.; Didham, R. K.; Fahrig, L.;
Batary, P. et al. (2012).
Landscape moderation of biodiversity patterns and processes -
eight hypotheses. In: *BIOLOGICAL REVIEWS* 87 (3), S. 661-685.

Walz, U.; Hou, W. (2011).
Charakterisierung der Landschaftsvielfalt mit RapidEye-Daten -
Erste Ergebnisse und Erfahrungen. In: Erik Borg (Hg.):
RapidEye Science Archive - erste Ergebnisse. Tagungsband ;
Neustrelitz, 23. - 24. März 2011, Orangerie Neustrelitz. Berlin: Gito,
S. 75-88.

Westphal, C.; Steffan-Dewenter, I.; Tscharntke, T. (2006).
Bumblebees experience landscapes at different spatial scales: possible
implications for coexistence. In: *OECOLOGIA* 149 (2), S. 289-300.

Object-Based Analysis of Multi-Temporal RapidEye Images for Landscape Monitoring
(Project ID: 441)

Wei Hou, Ulrich Walz
Leibniz Institute of Ecological Urban and Regional Development (IOER),
Dresden, D-01217, Germany

E-Mail: w.hou@ioer.de, u.walz@ioer.de

Object-Based Analysis of Multi-Temporal RapidEye Images for Landscape Monitoring

Wei Hou, Ulrich Walz

The main aim of this study is to develop methods for detecting landscape patterns using multi-temporal RapidEye data and a high resolution digital elevation model derived from Airborne Laser Scanning (ALS). Our study implements an object-based classification methodology on two spatial scales. The main classes were first classified using RapidEye time series data, including forest, grassland, farmland, water bodies, and settlement. Small-scale habitats, e.g. hedges, copses, tree rows and single trees, were then detected by integrating the main scale classification results into high resolution elevation data. The results show that the strategy is effective for detecting small-scale habitats. The incorporation of the third (altitude) dimension can enhance landscape structure monitoring. The next step is to test the methodology in a larger area and on different acquisition dates.

1. Introduction

Monitoring habitats is a critical component in an informed process for assessing not only the conservation status of protected areas (Kremen et al. 1994), but also the threat to biodiversity at landscape scale (United Nations 1993: Article 7). Indices on land cover and landscape structure can be used as indicators for biodiversity (Tasser et al. 2008; Turner et al. 2003; Walz 2011). Detecting and monitoring small-scale landscape elements is a challenge in regular monitoring. Nevertheless, these elements play an important role as habitats and elements of biotope networks. Remotely sensed images have frequently been used to map and monitor changes in vegetation patterns and land cover (Kennedy et al. 2009; Turner et al. 2003; Xie et al. 2008). Nowadays, the spatial and spectral resolutions of remote sensing data are much improved, and data processing software has advanced rapidly. Since 2008, new remote sensing data from the RapidEye satellite has became available, providing a new band with a wavelength of between 690nm-730nm, called Red Edge. RapidEye is a German, five satellite constellation; each satellite has five spectral bands (blue, green, red, red edge and near infrared) with a 6.5 meter nominal ground resolution. The red edge band has proved sensitive for the chlorophyll content of vegetation (Gitelson et al. 1996; Munden et al. 1994) and studies have been conducted to test the red edge band for improved variance measurement in vegetation, e.g. species separation and land-cover classification (Bindel et al. 2011; Schuster et al. 2012). The ability of RapidEye to capture multi-temporal images within a brief space of time can significantly improve the accuracy of classifying, for example, farmland (Tapsall et al. 2010). In addition, the integration of high resolution digital elevation data with RapidEye data provides new possibilities for monitoring landscape pattern including the third, altitude dimension.

In our project, a combination of different data sources and different classification algorithms were integrated in an object-based environment to develop methods for data analysis as a basis for regularly monitoring landscape structure. The focus is on data evaluation and the extraction of landscape elements from image and elevation data. The methodology was developed using eCognition software. Both object- and pixel-based algorithms were used on two spatial scales in the classification process. We adopted a multi-temporal approach to classify different crop plots and used high resolution digital elevation models to detect small-scale habitats. Furthermore, we tested a new vegetation index (REVI) based on red edge and near infrared bands for vegetation classification, especially for the extraction of forest areas.

2. Study area and data

The study area is located in south-eastern Germany, forming part of the German national park region "Saxon Switzerland". It is a mountainous area encompassing several types of land use structures and classes, including rural settlements and surrounding agriculture, forests, and others. It comprises a wide range of land-use types, but most of the area is covered by forests and fields. The River Elbe divides the area into a more forested area to the north and a more agricultural area to the south. In this test site it was possible to acquire sufficient ancillary data to implement and verify our methodology.

In this paper, RapidEye images from May 25 and August 1/31 2009 were used. The scenes were ordered as Level 3A without cloud or haze, resampled from the original ground sampling distance of 6.5m to 5m. Radiometric, sensor and geometric corrections have been applied to the data. A high resolution (1 m) digital elevation model (DEM) and a digital surface model (DSM) from airborne laser scanning (ALS) are available for this test site. While the DEM shows the height of the ground surface, DSM also contains vegetation and human artefacts such as buildings. To obtain object height information, we calculated the normalized digital surface model (nDSM) simply by subtracting the DEM from the DSM. For spectral testing samples and classification training, ancillary data was used, including a 2005 digital biotope map at scale 1:10.000 and ATKIS data from 2009 at scale 1:25.000.

3. Methodology

3.1 Image segmentation

Segmentation is the first step in object-based image classification. Generating meaningful image segments directly affects the post-classification process (Neubert et al. 2008). Among the many existing segmentation algorithms, the 'Multi-Resolution Image Segmentation' (MRIS) algorithm is frequently used in the Earth sciences. But the selection of appropriate scale parameters for segmentation depends strongly on trial and error. In order to evaluate the scale effect on RapidEye data, the additional tool 'Estimation of Scale Parameter' (ESP) was used for calculating the most suitable scale parameters for MRIS. In ESP tool local variance (LV) graphs are used to reveal the spatial structure of images. LV equals to the average value of standard deviation in all image segments (for details of ESP see Drăguţ et al. 2010). All bands from the May 25 image were individually tested in the ESP algorithm, while other parameters were held constant (compactness 0.5 and shape 0.1). In this study the initial process was to segment the whole image into the smallest homogeneous objects, and then to link all image objects to two organizational levels. The finest scale value of 22 was set in MRIS, which was obtained from the blue and red edge band. In order to eliminate the ambiguous border of settlement, an ATKIS layer with the settlement area was integrated into the segmentation process.

3.2 Image objects classification

Two classification scales

A hierarchical classification approach was implemented in this study, in which image objects are linked to specific operational levels. All land-use classes were organized top-down on two scales. An overview of the proposed methodology used for classification and detection can be seen in figure 1. On main scale, the focus is on a consistent strategy of land use classification which is transferable to RapidEye scenes from different time series. The classification process is mainly affected by the acquisition dates of RapidEye data. On detailed scale, special focus is on developing methods for detecting small-scale habitats from the high resolution normalized digital surface model (nDSM).

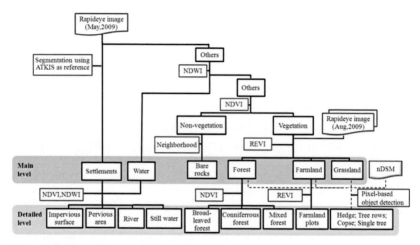

Figure 1: Scheme of the proposed methodology.

Classification of main classes with image indices

At first ATCOR2 was used for atmospheric correction to make the multi-temporal datasets comparable, (Richter/Schläpfer 2009). Then two indices frequently used in vegetation and water classification were calculated: the Normalized Difference Vegetation Index NDVI and the Normalized Difference Water Index NDWI (McFeeters 1996). To broaden the feature space, another index based on red edge band was developed: the Red Edge Vegetation Index (REVI, Equation 1).

Equation 1: REVI= $(\rho NIR) / (\rho RE)^{2}$; where ρ= reflectance value

In order to compare the spectral reflectance patterns between forest and grassland, the land use classes of forest and grassland from ATKIS were chosen as samples. The average value of the REVI and NDVI was calculated on a multi-temporal layerstack from 3 RapidEye images for forest and grassland, and the standard deviation values were shown as error bars (Fig. 2). The separability based on Jeffries–Matusita distances between forest and grassland classes were calculated in ERDAS. The average divergence using three REVI layers is 1350 and average divergence using NDVI layers is 1090. The measures of separability and figure 2 reveal that there is significant difference on REVI between forest and grassland in May and August; on the other hand, the NDVI value of grassland is not as stable as REVI, even mixed with forest classes in May.

However, the REVI values on multi-temporal images for the samples of forest sub-classes (broad-leaved forest, coniferous forest, and mixed forest) were overlapped. So the optimal solution is to use REVI firstly to differentiate forest and grassland on main scale and then to use NDVI to classify forest sub-classes on the detailed scale.

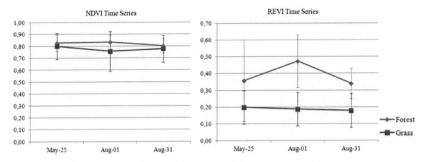

Figure 2: Comparing of REVI and NDVI value for forest and grassland.

Multi-temporal farmland classification

Because of seasonal changes in plants, a multi-temporal approach could be used to classify crops according to changes in spectral signals. In our study area, three types of farmland can be visually identified by false color composition with band 5, 4, 2 (Fig. 3). Since every year different crops will be planted in this region, we didn't look further into the crop types. Both NDVI and REVI can indicate the seasonal changes of farmland plots. From every farmland plot typical samples were chosen for the calculation of average and standard deviation of NDVI and REVI. In figure 3 we can see, from May to August both NDVI and REVI signal for farmland1 show an increasing trend contrary to the decreasing trends for farmland2 and farmland3, which makes farmland1 easier to differentiate. In May there is more REVI signal difference to distinguish farmland2 and farmland3 comparing to NDVI. The varying REVI in May and August is a significant feature, which enables farmland classes to be distinguished. In our research REVI was used to indicate change trends for farmland classes.

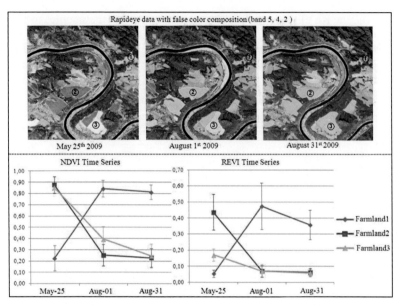

Figure 3: Comparison of the REVI pattern for differentiating farmland classes.

Detection of small-scale landscape elements from high resolution nDSM

Small vegetation elements like hedges, copses, tree rows, and single trees can be considered important biotopes in agricultural landscapes. They are defined by an area less than 0.5-1 hectare, a minimum width of 5 m and occurrence in open landscape, isolated from forest (BfN 2002). Hedges are defined as shrub-dominated structures in crop fields or meadows/pastures, while a copse is characterized by several or dominating trees in the vegetation stand and the covering of trees exceeds 40%. The definition of a tree row is a line of trees outside a closed wood stock. The average height of forest in the study area is about 16 m, and 40% of the average height of forest is 6.4m. From the definitions we see that their spectral characteristics are very similar, because they are all vegetation stocks with differing inner structures. They can be differentiated in terms of shape and height. Hedges are relatively lower than other elements because they consist mostly of shrubs. While copses contain trees and shrubs, tree rows consist only of trees. Tree rows are long and narrow in shape, so that this characteristic can be used to distinguish them from the two other types of landscape element. According to the definitions and experience in this test site, the distinguishing conditions for these small-scale elements can be summed up as follows (Table 1):

Biotope type	Hedge	Single tree	Copse	Tree row
Area	< (0.5-)1 ha	< (5-)10 m²; area of a single tree estimated about 5-10 m²	10 m² < area < (0.5-)1 ha;	< (0.5-)1 ha
Average Height	< 6.4 m	> 6.4 m	> = 6.4 m	> 6.4 m
Shape				length/width > 3 length >25 m width > 5m

Table 1: Concluded description of small-scale biotopes.

These features were translated into membership functions for each biotope class using fuzzy logic. Overlaying the classification result on the main scale with nDSM data, small-scale biotopes could be detected in open fields (farmland and grassland) on a detailed scale. However, the nDSM data allowed tree rows to be detected only as single trees. This being the case, the linearity of tree rows could not be used to distinguish them. For this reason, the pixel-based object resizing algorithm was used to create buffers according to the assumed distance between objects to be considered as constituting a row. Afterwards all candidates' pixels and the buffer around them were merged in order to connect up the single trees. In a next step, the length and length/width of features were used to differentiate tree rows, and, finally, the border of tree rows was smoothed and all candidate objects shrunk back to the original size.

4. Results

To assess classification result, ATKIS and the digital biotope map were consulted as ground-truth data. To assess the accuracy of each class the F1-measure was used. It represents the harmonic mean between precision (p) and recall(r) for each class i, because recall and precision are evenly weighted (Anindya et al. 2009). It is defined as equation 2.

Equation 2:

$$(F_1)_i = \frac{2 \times p_i \times r_i}{p_i + r_i}$$

p_i = *objects correctly classified as class i /*
(objects correctly classified as class i+
objects falsely classified as class i);
r_i = *objects correctly classified as class i /*
ground reference objects in class i.

On the main scale, the classification result was compared with ATKIS. Since settlements are extracted from ATKIS data, we didn't assess settlement classification accuracy. The assessment result (Table 2) shows relatively high accuracy on main scale. Grassland is considered in the classification process as consistent vegetation without seasonal change, but in reality some grassland plots have been moved during this period. This may lead to the misclassification as farmland. In this study area most bare areas are located in hilly forest and interspersed with trees, which explains the low recall of the bare rock classification. In order to assess the classification result on detailed scale, 500 stratified random points were selected as reference according to the high resolution aerial photo. The overall accuracy on main scale are higher than on detailed scale (Table 2), which means RapidEye data is more suitable for land-use classification on a medium scale (grain size). In figure 4 we see that the farmland plots detected and some small-scale landscape elements are also visible in the aerial image.

On main scale	Bare rock	Grassland	Farmland	Water	Forest
Recall	0.63	0.83	0.97	0.97	0.96
Precision	0.83	0.87	0.95	0.85	0.95
F1	0.72	0.85	0.96	0.91	0.95
Overall accuracy	0.92				

On detailed scale	Pervious area	Impervious area	Farmland plots	River	Still water	Coniferous forest	Broad-leaved forest	Mixed forest
Recall	0.96	0.62	1	0.95	0.58	0.88	0.89	0.79
Precision	0.86	0.80	1	1	1	0.96	0.76	0.87
F1	0.91	0.70	1	0.97	0.73	0.92	0.82	0.83
Overall accuracy	0.89							

Table 2: Accuracy measurements for classification on main and detailed scale.

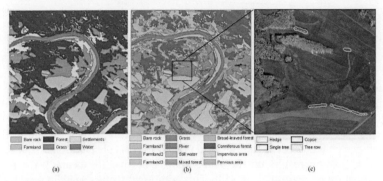

Bare rock	Forest	Settlements
Farmland	Grass	Water

Bare rock	Grass	Broad-leaved forest
Farmland1	River	Coniferous forest
Farmland2	Still water	Impervious area
Farmland3	Mixed forest	Pervious area

Hedge	Copse
Single tree	Tree row

(a) (b) (c)

Figure 4: (a) Classification result on main scale.
(b) Classification result on detailed scale.
(c) Small-scale landscape elements detection overlaid with aerial image.

After the classification, we used all forest and grassland segments to compare the feature distribution of REVI and NDVI (Fig. 5). In figure 5 we can see the roughly spectral boundaries between forest and grass on REVI layer. In our research, REVI index works better than NDVI for vegetation classification, especially for the extraction of forest mask. The possibility of acquiring multi-temporal images with short repetition interval and high-resolution makes RapidEye the ideal data source for regular agriculture monitoring. To expand the use of RapidEye data to a detailed scale, integrating high resolution DEM data could be a good choice. If vegetation is considered as part of the surface (relief and vegetation from the DSM), "surface roughness" can be used as a structural attribute, which can help enhance further land cover classifications. To improve the results, a further field inspection will be necessary to acquire more reliable ground truth data.

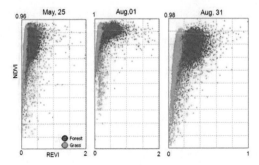

Figure 5: NDVI and REVI features space plot for forest and grassland.

5. Conclusions

Our work demonstrates the benefits and gains in information afforded by integration of multi-temporal RapidEye data and high resolution nDSM data in the segmentation and classification process. For the main land-use classes, the results show high overall accuracy up to 0.92, especially for vegetation classes. This is due to the newly incorporated red edge band and the multi-temporal approach. The comparison of signal reflectance patterns on REVI and NDVI reveals that incorporation of the red edge channel can greatly enlarge feature difference on REVI between forest and grassland. This observation is supported by classification results on the main scale. The overall accuracy for forest classification on main scale is 95%. This additional feature made it possible to extract a coincident forest mask with the ATKIS layer. In a next step, this vegetation index will be tested in a larger area and on a different acquisition date. On detailed scale, a promising pixel-based object detection concept was chosen to directly identify these small-scale landscape elements. The results fit very well with aerial photography, but to confirm the method, further field inspection is needed for small-scale habitats. The results can be used as a basis for indicators in the regular monitoring of changes in land cover and landscape structure and the evaluation of biodiversity on the landscape level.

Acknowledgements

The authors wish to thank the China Scholarship Council (CSC) for funding the PhD-work of Wei Hou. We also thank the German Aerospace Research Center (DLR) for enabling us to use the RapidEye-data.

References

Anindya, H., Ashish, G., Susmita, G., 2009.
Aggregation Pheromone Density Based Pattern Classification.
Fundam. Inf. 92, 345-362.

Bindel, M., Hese, S., Berger, C., Schmullius, C., 2011.
Evaluation of red-edge spectral information for biotope mapping using
RapidEye. In: Neale, C., Maltese, A. (Eds.), Proceedings of SPIE 8174,
Remote Sensing for Agriculture, Ecosystems and Hydrology XIII,
Prague, Volume 8174, 81740X-81740X-9.

BfN (Bundesamt für Naturschutz [Federal Agency for Nature Conservation]),
2002.
A system for the survey of biotope and land use types,
Bonn-Bad Godesberg 166 p.

Drăguț, L., Tiede, D., Levick, S.R., 2010.
ESP: a tool to estimate scale parameter for multiresolution image
segmentation of remotely sensed data. International Journal
of Geographical Information Science 24, 859-871.

Gitelson, A.A., Merzlyak, M.N., Lichtenthaler, H.K., 1996.
Detection of Red Edge Position and Chlorophyll Content
by Reflectance Measurements Near 700 nm. Journal of Plant
Physiology 148, 501-508.

Kennedy, R.E., Townsend, P.A., Gross, J.E., Cohen, W.B., Bolstad, P.,
Wang, Y.Q., Adams, P., 2009.
Remote sensing change detection tools for natural resource managers:
Understanding concepts and tradeoffs in the design of landscape
monitoring projects. Remote Sensing of Environment 113, 1382-1396.

Kremen, C., Merenlender, A.M., Murphy, D.D., 1994.
Ecological Monitoring: A Vital Need for Integrated Conservation
and Development Programs in the Tropics. Conservation Biology
8, 388-397.

McFeeters, S.K., 1996.
The use of the Normalized Difference Water Index (NDWI) in the
delineation of open water features. International Journal of Remote
Sensing 17, 1425-1432.

Munden, R., Curran, P.J., Catt, J.A., 1994.
The relationship between red edge and chlorophyll concentration in the Broadbalk winter wheat experiment at Rothamsted. International Journal of Remote Sensing 15, 705-709.

Neubert, M., Herold, H., Meinel, G., Blaschke, T., Lang, S., Hay, G.J., 2008.
Assessing image segmentation quality – concepts, methods and application. In: Cartwright, W., Gartner, G., Meng, L., Peterson, M.P. (eds.). Object-Based Image Analysis. Springer Berlin Heidelberg, 769-784.

Richter, R., Schläpfer, D. (eds.) 2009.
Atmospheric / Topographic Correction for Satellite Imagery (ATCOR-2/3 User Guide, Version 8.2, August 2012).

Schuster, C., Förster, M., Kleinschmit, B., 2012.
Testing the red edge channel for improving land-use classifications based on high-resolution multi-spectral satellite data. International Journal of Remote Sensing 33, 5583-5599.

Tapsall, B., Pavel, M., Kadim, T., 2010.
Analysis of rapideye imagery for annual landcover mapping as an aid to European Union (EU) common agricultural policy. In: Wagner W., Székely, B. (Eds.), ISPRS Technical Commission VII Symposium - 100 Years ISPRS Advancing Remote Sensing Science. IAPRS, Vienna, 568-573.

Tasser, E., Sternbach, E., Tappeiner, U., 2008.
Biodiversity indicators for sustainability monitoring at municipality level: An example of implementation in an alpine region. Ecological Indicators 8, 204-223.

Turner, W., Spector, S., Gardiner, N., Fladeland, M., Sterling, E., Steininger, M., 2003.
Remote sensing for biodiversity science and conservation. Trends in Ecology Evolution 18, 306-314.

Walz, U., 2011.
Landscape Structure, Landscape Metrics and Biodiversity. Living Reviews in Landscape Research 5, 1-35.

United Nations, 1993.
  Multilateral Convention on Biological Diversity (with annexes).
  Concluded at Rio de Janeiro on 5 June 1992. – United Nations -
  Treaty Series, 1760: 142-382.

Xie, Y., Sha, Z., Yu, M., 2008.
  Remote sensing imagery in vegetation mapping: a review. Journal
  of Plant Ecology 1, 9-23.

Littoral bottom mapping in lakes using multitemporal RapidEye data
(Project ID: 455_2)

Sebastian Rößler, Patrick Wolf, Thomas Schneider, Arnulf Melzer
Technische Universität München, Limnologische Station,
82393 Iffeldorf, Germany

E-Mail: sebastian.roessler@mytum.de

Littoral bottom mapping in lakes using multitemporal RapidEye data

Sebastian Rößler, Patrick Wolf, Thomas Schneider, Arnulf Melzer

Global warming increases the water temperatures of the Central European lakes. This may alter the composition of optical active water constituents – the inherent optical properties (IOPs) of the water column, but can also lead to change in species composition of submersed aquatic macrophytes. In Bavaria (Southern Germany), an increasing spread of endemic species like Najas marina and invasive plants like Elodea nuttallii can be observed which supports the assumption that these species benefits from rising water temperatures. Spatial and temporal high-resolution spaceborne sensors like RapidEye can be used to observe the seasonal highly variable growth of macrophytes on littoral areas. During the growing season 2011, RapidEye imagery was acquired monthly and processed towards littoral bottom coverage and IOPs using the bio-optical inversion model BOMBER and additional spectro-radiometrical in situ measurements carried out with RAMSES underwater spectrometers. The results show a good performance for the separation between vegetated areas and bare sediment, however a discrimination of species is still challenging.

1. Introduction

The water quality (nutrient conditions) of lakes can be coupled to the occurrence of specific macrophytes (Melzer 1999), and thus monitoring of these indicators for the trophic state are useful to detect changes in entire lake ecosystems at an early stage. Some invasive submersed aquatic plants are suspected to benefit from rising water temperatures due to global warming (Rahel/Olden 2008) and therefore offer the possibility to monitor these thermal changes as well. In the freshwater lakes of Bavaria (Southern Germany), an increased spread of invasive species like *Elodea nuttallii* and the expansion of indigenous species like *Najas marina* can be observed.

The spatially and temporally highly variable growth of these plants requires monitoring methods to cover large areas and rapid deployment. Until now, the identification of submersed macrophytes by remote sensing is only possible using hyperspectral airborne sensors (e.g. HyMap, ROSIS, APEX, HySpex) which offer the needed spectral and geometric resolution (Heege et al. 2003; Pinnel 2007).

Multispectral spaceborne imagery has been used successfully for bathymetric applications using Landsat TM (Bierwirth et al. 1993; Philpot 1989), IKONOS (Mishra et al. 2004; Stumpf et al. 2003) or SPOT (Lafon et al. 2002). The mapping of benthic habitats by using multispectral data is mainly focussed on coral reefs (Andréfouët et al. 2003; Kanno 2011; Mumby et al. 1997) and marine macrophytes (Phinn et al. 2008). Only few works were performed on the littoral bottom mapping of lakes (Ackleson/Klemas 1987; Dogan et al. 2009; Sawaya et al. 2003). The integration of field investigations and spatially high resolution satellite imagery for the monitoring of macrophytes development with focus on the EU water framework directive has also been discussed (Malthus/Karpouzli 2003).

In this study, multi seasonal RapidEye data in combination with multi seasonal field investigations were used to derive bottom information like coverage and colonization of submerged macrophytes as well as inherent optical properties (IOPs) of the water column throughout the year. For this, *in situ* measured bottom reflectances were implemented in the bio-optical software BOMBER (Giardino et al. 2012) which corrects for the exponential decrease of light intensity due to the optically active water constituents Phytoplankton (CHL), suspended particulate matter (SPM) and coloured dissolved organic matter (cDOM) and finally performs a depth retrieval as well as spectral bottom unmixing.

2. Methods and Material

2.1 Study area

The study area is Lake Starnberg (47°55'N, 11°19'E) in Bavaria, southern Germany (Fig. 1) covering an area of 56 km². The lake was formed by the Isar-Loisach-Glacier during last glacial period (Fesq-Martin et al. 2008), which explains its great depth of 127.8 meters (on average 53.2 m). Spacious littoral terraces lie on the western shore of the lake and guided the selection of the test sites. For the demonstration purposes of this study an area near the municipality of Bernried was chosen due to dense coverage of *Najas marina* in depth from 1 to 5 meters. In shallow water areas, large populations of *Chara* spec. occur and are therefore also subject in this study for comparison of low and high growing macrophytes and as competitors within the ecosystem.

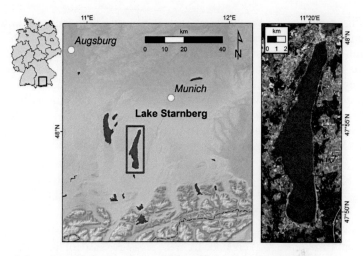

Figure 1: Location of Lake Starnberg and RapidEye image from 03/09/11

According to the nutrient content, Lake Starnberg can be classified as oligotrophic with an average primary production of 889 g C m^{-2} y^{-1}. Phytoplankton concentrations range between 2.4 to 4.8 µg l^{-1} in winter and 6 to 12 µg l^{-1} in summer, respectively (Pinnel 2007).

2.2 In situ data collection and processing

Spectro-radiometrical *in situ* measurements were performed in 2011 during the growing period of submersed aquatic plants (May to October) using three submersible RAMSES spectrometers (TRIOS). Two irradiance devices (ACC) and a radiance sensor (ARC), covering a spectral range from 320 to 950 nm with 3.3 nm intervals were used to measure hemispherical the upwelling (E$_u$) and downwelling irradiance (E$_d$) as well as the upwelling radiance (L$_u$) with a field of view of 7°.

Besides the mentioned invasive and expanding indigenous species, two other common macrophytes in Lake Starnberg were observed. Above (0+) and just below the water surface (0-), as well as just above the vegetation patches (b) simultaneous measurements of all three sensors were made from populations of *Chara* spec., *Elodea nuttallii*, *Potamogeton perfoliatus* and *Najas marina* as well as from uncovered sediment. The data was further processed to calculate subsurface remote sensing reflectance (r$_{rs}$), irradiance reflectance (r) of plants and the anisotropy of the underwater light field (Q).

The measurements below the water surface were made to include the water column and to obtain variations of concentration and of the IOPs during the year. Therefore, the E_d-measurements were inverted using the software WASI (Gege 2012) which is mainly based on the bio-optical model of Albert and Mobley (2003) for the radiative transfer in shallow waters. From r_{rs} measurements just below the water surface and directly above the macrophytes $r_{rs}{}^b$ (with nearly no water column in between) the deep-water remote sensing reflectance $r_{rs}{}^{dp}$ was estimated. For the latter, the equation of Lee et al. (1998) is solved for $r_{rs}{}^{dp}$ according to Eq. 1:

$$r_{rs}^{dp} = \frac{r_{rs} - r_{rs}^b \exp(-2K\Delta z)}{1 - \exp(-2K\Delta z)} \tag{1}$$

The depth difference Δz is obtained from the pressure sensor of the RAMSES E_d device (SN: 8109). The attenuation coefficient K is calculated from E_d-measurements in different depths (z_1 and z_2) using Eq. 2 (Maritorena 1996):

$$K = \frac{1}{\Delta z} \ln \frac{E_d(z_1)}{E_d(z_2)} \tag{2}$$

To evaluate the spectral separability of common macrophytes, their seasonal changing reflectances obtained by the above described RAMSES measurements were resampled to the spectral resolution of RapidEye and the M-statistic of Kaufman and Remer (1994) was used to calculate separability for all possible combinations of macrophyte classes. This index has been used in other studies for benthic mapping (O'Neill et al. 2011). μ is the mean and σ the standard deviation of r_{rs} for each spectral band of the classes 1 and 2 (Eq. 3):

$$M = (\mu_1 - \mu_2)/(\sigma_1 - \sigma_2) \tag{3}$$

To account for the seasonal development of different macrophyte reflectance (related to phenology), a wavelength dependent polynomial fit (2nd degree) was applied to the r_{rs}-spectra of vegetation. The time was used as x-value, each wavelength of the corresponding r_{rs}-spectra as y-value. Reliable bottom r_{rs}-spectra for each day of the year (DOY) were obtained as required for multi-seasonal RapidEye data processing.

2.3 RapidEye data and pre-processing

Within the RapidEye Science Archive (RESA) project no. 455, several scenes were acquired between May and October 2011 covering Lake Starnberg. The data were delivered as level 3A product tiles including standard radiometric correction and geocoding. The images were further normalized to top-of-atmosphere (TOA) reflectance using the recommendation given in the Product Specifications (RapidEye 2011) and subsequently mosaicked.

A simple atmospheric correction was applied assuming that the TOA-reflectance is the sum of contributions from Rayleigh scattering, aerosol scattering and the water leaving reflectance (R_w) lowered by the transmittance of the atmosphere (Gordon/Clark 1981). The wavelength dependent Rayleigh scattering was computed using the Rayleigh optical thickness (Hansen/Travis 1974), the Rayleigh scattering phase function (Doerffer 1992) and its relation to the forward/backward scattering angle (Gordon et al. 1983) depending on viewing and solar illumination directions (Mishra et al. 2005). The contribution of the aerosol was computed assuming that the water leaving reflectance in the near infrared (RapidEye Band 5) is essentially zero. The aerosol contribution to the other bands is calculated pixel based from the NIR-value using empirically defined factors from Gordon and Wang (1994) and has been developed on the combination of maritime and continental aerosol. Atmospheric correction was only applied to water areas which were extracted from the whole image using a threshold of the normalized difference water index (McFeeters 1996) greater than zero.

2.4 The bio-optical model BOMBER

The ENVI add-on BOMBER (Bio-Optical Model Based tool for Estimating water quality and bottom properties from Remote sensing images) has recently been published by Giardino et al. (2012) and relies on the model developed by Lee et al. (1998, 1999) with HYDROLIGHT (Mobley 1994) simulations. It can be run in a shallow water and a deep water mode. The shallow water mode requires additional bottom albedos for spectral unmixing as well as the apparent underwater sun zenith angle. Equation 4 summarizes the different contributions of the IOPs and the bottom reflectance (r_{rs}^{b}) as well as the attenuation coefficients for the up- and downwelling light to the subsurface remote sensing reflectance (r_{rs}) at a given depth (z) which are implemented in the shallow water model of BOMBER:

$$r_{rs} = r_{rs}^{dp}\left(1 - A_0 \exp\left[-\left(K_d + K_{uw}\right)z\right]\right) + A_1 r_{rs}^{b} \exp\left[-\left(K_d + K_{ub}\right)z\right] \qquad (4)$$

The contribution of the deep water (r_{rs}^{dp}) depends only on the IOPs (Lee et al. 1999), the factors A_0 and A_1 are weighting factors for the contribution of the water and the bottom to the received overall signal (Albert/Mobley 2003). The parameterization of the attenuation of downwelling irradiance (K_d) and the upwelling radiance coming from the water (K_{uw}) and the bottom (K_{ub}) is adapted from Lee et al. (1999). The transformation from the reflectance above (R_{rs}) to below the water surface (r_{rs}) is based on Lee et al. (1998).

BOMBER was only applied on shallow water areas. Land was masked using the normalized difference water index (NDWI) according to McFeeters (1996), values greater than 0 were assigned to water. Deep water was excluded based on a R_{rs}-threshold of 3% in the green wavelength region, lower values were masked. This masking results in different masks for each scene, thus only percent coverage was compared using the subpixel abundance of every pixel.

3 Results and discussion

3.1 In situ measurements

In situ measurements over different common macrophytes (*Chara* spec., *Elodea nuttallii*, *Potamogeton perfoliatus* and *Najas marina*) were carried out at Lake Starnberg during 2011 (Fig. 2 shows the reflectance development for three selected months).

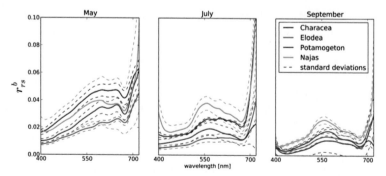

Figure 2: Seasonal variability of bottom r_{rs} of different macrophytes from May to September measured with RAMSES. The solid line shows the mean values, the dashed line shows the mean ± standard deviation.

In May, the differences in reflectance are caused mainly by the sediment since plants occur only sparsely. Regarding the standard deviations and the spectral shape, the curves are very similar. In July and September the coverage of *Characea, Elodea* and *Najas* was dense; only *Potamogeton perfoliatus* grows sparsely. The M-statistic (according to Eq. 3) was calculated for spectra shown in Fig. 2 (resampled to the spectral resolution of RapidEye) and compared in terms of species differentiation (Table 1, values greater than 1 indicate good separability, smaller values bad separability).

		Characea/ Elodea	*Characea/ Potamogeton*	*Characea/ Najas*	*Elodea/ Potamogeton*	*Elodea/ Najas*	*Potamogeton / Najas*
		May					
RapidEye Band	1	7.32	11.29	0.49	3.66	1.22	0.91
	2	10.16	694.18	0.57	4.13	1.37	0.76
	3	6.20	108.04	0.74	2.72	0.63	0.14
	4	5.10	1.56	0.37	2.91	0.74	0.45
	5	3.10	5.09	0.84	4.61	0.92	0.30
		July					
RapidEye Band	1	10.44	1.70	1.29	2.72	4.79	7.79
	2	8.04	1.94	2.73	3.37	10.14	35.54
	3	6.80	2.96	0.62	0.67	3.21	4.71
	4	42.72	9.78	0.42	1.94	2.38	3.41
	5	18.56	52.46	26.70	4.96	4.04	10.06
		September					
RapidEye Band	1	0.67	1.13	2.25	199.42	11.30	8.59
	2	0.53	1.23	2.59	12.26	50.11	16.19
	3	0.55	0.31	1.17	4.39	3.88	6.21
	4	0.08	1.62	3.07	7.74	1.66	2.31
	5	9.17	6.42	1.73	4.36	2.81	3.06

Table 1: M-statistic for all possible combinations of measured macrophytes reflectances (resampled to RapidEye), grey areas indicate bad separability (M < 1).

The following results concentrate on monitoring aspects for *Najas marina* and the competing *Chara* spec. population at the Bernried demonstration site since they are the dominant species at this littoral region of Lake Starnberg and BOMBER supports only three endmembers (including uncovered sediment) for spectral unmixing. According to the M-statistic, a best differentiation between *Chara* spec. and *Najas marina* can be made in September when all bands show a good separability.

For the application of BOMBER at the demonstration site Bernried, all measurements above *Najas marina* (19/05/11, 28/06/11, 27/07/11, 12/08/11, 03/09/11, 16/09/11 and 18/10/11) were interpolated according to the methods described above to derive bottom reflection for each day of the year (Fig. 3, right).

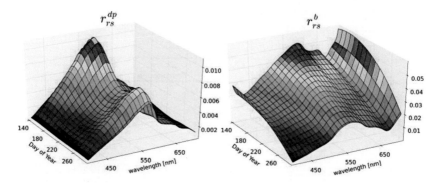

Figure 3: interpolated deep water r_{rs}^{dp}-spectra (left) and bottom r_{rs}^b-spectra of Najas marina (right) during growing season 2011 (based on in situ measurements).

The r_{rs}^{dp}-spectra (Fig. 3, left) were used to evaluate the atmospheric correction results (see 3.2). From the interpolated bottom reflectances of *Najas marina* for the growing period 2011 the spectra corresponding to the acquisition dates of RapidEye were resampled to the spectral resolution of RapidEye and included as possible endmember for the unmixing within the BOMBER processing. In the shallow water model of BOMBER, only three endmembers can be selected for bottom unmixing, thus only the dominant species for the test site were chosen next to a measured spectrum of pure sediment. In BOMBER, two bottom types (endmembers) are treated as fit-parameters, the third bottom type is adjusted that the sum equals 1 (100% coverage). Besides *Najas marina*, the low growing *Chara* spec. was chosen as endmember to be fitted. The adjusted third endmember was uncovered sediment (silty sand) measured at the test site in spring 2011 (Fig. 4).

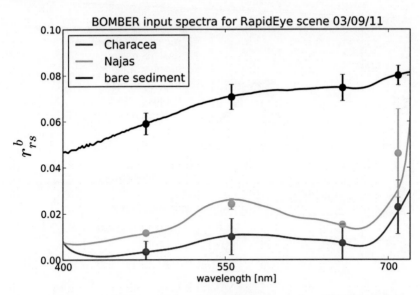

*Figure 4: Bottom r_{rs} used for unmixing of the RapidEye Scene from 03/09/11, circles
show the spectra resampled to RapidEye, error bars show standard deviation.*

3.2 RapidEye data

The performance of the atmospheric correction was tested on the result of the
RapidEye scene from 3rd September 2011. R_{rs} spectra were measured
simultaneously to image acquisition over shallow water and the associated deep
water reflection R_{rs}^{dp} was estimated from measured subsurface reflectance (r_{rs})
using Eq. 1. Both spectra were compared to image derived RapidEye spectra
after atmospheric correction (Fig. 5). The image derived R_{rs} are slightly higher
than the in situ measured ones (mean difference of +0.13% reflectance for all
bands).

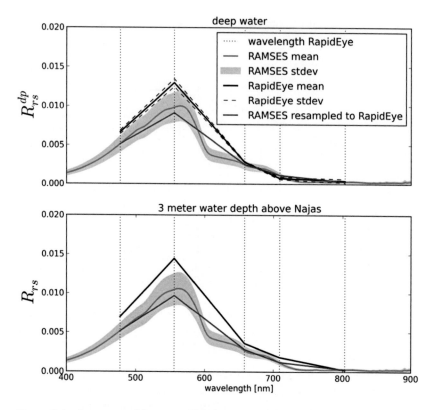

Figure 5: in situ measured R_{rs} over a Najas marina patch in 3 meter water depth (below) and derived deep water reflectance $R_{rs}{}^{dp}$ (above) were resampled to the spectral resolution of RapidEye (red curves) and compared to the image derived R_{rs} spectra after atmospheric correction (black lines). For the shallow water area only one pixel centered at the measurement site was used, the deep water reflection is the mean of 100 pixels (shown ± standard deviation) located nearby the test site.

For the shallow water mode of BOMBER, endmember spectra for *Najas marina* are taken from modelled reflectance spectra (Fig. 3, right) corresponding to the acquisition date. The resulting inversion and bottom unmixing result of the three allowed endmembers (in this case *Najas marina*, *Chara* spec., and uncovered sediment) is shown in Fig. 6 for three selected scenes acquired in 2011.

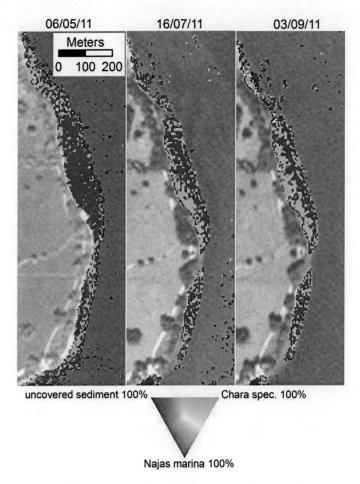

06/05/11 16/07/11 03/09/11

Meters
0 100 200

uncovered sediment 100% ———— Chara spec. 100%

Najas marina 100%

*Figure 6: result of bottom unmixing for three selected RapidEye subsets showing
the test site Bernried.*

A decreasing proportion of uncovered sediment can be observed from May to
September: the sum of subpixel abundance of uncovered sediment multiplied
with pixel area and divided with the whole classified area changed from 69.9% in
May to 60.1% in September. Consequently, the fractions of submersed
macrophytes increase (*Najas marina*: 16% to 17.1%; *Chara* spec.: 14.8% to
22.9%). *Chara* spec. occurs predominantly sparsely at lower water depths
(cyan areas in Fig. 6) and interspersed in *Najas marina* patches. Areas classified

as *Chara* spec. in greater depths (2-5m) are incorrectly classified *N. marina* patches which are known here to cover the whole shore area at this depth (mapped by diving). This misclassification of macrophytes with multispectral sensors has also been observed in other studies (Vahtmäe/Kutser 2007).

The resulting BOMBER derived concentrations for the shallow water area at the test site Bernried were compared to the concentrations derived by E_d-measurement inversions with WASI (Fig. 7). An overestimation of CHL and simultaneous underestimation of cDOM can be explained by their overlapping absorption bands in the blue wavelength domain (Mobley 1994). The large standard deviations show that an accurate estimate of water constituent concentrations is not possible. The WASI derived concentrations show lower errors and a seasonal development (expect for SPM).

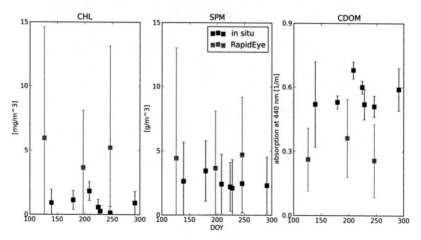

Figure 7: seasonal variability of the concentrations of phytoplankton (CHL), suspended particulate matter (SPM), and coloured dissolved organic matter (cDOM) from WASI inverted E_d-measurements (black squares) and BOMBER processed RapidEye images (red squares), error bars show standard deviation.

4. Conclusion

In this study, it has been shown that the bio-optical inversion model BOMBER (originally designed for hyperspectral images) can be applied on RapidEye imagery for littoral bottom mapping and the observation of seasonal changes in littoral coverage. In this study, this was achieved by building time dependent spectral libraries for *Chara* spec. and *Najas marina* for the growing season 2011.

Applying BOMBER to multitemporal RapidEye imagery can help to monitor the seasonal development from sparsely vegetated areas (May) to larger vegetated areas (September). In 2011, the maximum of macrophytes growth was assessed in September (mapped by diving). The retrieval of concentrations of water constituents using BOMBER didn't reveal good results. The derived concentrations showed strong deviations to the WASI inverted *in situ* measurements of E_d and the standard deviations were very high.

The main limitation of multispectral sensors like RapidEye is the spectral resolution which prevents a differentiation between different macrophytes. Here, the combination of multitemporal imagery and a phenological reflectance database presented in this study can be used to find a moment where the plants are best separable even on a multispectral image with broad bands. Another limitation of the BOMBER algorithm is caused by the attenuation which depends on IOPs and illumination conditions and controls the maximal depth of application due to scattering and absorption of the water body (approximately 5 meters in the case of Lake Starnberg). However this limitation also offers new possibilities. The *in situ* observations let expect a good separability chance when depth is used as decision threshold for species differentiation of *Chara* and *Najas*. This approach may be useful for implementation in object-based image analysis (OBIA) knowledge based rule sets.

Further works will focus on the investigation of water constituent concentrations by laboratory analysis to evaluate inversion results and to regionalize existing radiative transfer models. Echo sounders will be used to validate retrieved depths and to estimate biomass by distinguishing between vegetation surface and the bottom echo. A combination of the presented method with semi-empirical models based on logarithmic transformation (Rößler et al. 2012, 2013) is envisaged in order to include the biomass of invasive aquatic plants as well.

5. Acknowledgements

This project is funded by the Bavarian State Ministry of the Environment and Public Health under the number ZKL01Abt7_18457. Thanks to the RapidEye Science Archive (RESA) who provided us with data within the project no. 455. A special thanks to Claudia Giardino for providing the software BOMBER and to all colleagues from the Limnological Institute who helped us during field work.

6. References

Ackleson, S. G., Klemas, V., 1987.
Remote sensing of submerged aquatic vegetation in lower chesapeake bay: A comparison of Landsat MSS to TM imagery. Remote Sensing of Environment, 22(2):235-248.

Albert, A., Mobley, C., 2003.
An analytical model for subsurface irradiance and remote sensing reflectance in deep and shallow case-2 waters. Optics Express, 11(22):2873-2890.

Andréfouët, S., Kramer, P., Torres-Pulliza, D., Joyce, K. E., Hochberg, E. J., Garza-Pérez, R., Mumby, P. J., Riegl, B., Yamano, H., White, W. H., Zubia, M., Brock, J. C., Phinn, S. R., Naseer, A., Hatcher, B. G., Muller-Karger, F. E., 2003.
Multi-site evaluation of IKONOS data for classification of tropical coral reef environments. Remote Sensing of Environment, 88:128-143.

Bierwirth, P. N., Lee, T. J., Burne, R. V., 1993.
Shallow sea-floor reflectance and water depth derived by unmixing multispectral imagery. Photogrammetric Engineering and Remote Sensing, 59(3):331-338.

Doerffer, R., 1992.
Imaging spectroscopy for detection of chlorophyll and suspended matter. In: Toselli, F., and Bodechtel, J., (Eds.). Imaging Spectroscopy: Fundamentals and Prospective Applications, Kluwer Academic Publishers, pp. 215-257.

Dogan, O. K., Akyurek, Z., Beklioglu, M., 2009.
Identification and mapping of submerged plants in a shallow lake using quickbird satellite data. Journal of Environmental Management, 90(7):2138-2143.

Fesq-Martin, A., Lang, A., Peters, M., 2008.
Der Starnberger See - Natur- und Vorgeschichte einer bayerischen Landschaft. Pfeil-Verlag, p.

Gege, P., 2012.
Estimation of phytoplankton concentration from downwelling irradiance measurements in water. Israel Journal of Plant Sciences, 60(1-2):193-207.

Giardino, C., Candiani, G., Bresciani, M., Lee, Z., Gagliano, S., Pepe, M., 2012.
    BOMBER: A tool for estimating water quality and bottom properties from remote sensing images. Computers & Geosciences, 45:313-318.

Gordon, H. R., Clark, D. K., 1981.
    Clear water radiances for atmospheric correction of coastal zone color scanner imagery. Applied Optics, 20(24):4175-4180.

Gordon, H. R., Clark, D. K., Brown, J. W., Brown, O. B., Evans, R. H., Broenkow, W. W., 1983.
    Phytoplankton pigment concentrations in the Middle Atlantic Bight: comparison of ship determinations and CZCS estimates. Applied Optics, 22(1):20-36.

Gordon, H. R., Wang, M., 1994.
    Retrieval of water-leaving radiance and aerosol optical thickness over the oceans with SeaWiFS: a preliminary algorithm. Applied Optics, 33(3):443-452.

Hansen, J. E., Travis, L. D., 1974.
    Light scattering in planetary atmospheres. Space Science Reviews, 16(4):527-610.

Heege, T., Bogner, A., Pinnel, N.
    Mapping of submerged aquatic vegetation with a physically based processing chain, in Proceedings SPIE-The International Society for Optical Engineering, Barcelona, Spain, 2003, Volume 5233, pp. 43-50.

Kanno, A., 2011.
    Coral Reef Bathymetry using Satellite Imagery - Validation of Accuracy Improvement with Doubled Bands. Journal of Japan Society of Civil Engineers, Series B2 (Coastal Engineering), 67(2):1341-1345.

Kaufman, Y. J., Remer, L. A., 1994.
    Detection of forests using mid-IR reflectance: an application for aerosol studies. Geoscience and Remote Sensing, IEEE Transactions on, 32(3):672-683.

Lafon, V., Froidefond, J. M., Lahet, F., Castaing, P., 2002.
    SPOT shallow water bathymetry of a moderately turbid tidal inlet based on field measurements. Remote Sensing of Environment, 81(1):136-148.

Lee, Z., Carder, K. L., Mobley, C. D., Steward, R. G., Patch, J. S., 1998.
Hyperspectral Remote Sensing for Shallow Waters. I. A Semianalytical
Model. Applied Optics, 37(27):6329-6338.

Lee, Z., Carder, K. L., Mobley, C. D., Steward, R. G., Patch, J. S., 1999.
Hyperspectral Remote Sensing for Shallow Waters. 2. Deriving
Bottom Depths and Water Properties by Optimization. Applied Optics,
38(18):3831-3843.

Malthus, T. J., Karpouzli, E., 2003.
Integrating field and high spatial resolution satellite-based methods
for monitoring shallow submersed aquatic habitats in the Sound of
Eriskay, Scotland, UK. International Journal of Remote Sensing,
24(13):2585-2593.

Maritorena, S., 1996.
Remote sensing of the water attenuation in coral reefs: a case study
in French Polynesia. International Journal of Remote Sensing,
17(1):155 - 166.

McFeeters, S. K., 1996.
The use of the Normalized Difference Water Index (NDWI) in the
delineation of open water features. International Journal of Remote
Sensing, 17(7):1425 - 1432.

Melzer, A., 1999.
Aquatic macrophytes as tools for lake management. Hydrobiologia,
396:181-190.

Mishra, D., Narumalani, S., Lawson, M., Rundquist, D., 2004.
Bathymetric Mapping Using IKONOS Multispectral Data.
GIScience & Remote Sensing, 41(4):301-321.

Mishra, D. R., Narumalani, S., Rundquist, D., Lawson, M., 2005.
Characterizing the vertical diffuse attenuation coefficient
for downwelling irradiance in coastal waters: Implications for water
penetration by high resolution satellite data. ISPRS Journal
of Photogrammetry and Remote Sensing, 60(1):48-64.

Mobley, C. D., 1994.
Light and Water. Academic Press, 592 p.

Mumby, P. J., Green, E. P., Edwards, A. J., Clark, C. D., 1997.
Coral reef habitat mapping: how much detail can remote sensing
provide? Marine Biology, 130(2):193-202.

O'Neill, J. D., Costa, M., Sharma, T., 2011.
Remote Sensing of Shallow Coastal Benthic Substrates: In situ Spectra
and Mapping of Eelgrass (Zostera marina) in the Gulf Islands National
Park Reserve of Canada. Remote Sensing, 3(5):975-1005.

Philpot, W. D., 1989.
Bathymetric mapping with passive multispectral imagery.
Applied Optics, 28(8):1569-1578.

Phinn, S., Roelfsema, C., Dekker, A., Brando, V., Anstee, J., 2008.
Mapping seagrass species, cover and biomass in shallow waters:
An assessment of satellite multi-spectral and airborne hyper-spectral
imaging systems in Moreton Bay (Australia). Remote Sensing
of Environment, 112(8):3413-3425.

Pinnel, N., 2007.
A method for mapping submerged macrophytes in lakes using
hyperspectral remote sensing. Ph.D. Thesis, Technische Universität
München, 164 p.

Rahel, F. J., Olden, J. D., 2008.
Assessing the Effects of Climate Change on Aquatic Invasive Species.
Conservation Biology, 22(3):521-533.

RapidEye, 2011.
Satellite Imagery Product Specifications, Version 3.2, 47 p.

Rößler, S., Wolf, P., Schneider, T., Melzer, A., 2012.
Identifizierung und Überwachung invasiver Wasserpflanzen mit
RapidEye. In: Borg, E., Daedelow, H., and Johnson, R., (Eds.).
RapidEye Science Archiven (RESA) - Vom Algorithmus zum Produkt,
GITO Verlag, pp. 73-91.

Rößler, S., Wolf, P., Schneider, T., Melzer, A., 2013.
Multispectral Remote Sensing of Invasive Aquatic Plants Using
RapidEye. In: Krisp, J. M., Meng, L., Pail, R., and Stilla, U., (Eds.).
Earth Observation of Global Changes (EOGC), Springer Berlin
Heidelberg, pp. 109-123.

Sawaya, K. E., Olmanson, L. G., Heinert, N. J., Brezonik, P. L., Bauer, M. E.,
2003.
Extending satellite remote sensing to local scales: land and water
resource monitoring using high-resolution imagery. Remote Sensing
of Environment, 88(1-2):144-156.

Stumpf, R. P., Holderied, K., Sinclair, M., 2003.
Determination of Water Depth with High-Resolution Satellite Imagery
over Variable Bottom Types. Limnology and Oceanography,
48(1):547-556.

Vahtmäe, E., Kutser, T., 2007.
Mapping Bottom Type and Water Depth in Shallow Coastal Waters
with Satellite Remote Sensing. Journal of Coastal Research,
SI 50:185-189.

Application of RapidEye data for the derivation of urban Geo-information products – an overview of first results (Project ID: 340)

Hannes Taubenböck, Thomas Esch, Michael Wurm, Wieke Heldens

German Aerospace Center (DLR)
Earth Observation Center (EOC)
German Remote Sensing Data Center (DFD)
Oberpfaffenhofen
82234 Wessling

Application of RapidEye data for the derivation of urban geo-information products – an overview of first results

Hannes Taubenböck, Thomas Esch, Michael Wurm, Wieke Heldens

Urbanization is a global change issue. Virtually all of the world's population growth over the next 30 years will be absorbed by urban areas. The challenges for sustainable urban development are immense. New data, applications and ideas are needed to meet these challenges. This paper provides insight into recently developed geo-information products for urbanized areas using RapidEye data. The multi-scale products – from the coarse delineation of urbanized areas to non-urbanized areas to higher resolved thematic classification such as land cover or vegetation fraction – aim to support the complex task of monitoring and decision-making with manifold up-to-date and area-wide spatial information.

1. Introduction

1.1 The urban information crisis

The population development of the world is expected to increase continuously from currently 6.7 billion to 9.3 billion in 2050. And trends imply that almost all the expected future world population growth will be absorbed by urban areas (UN, 2011). The massive dynamics of urbanization naturally effect immensely the spatial configuration of cities, often described as urban sprawl. The dynamics often overcharge the capability to govern, organize and plan new settlements. It is often even a difficult task to document and measure what has already happened spatially (Taubenböck et al., 2012).

In the last decade, earth observation sensors developed to a stage where the availability, geometric resolution and spatial coverage of data allows new possibilities for measuring and analyzing urban areas from a global scale (Potere & Schneider, 2009) to a local scale (e.g. Seifert, 2009). Approaches reach from binary masks of the world's urbanized areas (e.g. Elvidge et al. 2001) to multi-temporal documentation of urban sprawl at regional level (e.g. Angel et al., 2005; Taubenböck et al., 2012) to highly detailed 3-D city models (e.g. Sohn & Dowmann, 2007; Wurm et al., 2011) and related applications in various thematic domains such as population assessment, risk analysis or energy-related questions.

This paper provides insight into recently developed geo-information products using RapidEye data, with the aim to support monitoring and decision-making with manifold up-to-date and area-wide spatial information. Geo-information products from the generalized urban footprint mapping result, to the classification of percentages of impervious surfaces to a thematically highly resolved land cover classification and to the derivation of structural urban parameters are presented.

1.2 The RapidEye constellation

The RapidEye space segment consists of a constellation of five identical sun-synchronous earth observation satellites. Due to this constellation the global revisit time is one day, which makes the RapidEye system very attractive for applications such as crisis mapping (RapidEye, 2012).

With its swath of 77km and its ground sampling of 5 meter it enables, from an urban perspective, to cover entire city regions and at the same time providing a geometric resolution which enables differing small-scale urban objects such as buildings. This capability is supported by five spectral bands (blue, green, red, red edge, near infrared) and a radiometric resolution of 12bit.

2. Geo-information for urban areas

2.1 Urban footprint

The term 'urban footprint' is widely used in literature and basically refers to the spatial extent of urbanized areas on a regional scale (Cahn, 1978; Taubenböck et al., 2011a); it represents spatial information which is especially in dynamically sprawling cities often not available or up-to-date. However, the 'urban footprint' should not be misunderstood as a spatially and thematically exact measurement of individual urban objects, and their detailed spatial arrangements, but as abstract delineation of the physical man-made structures of cities.

The approach applied to the RapidEye data is based on an object-based procedure with two modules: segmentation and classification. The basic task of the segmentation is to merge homogenous pixels into image objects to enable the differentiation between heterogeneous neighboring regions (Benz et al. 2004). The applied multi-resolution segmentation algorithm is a bottom-up region-growing technique, starting at the pixel level. From it, the resulting segments differ significantly in shape between spectrally homogeneous areas such as water or grassland and spectrally heterogeneous areas such as built-up areas.

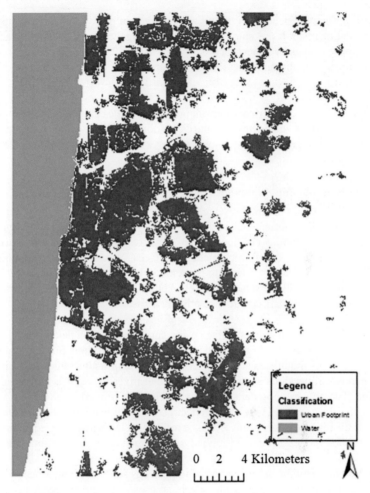

Figure 1: Urban footprint classification for Tel Aviv, Israel.

The classification module is a combination of these resulting spatial features of the segments and a simple threshold procedure based on spectral values. Especially the band ratio 'normalized difference vegetation index' (NDVI) is used to distinguish built from the natural environment. The combination of these features – size, shape and spectral information –is based on a fuzzy logic methodology for classification. Thus, every segment has a certain probability of class membership based on the particular features.

The result is a delineation of the urbanized areas of a city. An urban footprint classification result is presented in figure 1 showing the city of Tel Aviv, Israel as an example. A visual verification process based on 150 sample pixels distributed randomly for the thematic class "urban" results in 84.6 % correctly classified pixels.

On a regional scale the urban footprint product provides insight into dimension, directions, patterns and location of the city. Additionally, the urban footprint and hence, the urban growth, can be monitored over time using multi-temporal earth observation data.

2.2 Derivation of impervious surfaces

In policy and environmental research, the quantification of impervious surface has become an important indicator for estimating and assessing the negative effects of the ongoing consumption of land resources. Impervious surface describes the entirety of impermeable surfaces including roads, buildings, parking lots, railroads or other infrastructural elements of urban areas such as squares and sidewalks (Esch et al., 2009). Thus, the urban footprint classification presented in chapter 2.1 can be thematically refined.

The modeling of impervious surface using earth observation data is based on a technique introduced by Esch et al. (2009) – the Impervious Surface Analyst (iSurf-A). This module uses Support Vector Regression algorithms to estimate the percent impervious surface (PIS) for each pixel of a given multispectral image. Thereby, training data, being available for a limited area (e.g. a city or parts of a city), are used to relate the spectral information of the earth observation data to the real impervious surfaces. The resulting relationship is saved in form of a regression model that can be applied to additional earth observation data.

The methodology for the derivation of impervious surfaces is implemented in a fully operational processing chain, where no user interaction is needed.

Figure 2 presents the PIS derived fully automatic from a mosaic of RapidEye data for the entire area of the federal state of Bavaria in Germany. It shows the distribution of urbanized areas with the three spatially dominating urban centers: Munich, Nuremberg and Augsburg. Beyond this, the detailed view of a part in Munich shows the differentiation of various percentages of impervious surfaces in a part of the city. In order to eliminate confusions with bare soil, the PIS modeling was focused on built-up areas by using a corresponding mask derived from official topographic data.

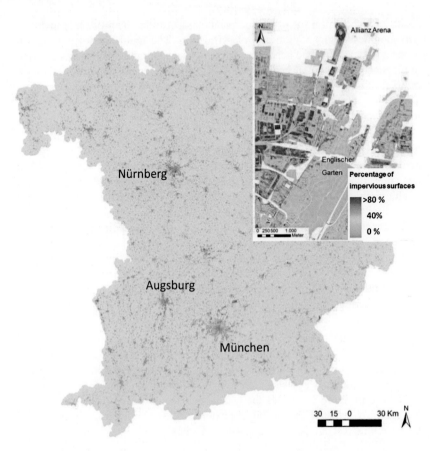

*Figure 2: Percentage of impervious surfaces mapped for the Bavaria, Germany
and detailed view for a part of Munich.*

2.3 Land cover classification

The geometric resolution of RapidEye data enables deriving a higher thematic
detail for land cover classifications as shown in chapter 2.1 and 2.2. Therefore,
an object-based classification approach, originally developed for the
classification of very high resolution satellite data such as Ikonos or QuickBird,
has been adjusted and tested on RapidEye data.

As already shown for the urban footprint classification, the procedure includes two modules: segmentation and classification. The multi-level segmentation process basically aims to generate class dependent appropriate segments for large homogeneous and small heterogeneous areas of the land surface. Therefore a multi-resolution, bottom-up, region-growing segmentation approach is applied. The scale parameter and the amount of necessary segmentation levels can interactively be determined by the user.

The subsequent classification procedure is based on a hierarchical, multi-level decision tree system using spectral features as well as spatial features and has been presented in detail by Taubenböck et al. (2011b). In general, the procedure is a hierarchical elimination of non-building areas. Based on the assumption that the spatially and spectrally heterogeneous urban areas show significantly small and geometrical segments, shape features support the classification. Vice versa homogenous zones such as water or grassland show larger and shapeless segments, thus these spatial features are combined with the spectral feature NDVI to start the classification. The NDVI is the only spectral feature used to reduce interactive adjustments for classification with other RapidEye scenes having differing atmospheric conditions or land cover classes.

The configuration of the chronological framework allows the user to initialize all or selected classes for classification at the appropriate segmentation level. The classification procedure allows for 6 land cover classes, namely 'buildings', 'impervious surfaces', 'water', 'trees', 'grassland' and 'open soil'. The result visualized in figure 3 presents the geo-information product for the suburbia of Wuppertal, Germany. The city outline extends along a valley from the north-east to the south-west surrounded by afforested areas.

The accuracy of the classification has been checked by a visual verification process with the RapidEye data. For every thematic class 200 randomly distributed sample points have been compared to the optical data. The resulting confusion matrix shows an overall accuracy of 90.17 %. The accuracy of the small-scale built-area has been measured with a 84.2 % user accuracy and a 87.7 % producer accuracy.

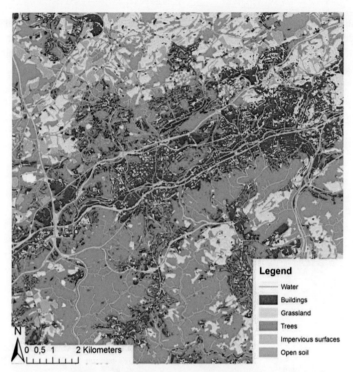

Legend

— Water
■ Buildings
Grassland
Trees
Impervious surfaces
Open soil

N
0 0,5 1   2 Kilometers

Figure 3: Land cover classification for the suburbia of Wuppertal, Germany.

2.4 Derivation of structural urban parameters

Cities are a heterogeneous morphological configuration of urban objects such as buildings, streets or open spaces. The aggregation of individual thematic classes, as classified in figure 3, to a superordinate class allows to quantitatively capturing the physical urban structure based on parameters such as building density (Wurm et al., 2010).

To do so different reference units can be used: From the entire city, to administrative units such as districts or sub-districts, natural spatial units such as blocks defined by a closed meshed street network or artificial units such as a chessboard network with a defined length of the edge.

In our case we use the blocks defined by the street network in the suburbia area of Wuppertal in Germany. Based on the land cover classification (cp. 2.3) structural parameters such as vegetation fraction, percentages of impervious surfaces or building density can be calculated on the block level. The latter one is calculated as the spatial ratio of the sum of all building ground floors per block to the area of the particular block.

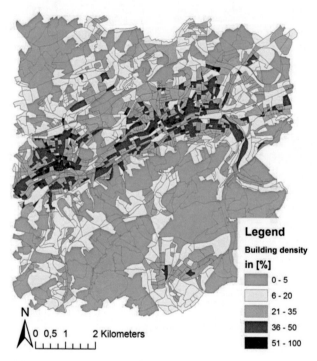

Figure 4: Building density per block area for the suburbia of Wuppertal, Germany.

The thematic indicators such as building density, vegetation fraction, and percentage of impervious surfaces can also serve as input for the derivation of urban structure types. This concept of urban structure types is a common approach for monitoring in German cities (Pauleit, 1998).

The result in figure 4 presents the distribution of building densities based on the block areas in the suburbia in Wuppertal. The drawn-out urban structure is again represented by the higher building density values along the valley. Beyond this, the clustering of areas with density values of higher than 50% in the west and northeast allows to infer two urban centers.

Conclusion and outlook

The constantly increasing availability and accessibility of modern remote sensing technologies provides new opportunities for a wide range of urban applications. The constellation of the RapidEye system allows for an independent, up-to-date and large-area availability of optical satellite data with a relatively high geometric resolution.

The overview of methodologies and the respective geo-information products show the capabilities to provide spatial information at various thematic details for the complex urban areas based on RapidEye data. The products are also reproducible and thus consistent and comparable. Especially in developing countries, remote sensing data often are the only data source.

Thus, these geo-information products allow to significantly improve the availability of spatial information for mapping, analyzing and understanding cities and their dynamics across the globe.

However, the investment in processing is still comparatively high due to a lack of fully automated classification procedures. During processing, adjustments are needed due to different atmospheric conditions, land cover types or different user requirements. Algorithms are also still in experimental status; the need for operationalization becomes obvious.

Beyond this, the accuracy is compared to cadastral data sets limited. On the one hand, accuracies of 80-90 % and sometimes even higher provide an objective basis for decisions. On the other hand, these Earth observation products are not established at the current legal foundation and now need to find juristic acceptance (Taubenböck & Esch, 2011).

However, RapidEye data prove to be an effective data source for monitoring urban areas across the globe.

Acknowledgements

The authors would specifically like to thank the RESA – RapidEye science team for providing data on the following accepted proposals: '340 Urbane Strukturanalysen mit RapidEye (USARE)', '475 Bundesweite Versiegelungs-kartierung mit Rapid Eye' and '504 Exploiting the potential of Rapid Eye data for sustainable urban planning and land management'.

The authors would also like to thank the Federal Office of Civil Protection and Disaster Assistance (BBK) of Germany for funding the KIBEX-Project (Reference number: AZ III.1-413-10-00-368), where part of this work has been carried out. In addition, the authors thank the European Commission for the funding in the context of the GEOURBAN project (FP7 - ERA.Net-RUS-033), that was basis for parts of the works.

Literature

Angel, S., Sheppard, S. C., & Civco, D. L. (2005).
The dynamics of global urban expansion (pp. 102). Washington, D.C.:
Transport and Urban Development Department, the World Bank.

Benz, U., Hofmann, P., Willhauck, G., Lingenfelder, I., & Heynen, M. (2004).
Multi-resolution, objectoriented fuzzy analysis of remote sensing data
for GIS-ready information. ISPRS Journal of Photogrammetry and
Remote Rensing, 58, 239-258.

Cahn, R. (1978).
Footprints on the planet: A search for an environmental ethic. ISBN:
0876633246, p. 277.

Esch, T., Himmler, V., Schorcht, G., Thiel, M., Wehrmann, T., Bachofer, F.,
Conrad, C., Schmidt, M., Dech, S. (2009).
Large-area assessment of impervious surface based on integrated
analysis of single-date Landsat-7 images and geospatial vector data.
Remote Sensing of Environment.

Pauleit, S. (1998).
Das Umweltwirkgefüge städtischer Siedlungsstrukturen: Darstellung
des städtischen Ökosystems durch eine Strukturtypenkartierung
zur Bestimmung von Umweltqualitätszielen für die Stadtplanung,
PhD Thesis, Technische Universität of München.

Potere, D., & Schneider, A. (2009).
Comparison of global urban maps. In P. Gamba, &M. Herold (Eds.),
Global mapping of human settlements: Experiences, data sets, and
prospects (pp. 269-308). Taylor & Francis Group.

RapidEye (2012).
RapidEye System Specifications
http://www.rapideye.com/about/satellites.htm.

Seifert, F. M. (2009).
Improving urban monitoring toward a European urban atlas. In
P. Gamba, & M. Herold (Eds.), Global mapping of human settlements:
Experiences, data sets, and prospects (pp. 231-249). Taylor & Francis
Group.

Sohn, G. & Dowman, I. (2007).
Data fusion of high-resolution satellite imagery and LiDAR data for automatic building extraction. ISPRS Journal of Photogrammetry and Remote Sensing, 62 (1), 43-63.

Taubenböck H., Esch T., Felbier A., Roth A. & Dech S. (2011a).
Pattern-based accuracy assessment of an urban footprint classification using TerraSAR-X data. In: IEEE Geoscience and Remote Sensing Letters. Vol. 8; No. 2; pp. 278-282.

Taubenböck H., Wurm M., Klein I. & Esch T. (2011b).
Verwundbarkeitsanalyse urbaner Räume: Ableitung von Indikatoren aus multisensoralen Fernerkundungsdaten. In: Proceedings of the REAL Corp. ISBN: 978-3-9503110-0-6. pp. 1107-1118.

Taubenböck H & Esch T (2011).
Remote sensing – An effective data source for urban monitoring. In: Earthzine IEEE Magazine.

Wurm M., Taubenböck H., & Dech S. (2010).
Quantification of urban structures on building block level utilizing multisensoral remote sensing data. SPIE Europe Conference, Toulouse, France. pp. 13.

Wurm, M., Taubenböck, H., Schardt, M., Esch, T. & Dech, S. (2011).
Object-based image information fusion using multisensor earth observation data over urban areas, International Journal of Image and Data Fusion, Vol. 2, Issue 2, p. 121-147.

United Nations Department of Economic and Social Affairs (2011).
Population Division. United Nations publications.

Analyzing the seasonal relations between *in situ* fPAR / LAI of cotton and spectral information of RapidEye (Project ID: 461)

Sylvia Lex, Christopher Conrad, Gunther Schorcht
Department of Remote Sensing, Institute for Geography and Geology, University of Wuerzburg

E-Mail: sylvia.lex@uni-wuerzburg.de

Analyzing the seasonal relations between *in situ* fPAR / LAI of cotton and spectral information of RapidEye

Sylvia Lex, Christopher Conrad, Gunther Schorcht

Leaf Area Index (LAI) and the fraction of absorbed Photosynthetically Active Radiation (fPAR) are frequently used for biophysical modeling of crop growth and yield prediction. This study examines the calculation of LAI and fPAR of cotton using statistical regression with spectral information of RapidEye. Based on the knowledge that commonly used vegetation indices (NDVI, SAVI, EVI) may underperform in the situation of dense vegetation the growing season was divided into main growth and reproductive phases. To account for saturation effects indices including the curvature in the red edge part of the spectra were tested. Field measurements on LAI and fPAR were carried out during the vegetation period of 2011 on cotton fields in Uzbekistan. The LAI/fPAR results for RapidEye data will be used as input for an upscaling to TERRA-MODIS time series and transfer to larger areas of Central Asia.

1. Introduction

Regression analysis of vegetation indices for LAI and fPAR often faces the problem of saturation for high LAI values. This means that high LAI values are difficult to predict with well-established indices like the *NDVI* (Huete, 1997). In case of agricultural crops, this situation mainly occurs in later parts of the season, when the canopy is closed but biomass is still increasing. This is also valid for cotton, when canopy closure can be assigned to the reproductive growth phase.

The recently proposed measures *Length*, *Relative Length* and *Curvature* which utilize the REDEDGE band of RapidEye indicated their ability to reduce this effect (Conrad et al. 2012). The focus of this study is a more detailed examination of these REDEDGE indices for the statistical derivation of fPAR and LAI. A case study has been conducted on cotton fields in Central Asia where multi-temporal RapidEye data and corresponding field measurements were available for the cropping season 2011. It is assumed that the relation of LAI and fPAR to vegetation indices differs between the main growing phase and the reproductive phase. Thus, regression analysis is tested for both phases as well as for the whole period which ranged from June to September.

2. Study Area

The Fergana valley is located in the eastern part of Uzbekistan and comprises some parts of Kirgizstan and Tajikistan, as shown in Figure 1. It belongs to the Syr Darya catchment, which is part of the Aral Sea Basin in Central Asia. Main crops are cotton, winter wheat, maize, rice and fruit trees. After harvesting of winter wheat mainly the vegetables carrots and beans are planted. Because of the arid climate with an annual mean temperature of 13°C and a precipitation of 500 mm only irrigation enables agricultural use of the landscape (Abdullaev et al, 2009). The observed cotton fields are in the South Fergana Channel and Main Fergana Channel irrigation systems.

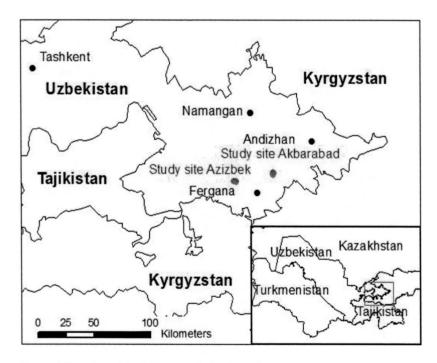

Figure 1: Location of the Fergana valley in Central Asia
(data source: GIS Center Urgench, ZEF UNESCO Khorezm Project.)

3. Data and methods

3.1 Multi-temporal RapidEye data

For this study, 28 RapidEye scenes covering parts of the Fergana valley were available. The RapidEye data was radiometrically corrected with the process chain CATENA (Reinartz, 2010) developed by the German Aerospace Center and geometrically corrected using the *Autosync* function of the software ERDAS IMAGINE. Radiometric correction was necessary to get comparable conditions for the derivation of the biophysical parameters fPAR and LAI.

3.2 Field measurements

Leaf Area Index and fPAR measurements were conducted in the period from the beginning of June until the end of August 2011 on cotton fields. Two study areas Azizbek and Akbarabad in the vicinity of Fergana city were selected (Figure 1).

With the Ceptometer AccuPAR LP 80, provided by Decagon Devices, nine cotton fields were observed with three measuring plots on each field. Each plot covered an area of approximately 320m². It consisted of twelve measurements which were arranged in a cross in a homogeneous surrounding as proposed by Ehammer et al (2010). Five fields were located in the vicinity of Akbarabad and four fields were chosen in the region Azizbek. The 80 cm long sensor bar of the AccuPAR LP-80 was placed diagonal to the cotton rows as proposed by Tewolde et al. (2005). All points were measured six to eight times during the whole period.

3.3 Matching field and satellite measurements

Only those RapidEye data corresponding with field measurements were further analyzed. Vice versa, only field measurements with suitable satellite records were selected. Only those pairs of field and satellite measurements were included which show a maximum difference of eight days. For both study sites, each six matches were found. According to the selection rules and due to the fact that the field measurements were not carried out simultaneously the data pairs differ between the study sites. Table 1 shows the periods of suitable field measurements in comparison to the RapidEye recordings.

Akbarabad

RapidEye	Beginning of fieldwork	End of fieldwork
07.06.2011	08.06.2011	15.06.2011
24.06.2011	24.06.2011	28.06.2011
23.07.2011	15.07.2011	23.07.2011
29.07.2011	30.07.2011	01.08.2011
07.08.2011	10.08.2011	16.08.2011
31.08.2011	26.08.2011	05.09.2011

Azizbek

RapidEye	Beginning of fieldwork	End of fieldwork
15.06.2011	14.06.2011	16.06.2011
23.06.2011	25.06.2011	29.06.2011
07.07.2011	11.07.2011	13.07.2011
29.07.2011	21.07.2011	29.07.2011
07.08.2011	12.08.2011	15.08.2011
23.08.2011	24.08.2011	25.08.2011

Table 1: Field measurement periods and record times of selected RapidEye scenes.

3.4 Vegetation Indices

The vegetation indices *NDVI, SAVI, RDVI, EVI, NDVI$_{RedEdge}$, Length, Relative Length* and *Curvature* were derived from all selected RapidEye data. Table 2 gives an overview of the equations used for the calculation of the indices.

NDVI, SAVI, RDVI, NDVI$_{RedEdge}$ and *EVI* use the NIR and RED bands to obtain information through the increase between RED and NIR wavelengths (Huete et al., 1997). *SAVI* additionally considers soil reflectance (Huete, 1988). *Curvature* is the second derivative of the slope of the REDEDGE, represented by the wavelengths RED, REDEDGE, and NIR. Therefore, divided differences were used. The parameter *Length* figures up the Euclidean distances between both, the RED and REDEDGE and REDEDGE and NIR. The *Relative Length* relates the *Length* to the Length between RED and NIR. It describes the relation of the REDEDGE value to the direct line between RED and NIR (Conrad et al. 2012).

NDVI	$= \dfrac{\rho Nir - \rho Red}{\rho Nir + \rho Red}$	Birth and McVey (1968)
SAVI	$= (1 + L)\dfrac{\rho Nir - \rho Red}{\rho Nir + \rho Red + L}$	Huete (1988)
RDVI	$= \dfrac{\rho Nir - \rho Red}{\sqrt{\rho Nir + \rho Red}}$	Roujean (1995)
EVI	$= 2.5\dfrac{\rho Nir - \rho Red}{1 + \rho Nir + C1 * \rho Red - C2 * \rho Blue}$	Huete et al. (2002)
NDVIRededge	$= \dfrac{\rho NIR - \rho RE}{\rho NIR + \rho RE}$	Vina and Gitelson (2005)
Length	$= \sqrt{(\rho Nir - \rho RE)^2 + (\lambda Nir - \lambda RE)^2} + \sqrt{(\rho RE - \rho Red)^2 + (\lambda RE - \lambda Red)^2}$	Conrad et al. (2012)
Rel. Length	$= \dfrac{Length}{\sqrt{(\rho Nir - \rho RE)^2 + (\lambda Nir - \lambda Red)^2}}$	Conrad et al. (2012)
Curvature	$= \dfrac{\left(\frac{\rho Nir - \rho RE}{\lambda Nir - \lambda RE}\right) - \left(\frac{\rho RE - \rho Red}{\lambda RE - \lambda Red}\right)}{\lambda Nir - \lambda Red}$	Conrad et al. (2012)

Table 2: Overview of the calculated indices with equations.
(ρ: reflectance, λ: wavelength)

3.5 Regression analyses of LAI and fPAR

For correlation and regression of LAI and fPAR a homogeneous area around the field points was selected. By using this approach more representative results are expected than by correlating each field measurement to the corresponding RapidEye pixel, because of likely spatial mismatches between the GPS coordinates of field measurements and the pixel location. RapidEye data was segmented with the software Definiens eCognition using the parameters scale = 9, shape = 0.9 and compactness 0.9. The parameters were chosen according to the findings of Ehammer et al. (2010) who found scale parameters between 5 and 10 most suited for similar analyses. The resulting segments cover an average area of 0.49 ha. Within the homogeneous segments the mean value for each index was calculated in every time step and correlated to the measured fPAR and LAI.

The regression analysis was carried out with all indices. Linear regression was tested as well as power, exponential, and polynomial models. Multiple regressions were also conducted with the best correlating *SAVI, RDVI, EVI* and *Length*.

149

A regression analysis was done with all LAI/fPAR values for the whole period. According to the aims of the study, the data was split and the regression was calculated once for both phases, the main growth phase (time steps one, two and three) and the reproductive phase (time steps four, five and six).

4. Results

4.1 Results from field measurements

During the growing season an increase of fPAR and LAI could be measured. The main growing phase lasted until the mid/end of July. In this phase plants still grow and the vegetation density gets higher. The reproductive phase began by the end of July as Figure 2 shows. fPAR and LAI values stagnate and get lower again.

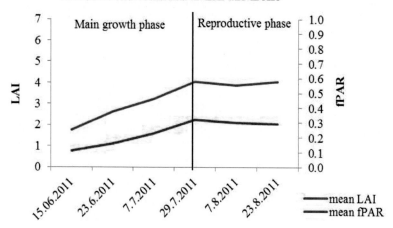

Figure 2: Seasonal trend of LAI and fPAR derived by field data.

4.2 Regression results

Statistical analyses showed the best correlations for LAI with *Length, SAVI, EVI* and *RDVI*. For fPAR, a linear model with *SAVI* fitted best ($R^2 = 0.87$) while for LAI a power model ($R^2 = 0.82$) suited better than the linear model with *SAVI*

(0.78). The results for LAI are shown in Table 3. A multiple regression with best fitting indices *SAVI* and *RDVI* for Leaf Area Index and *NDVI* and *Length* for fPAR did not show better results than the simple regression.

Correlations between RapidEye spectral information and fPAR performed in in general better than for LAI. This can be explained by differing height of cotton and not perfect corresponding field measurements to RapidEye recordings. Besides, irrigation times and moist or wet soil could also be a factor that corresponds not well enough to RapidEye recordings in not fully closed canopies.

Vegetation indices	Vegetation Period		Main growing phase		Reproductive phase	
	R^2	SE	R^2	SE	R^2	SE
NDVI	0.72	0.68	0.80	0.39	0.59	0.79
SAVI	**0.78**	**0.60**	**0.82**	**0.37**	0.75	0.62
EVI	0.79	0.58	0.81	0.38	0.78	0.59
RDVI	0.78	0.60	0.82	0.37	0.75	0.62
NDVI$_{rededge}$	0.73	0.66	0.81	0.37	0.65	0.74
Curvature	0.67	0.73	0.75	0.44	0.70	0.69
Length	**0.79**	**0.58**	0.79	0.40	**0.81**	**0.54**
Relative Length	0.56	0.85	0.58	0.57	0.67	0.72

Table 3: Overview of R^2 values and standard errors for the regression analyses of LAI with different vegetation indices.

For the derivation of LAI a saturation effect for high values occurred with all well-established vegetation indices (*SAVI, NDVI, EVI,* and *RDVI*). Figure 3 exemplarily shows the scatterplot between LAI and SAVI. Even though a non-linear model showed a high regression the division in two growth periods was beneficial. For the reproductive period, especially the parameter *Length* could increase and reduce R^2 and SE, respectively (lower part of Figure 3 and Table 3). For the main growth period analyses showed best results for *SAVI* ($R^2 = 0.82$). Also the standard error decreases for the first period. Moreover, using different linear models for the two growth periods appears superior to a single non-linear model for the entire season, as only linear models are valid for the whole range of values outside the measured range.

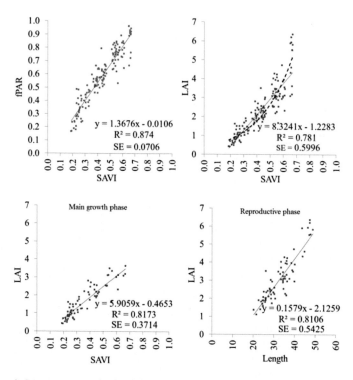

Figure 3: Regression results for fPAR and LAI of cotton derived by SAVI and 'Length'.

5. Conclusions

The case study showed a good linear agreement between the spectral indices *SAVI, NDVI, RDVI, Length* and fPAR on cotton fields. Also LAI could be modeled with satisfying accuracy, however, saturation effects for high LAI-values shown by vegetation indices like *NDVI* and *SAVI* could be avoided when using *Length*. The latter underlines the advantages from integrating the red edge information into vegetation indices, but also from utilizing the spectral curve between the red and NIR spectra for assessments of vegetation growth. The results of this study also suggest considering two parts of the growing season for regression analyses between LAI and spectral RapidEye measurements. R^2-values fitted better in the periods before shooting of cotton (main growth phase) and after shooting (reproductive phase).

Summary and Outlook

Multi-temporal RapidEye data was used to calculate Leaf Area Index (LAI) and the Fraction of absorbed Photosynthetically Active Radiation (fPAR) of cotton in the Fergana valley in Uzbekistan. Field measurements during the growing period 2011 and six time steps of RapidEye served as input data for the derivation of regression equations. Satellite recording time and field measurements fitted for six time steps between June and the end of August 2011. The field measurements comprised 26 plots on cotton fields with twelve sampling points each. Each plot was measured several times during the growing season. The vegetation indices *NDVI, SAVI, RDVI, EVI* and the REDEDGE indices $NDVI_{Rededge}$, *Length, Relative Length* and *Curvature* were used. All indices except *Relative Length* and *Curvature* show good results with R^2 values above 0.85 for fPAR and 0.79 for LAI. The results between the vegetation indices varied only slightly with *SAVI* and *Length* optimally corresponding for fPAR and for LAI, respectively. This shows that utilizing the soil line and additional spectral information like the RE band of RapidEye is beneficial for statistically deriving biophysical parameters on cotton fields. A division in the two vegetation periods main growth phase and reproductive phase was useful to optimize regression equations. For the first phase best results were obtained by *SAVI* and for the second phase *Length* fitted best. The findings underline the suitability of considering the soil line especially in the initial part of the vegetation season, when the vegetation coverage in the fields is still below 100%. Altogether, the results indicate the suitability of the high temporal resolution or additional red edge information of RapidEye and other upcoming sensor systems like Sentinel-2 for dedicated seasonal assessments of biophysical parameters.

Acknowledgement

This study is part of the CAWa project, funded by the Federal Foreign Office Germany (AA7090002). The authors thank the fiat panis foundation for enabling them to take field measurements. Much gratitude is given to the German Aerospace Center (DLR) for providing the RapidEye Data from RapidEye Science Archive in RESA project 461.

References

Abdullaev, I, Kazbekov, J., Manthritilake, H., Jumaboev, K. (2009).
Participatory watermanagement at the main canal: A case from
South Ferghana canal in Uzbekistan. Agricultural Water Management,
96, 317-329.

Birth, G. S. and McVey, G.,
"Measuring the Color of Growing Turf with a Reflectance
Spectrophotometer", Agronomy Journal 60, 640-643 (1968).

Conrad, C., Fritsch, S., Lex, S., Löw, F., Rücker, G., Schorcht, G.,
Sultanov, M., Lamers, J. (2012).
Potenziale des 'Red Edge' Kanals von RapidEye zur Unterscheidung
und zum Monitoring landwirtschaftlicher Anbaufrüchte am Beispiel
des usbekischen Bewässerungssystems Khorezm. In: E. Borg,
H. Daedelow, R. Johnson (Hrsg.): RapidEye Science Archive (RESA)
– Vom Algorithmus zum Produkt. 4. RESA Workshop, GITO Verlag,
Berlin, S. 203-217.

Delecolle, R., Maas, S.J., Guérif, M., Baret, F. (1992).
Remote sensing and crop production models: present trends. ISPRS
Journal of Photogrammetry and Remote Sensing, 47, 145-161.

Ehammer, A., Fritsch, S., Conrad, C., Lamers, J., Dech, S. (2010).
Statistical derivation of fPAR and LAI for irrigated cotton and rice
in arid Uzbekistan by combining multi-temporal RapidEye data and
ground measurements. In: Proc. SPIE 7824, 782409:10, 2010
(Remote Sensing for Agriculture, Ecosystems, and Hydrology XII).

Fritsch, S., Conrad, C., Manschadi, A., Machwitz, M., Rücker, G.,
Schorcht, G., Knöfel, P., Dech, S.
Regional field based yield prediction of irrigated cotton and rice
with multi-temporal RapidEye data and a light use efficiency model.
(in preparation).

Huete, A.R. (1988).
A Soil-Adjusted Vegetation Index (SAVI). Remote Sensing
of Environment. 25, 295-309.

Huete, A.R, Liu, H.Q., Batchily, K., Leeuwen, W. van (1997).
A comparison of Vegetation Indices over a Global Set of TM Images
for EOS-MODIS. Remote Sensing of Environment, 59, 440-451.

Huete, A., Didan, K., Miura, T., Rodriguez, E. P., Gao, X., and Ferreira, L. G.
"Overview of the radiometric and biophysical performance
of the MODIS vegetation indices," Remote Sensing of Environment
83, 195-213 (2002).

Kraft, P., Vaché, K.B., Frede, H.-G. Breuer, L. (2011).
A hydrological programming language extension for integrated
catchment models, Environmental Modelling & Software.

Kumar, M., and Monteith, J. L., (1981).
Remote sensing of crop growth. In: Plants and the Daylight Spectrum,
edited by H. Smith (London: Academic Press), pp. 133-144.

Löw, F., Schorcht, G., Michel, U., Dech, S., Conrad, C.
"Per-field crop classification in irrigated agricultural regions in middle
Asia using random forest and support vector machine ensemble",
Proceedings of SPIE (2012).

Machwitz, M. (2011).
Eine raum-zeitliche Modellierung der Kohlenstoffbilanz
mit Fernerkundungsdaten auf regionaler Ebene in Westafrika,
Dissertation, University of Wuerzburg.

Reinartz, P.(2010).
The CATENA Processing Chain - Multi-Sensor Pre-processing:
Orthorectification, Atmospheric Correction, Future Aspects.
geoland Forum_6, 24.-25. March 2010, Toulouse, France.

Roujean, J. and Breon, F.-M.
"Estimating PAR Absorbed by Vegetation from Bidirectional
Reflectance Measurements," Remote Sensing of Environment 51(3),
375-384 (1995).

Tewolde, H., Sistani, K.R., Rowe, D.E., Adelli, A., Tsegaye, T.
Estimating Cotton Leaf Area Index Nondestructively with a Light
Sensor (2005).Agronomy Journal 97, 1158-1163.

Tian, Y., Zhang, Y., Knyazikhin, Y., Myneni, R.B., Glassy, J.M., Dedieu, G.,
Running, S. (2000).
Prototyping of MODIS LAI and FPAR Algorithm with LASUR
and LANDSAT Data. IEEE Transactions on Geoscience
and Remote Sensing, 38, 5, 2387-2401.

Vina, A. and Gitelson, A. A.
"New developments in the remote estimation of the fraction of absorbed photosynthetically active radiation in crops", Geophysical Research Letters 32 (L17403), 1-4 (2005).

Validation of Leaf Area Index calculated on RapidEye imagery against in situ measurements in Rur Catchment, Germany (Project ID: 462)

Muhammad Ali*[1,2], Carsten Montzka[1], Anja Stadler[3], Harry Vereecken[1]

[1] Agrosphere (IBG-3), Forschungszentrum Jülich GmbH, Jülich, Germany
[2] National Centre of Excellence in Geology, University of Peshawar, Pakistan
[3] Institute of Crop Science and Resource Conservation, University of Bonn, Germany

Email: m.ali@fz-juelich.de

Validation of Leaf Area Index calculated on RapidEye imagery against in situ measurements in Rur Catchment, Germany

Muhammad Ali*, Carsten Montzka, Anja Stadler, Harry Vereecken

Abstract

Time series of Leaf Area Index (LAI) calculated on high spatial and temporal optical satellite imagery obtained by RapidEye, is validated against in situ LAI for vegetation season 2011-12. For in situ LAI, Delta-T SunScan, LiCor's LAI2200 and a destructive method were used at different places inside a winter wheat field. The availability of the unique red edge band was also tested in this paper for accurate estimation of LAI. Prior to the LAI estimation, RapidEye images are radiometrically normalized, that enhanced the quality of the product and made the results more reliable. Both LAI ground based sensors were also compared and LAI2200 vs destructive LAI gave a bit higher R^2 value ($R^2=0.75$) than SunScan vs destructive LAI ($R^2=0.55$). Better calculation of LAI will greatly help improve the estimation of soil moisture and evapotranspiration (ET).

1. Introduction

Hydrological cycle represents the continuous movement of water between earth and atmosphere where vegetation is of key importance providing water back to the atmosphere through the process of evapotranspiration (ET), (Lu et al., 2001). ET is one of the largest components in the soil water balance and it is strongly controlled by the hydrological status of the soil, the status of the vegetation canopy and the land use management (Thompson et al., 2011). Evapotranspiration from the plant bodies contribute about 70% of the total evapotranspiration from land surface while more than 70% of the total precipitation is processed by vegetation (Arora and Boer, 2002). Other factors that make vegetation important for the hydrological processes are infiltration and hydraulic redistribution as well as its impact on the soil water status through the generation of stem flow (Crockford and Richardson, 2000). Roots may enhance the process of infiltration and percolation through the generation of macro-pores. For these reasons, the detailed record of the spatial and temporal variability of vegetation is important for a good estimation of the hydrological fluxes.

Remote sensing is an economic and time saving method for getting time series of vegetation data with a continuous spatial coverage for large areas. In addition, data are obtained at different wavelengths ranging from visible to infra-red radiation providing the potential for the analysis of a broad range of research questions and interactions between different processes and compartments. These analyses and issues involve e.g. the role of climate as determinant of land surface characteristics such as vegetation phenology (Lu et al., 2001), relationships between vegetation communities and local climate (Weiss et al., 2004), utilization of satellite image derived leaf area index (LAI) in climatic models (Ge, 2009), vegetation impact over land atmosphere interaction and variation in hydraulic conductivity determines vegetation properties and soil moisture (Lakshmi et al., 2011). Weiss et al., 2004, Ge 2009 and Lakshmi et al., 2011, used satellite remote sensing data for correlating vegetation based analysis in their respective studies. Vegetation indices (NDVI, LAI and FPAR) are important variables for climatic and hydrological models (Sellers et al., 1997). Leaf Area Index, LAI, is a dimensionless variable (ratio of leaf area surface to a unit land surface area) that can be used for investigating variations in productivity and to study the impacts of climate on the surrounding environment (Zheng and Moskal, 2009). The LAI is the variable which is needed for most hydrological models, in order to consider plant-specific transpiration, infiltration, interception, etc. It is used to split evapotranspiration in soil evaporation and the water transpired by the vegetation. In addition, in situ measurements for the estimation of LAI, NDVI can be used as a good estimator for the indirect estimation of LAI (Lu et al., 2004).

Being the first operational satellite providing data in red-edge spectral band, RapidEye is one of the best choices for various disciplines involving time-series analysis of vegetation-based analysis. Vegetation indices with and without red-edge spectral channel may be checked for more accuracy of these indices. According to (Eitel et al., 2007), high spatio-temporal resolution of RapidEye[TM] with the availability of red-edge band, would be more useful for nitrogen (N) management of various crops. They evaluated the suitability of RapidEye[TM] derived chlorophyll indices to predict relative chlorophyll and N status in spring wheat. (Sprintsin et al., 2007) presented a methodology for determining LAI in a forest and analyzed results from a high spatial resolution (IKONOS, 4m) with moderate spatial resolution but temporally high resolution MODIS (250m) data. (Propastin and Erasmi, 2010) suggested an algorithm to estimate LAI over the Lore-Lindu National Park (Indonesia) using in situ measurements and a 16-day time series of MODIS 250m. They also evaluated fractional vegetation cover (FVC) and LAI estimated over high resolution

Quick-bird and Landsat ETM+ satellite data. (Ehammer et al., 2010) used RapidEye images in arid Uzbekistan for measuring the fraction of photosynthetically active radiation (FPAR) and LAI of cotton and rice with frequent and spatially accurate measurements. (Eitel et al., 2011) examined the utility of red-edge and non red-edge vegetation indices calculated on a time series of 22 RapidEye images of a piñon-juniper woodland in central New Mexico, for early stress detection.

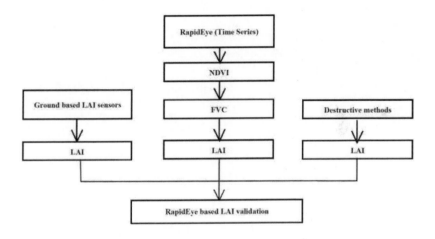

Figure 1: Processing workflow for the validation of RapidEye imagery against in situ vegetation observations.

Our present study aims at the improvement in acquisition of LAI on a high spatial scale of spaceborne remote sensing data and its subsequent validation against in situ LAI. Time series of LAI is of utmost importance to study seasonal and spatial variability of vegetation on the large scale. RapidEye has the potential to highlight variations of LAI at the scale of the field. The red-edge band in multi-spectral data of RapidEye is being tested for obtaining improved estimates of vegetation indices. Furthermore, both ground based LAI sensors are also validated against destructive measurements.

2. Study area

Area under investigation for this study is the Rur catchment, located in the German-Belgium-Netherlands border area, near the city of Aachen. Rur river has a length of 165 km and drains 2354 km² area (Montzka et al. 2008ab) with its origin in the mountains of Sauerland near the town of Winterberg and flows into lower river Rhine. This catchment is under investigation of Transregional Collaborative Research Centre 32—Patterns in Soil–Vegetation–Atmosphere Systems: Monitoring, modeling and data assimilation (http://tr32.uni-koeln.de/index.php) and TERENO (http://teodoor.icg.kfa-juelich.de/overview-de). The southern part of the catchment is covered by the bedrock of the Eifel mountains with a high long term annual precipitation and a moderate potential evapotranspiration, while the northern part receives relatively low annual precipitation and higher potential evapotranspiration (German Weather Service (DWD), Bogena et al 2005a). Winter wheat and sugar beet are main crops cultivated in the area. RapidEye data have been provided by the RapidEye Science Archive (RESA) for the two vegetation seasons during 2011 and 2012.

3. LAI time series/ Data & Methods

3.1 RapidEye based LAI

RapidEye satellites provide data in visible and near infra-red where clouds may hinder to see the earth while time-series analysis of LAI (this study) requires data on regular basis. For this study a total of 19 images were processed. These images were acquired during 2011 and 2012 in different dates (figure- 4). RapidEye is capable of providing information of large area in 5 days and have the ability to map any area on the earth surface once per day (Tyc et al.,- 2005), enhancing the possibility for more cloud-free scenes.

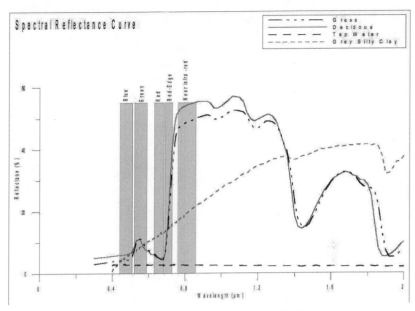

Figure 2: Spectral reflectance curve for various features of the land surface plotted against different RapidEye's spectral channels (Source for reflectance data is ASTER Spectral Library version 1.2)

In a time series analysis, different atmospheric conditions on RapidEye images during different observation times need to be normalized. Method used for this normalization was relative normalization by the Multivariate Alteration Detection (MAD) by (Canty et al., 2004; Canty and Nielsen, 2008). First of all, a time series of Normalized Difference Vegetation Index, [NDVI = (NIR – Red) / (NIR + Red)] is calculated using RapidEye images. NDVI has wide applications for vegetation, uses red and near Infrared bands. NDVI has good potential to extract useful information regarding dynamic changes in different vegetation types making NDVI a good indicator to investigate such changes temporally (Geerken et al., 2005; Xie et al., 2008). Generally NDVI has a range of 0-1 where high value exhibit concentration of vegetation (e.g. dense vegetation has value 0.3-0.8), bare soil and water has lowest values, while negative values indicate clouds and snow cover. Based on the NDVI, fractional vegetation cover, [FVC = (NDVI - NDVIs) / (NDVIv - NDVIs)] is calculated (Zeng et al., 2000; Zeng et al., 2003). In FVC equation, NDVIs represents NDVI values of soil with no vegetation while NDVIv represents NDVI of dense vegetation. Both, NDVIs and NDVIv are selected by thorough visual

163

analysis of the NDVI image with natural colour composite. FVC can also be calculated using measuring photosynthetically active radiation (PAR) above and below the canopy by [FVC = 1 – (PARb / PARa)], where PARa is PAR measured above canopy and PARb is PAR measured below canopy. LAI is then calculated via [LAI = -ln (1-FVC) / k(θ)] as (Norman et al., 1995, 1996) where k(θ) is light extinction coefficient for a solar zenith angle. Light extinction coefficient is the measure of attenuation of radiation in the canopy. Solar zenith angle (θ) depends on geometry of terrain, solar declination, solar elevation angle, latitudinal location and day of the year (Propastin and Erasmi, 2010). For general purpose the value of k(θ) may be taken as 0.54, which is an average value calculated by (Aubin et al., 2000). To investigate the potential of enhancing LAI, the red band (0.630 - 0.685 µm) was replaced with red-edge band (0.690 - 0.730 µm) in calculating NDVI. Outcome of both the LAI sets were compared to get more accurate and reliable results.

3.2 In situ LAI

In order to validate the accuracy of RapidEye based LAI data, two ground based LAI sensors (LiCor's LAI2200 and delta-T SunScan) and destructive methods were used for in situ LAI. In situ LAI was calculated on bi-weekly basis in selected winter wheat fields near test sites of the Forschungszentrum Juelich in Rur catchment, Germany. Direct Sun rays falling on the canopy can underestimate the LAI value through LAI2200. To estimate more accurate LAI, LAI2200 must be used, under overcast conditions, late afternoon or early in the morning, when sun rays are at low angle (Wilhelm et al., 2000).

Delta-T SunScan, was used exclusively during 2011 and parallel with LAI2200 during 2012. SunScan needs uniform light conditions during measurements. Rapidly changing light conditions are not favourable for SunScan use. The third in situ LAI method is more complicated and time consuming but more accurate. Time series of destructive LAI from winter wheat fields can be used to check for over- or underestimation of the LAI sensors due to changing weather conditions.

4. Results and discussion

Non-destructive in situ measurements of LAI are based on the principle of measuring light intensity trapped by the canopy. This may lead to an over-estimation of LAI by SunScan or LAI2200 (Wilhelm et al., 2000), it was also

observed during the parallel field campaign for in situ LAI via SunScan and
LAI2200. In this study LAI2200's and SunScan's LAI were linearly plotted
against destructive LAI (Figure 3). The coefficient of determination (R^2)
calculated for LAI2200 vs destructive (R^2= 0.75) gave better value than
SunScan' vs destructive LAI (R^2=0.55). So it is assumed that LiCor's
LAI2200 gave more promising results than SunScan. This assumption is also
supported by results from (Wilhelm et al., 2000) for Pioneer Hybrid 3394
(R^2= 0.94 for LAI2000 vs destructive LAI and R^2=0.79 for SunScan vs
destructive LAI).

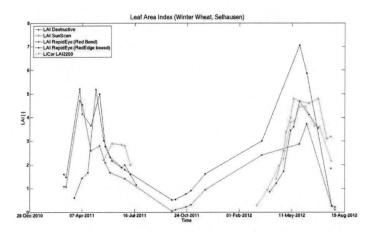

Figure 3: Comparison of destructive LAI against Delta-t SunScan and LiCor's LAI2200.

LAI calculated on RapidEye images with and without the red-edge spectral
band is plotted against all in situ LAI measurements in winter wheat field at
Selhausen (Figure 4). LAI2200's data was acquired only during vegetation
season of 2012, whereas the rest LAI data is covering two vegetation seasons
from 2011 to 2012. Figure 4 verifies our first assumption regarding LAI2200
against destructive LAI during 2012. During 2011, RapidEye based LAI (both
with and without red-edge band) representing best fit against destructive LAI.
During vegetation season of 2012, as a whole, both types of RapidEye based
LAI represents better curves with some degree of over and underestimation.
LAI (with red-edge band) shows an overestimation of LAI≈2 while LAI

(without red-edge band) shows an underestimation of LAI≈1 during 2012 as compared to in situ LAI. Thus LAI with red-edge band for 2012, does not show better curve as compared to LAI without red-edge band which supports (Ehammer et al., 2010) dissatisfaction regarding inclusion of Rapideye's red-edge band into vegetation indices for better results. But during the year 2011, red-edge based LAI shows better fit as compared to LAI without red-edge band (Figure 4).

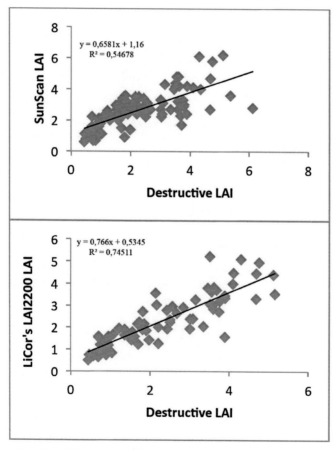

Figure 4: Plot of RapidEye based LAI (with & without red-edge band)
plotted against in situ LAI observations in winter wheat field at Selhausen,
Rur Catchment, Germany.

5. Conclusion and outlook

LAI acquisition via destructive method may be more precise as compared to ground based LAI sensors but it is more cumbersome and time consuming method. For validation of the satellite data, no doubt, it plays an imperative role. On the other hand ground based LAI sensors are non-destructive and less time consuming but they need calibration and are therefore site specific. But LAI acquired thus cannot be extrapolated outside the field where in situ measurements are taken. Therefore remote sensing based LAI acquisition derived from atmospherically and radiometrically corrected imagery via most optimized and generally accepted algorithms may provide an efficient mean of obtaining LAI data for large regions. Value of $k(\theta)$ used in this study is calculated by (Aubin et al., 2000), but for more accurate and reliable LAI, better estimates of the value of $k(\theta)$ are required. RapidEye data is comparatively new product and yet needs more precise validation. Due to the difference in spatial resolution between RapidEye and other remote sensing products, up- or downscaling of LAI is required (e.g. upscaling of RapidEye data to the pixel scale of MODIS). Generally coarse resolution imagery overestimate LAI due to increased homogeneity by larger pixels (Propastin and Erasmi, 2010), but using high resolution data, this overestimation might be corrected.

Acknowledgements

This study is supported by the Higher Education Commission (HEC) of Pakistan through German Academic Exchange Service (DAAD). It is incorporated in the German Research Foundation DFG Transregional Collaborative Research Centre 32—Patterns in Soil–Vegetation–Atmosphere Systems: Monitoring, modeling and data assimilation. RapidEye data have been provided by the RapidEye Science Archive (RESA).

Literature

Arora, V.K., and Boer, G.J., 2002.
A GCM-based assessment of simulated global moisture budget and the role of land-surface moisture reservoirs in processing precipitation. Climate Dynamics. 20(1), 13-29.

Aubin, I., Beaudet, M., Messier, C., 2000.
Light extinction coefficients specific to the understory vegetation of the southern boreal forest, Quebec. Can. J. For. Res.-Rev. Can. Rech. For. 30, 168-177.

Bogena, H., Hake, J.F., Herbst, M., Kunkel, R., Montzka, C., Putz, T., Vereecken, H., Wendland, F., 2005a.
MOSYRURdWater balance analysis in the Rur basin. Schriften des Forschungszentrums Juelich, Reihe Umwelt 52.

Canty, M.J., Nielsen, A.A., 2008.
Automatic radiometric normalization of multitemporal satellite imagery with the iteratively re-weighted MAD transformation. Remote Sens. Environ. 112, 1025-1036.

Canty, M.J., Nielsen, A.A., Schmidt, M., 2004.
Automatic radiometric normalization of multitemporal satellite imagery. Remote Sens. Environ. 91, 441-451.

Coops, N.C., Smith, M.L., Jacobsen, K.L., Martin, M., Ollinger, S., 2004.
Estimation of plant and leaf area index using three techniques in a mature native eucalypt canopy. Austral Ecol. 29, 332-341.

Crockford, R.H., Richardson, D.P., 2000.
Partitioning of rainfall into throughfall, stemflow and interception: effect of forest type, ground cover and climate. Hydrol. Process. 14, 2903-2920.

Ehammer, A., Fritsch, S., Conrad, C., Lamers, J., Dech, S., 2010.
Statistical derivation of fPAR and LAI for irrigated cotton and rice in arid Uzbekistan by combining multi-temporal RapidEye data and ground measurements. In: Neale, C.M.U., Maltese, A. (Eds.), Remote Sensing for Agriculture, Ecosystems, and Hydrology Xii. Spie-Int Soc Optical Engineering, Bellingham.

Eitel, J.U.H., Long, D.S., Gessler, P.E., Smith, A.M.S., 2007.
Using in-situ measurements to evaluate the new RapidEye (TM) satellite series for prediction of wheat nitrogen status. Int. J. Remote Sens. 28, 4183-4190.

Eitel, J.U.H., Vierling, L.A., Litvak, M.E., Long, D.S., Schulthess, U.,
Ager, A.A., Krofcheck, D.J., Stoscheck, L., 2011.
Broadband, red-edge information from satellites improves early stress
detection in a New Mexico conifer woodland. Remote Sens. Environ.
115, 3640-3646.

Ge, J.J., 2009.
On the Proper Use of Satellite-Derived Leaf Area Index in Climate
Modeling. J. Clim. 22, 4427-4433.

Geerken, R., Zaitchik, B., Evans, J.P., 2005.
Classifying rangeland vegetation type and coverage from NDVI time
series using Fourier Filtered Cycle Similarity. Int. J. Remote Sens.
26, 5535-5554.

Lakshmi, V., Hong, S., Small, E.E., Chen, F., 2011.
The influence of the land surface on hydrometeorology and ecology:
new advances from modeling and satellite remote sensing. Hydrol.
Res. 42, 95-112.

Lu, L., Li, X., Ma, M.G., Che, T., Huang, C.L., Bogaert, J., Veroustraete, F.,
Dong, Q.H., Ceulemans, R., ieee, 2004.
Investigating relationship between landsat ETM plus data and LAI
in a semi-arid grassland of northwest China. Ieee, New York.

Lu, L.X., Pielke, R.A., Liston, G.E., Parton, W.J., Ojima, D., Hartman, M.,
2001.
Implementation of a two-way interactive atmospheric and ecological
model and its application to the central United States. J. Clim.
14, 900-919.

Montzka, C., M. Canty, P. Kreins, R. Kunkel, G. Menz, H. Vereecken,
F. Wendland (2008a).
Multispectral remotely sensed data in modelling the annual variability
of nitrate concentrations in the leachate. Environmental Modelling
and Software 23(8), 1070 - 1081.

Montzka, C., M. Canty, R. Kunkel, G. Menz, H. Vereecken,
F. Wendland (2008b).
Modelling the water balance of a mesoscale catchment basin using
remotely sensed land cover data. Journal of Hydrology 353, 322 - 334.

Norman, J.M., Kustas, W.P., Humes, K.S., 1995.
SOURCE APPROACH FOR ESTIMATING SOIL AND
VEGETATION ENERGY FLUXES IN OBSERVATIONS
OF DIRECTIONAL RADIOMETRIC SURFACE-TEMPERATURE.
Agric. For. Meteorol. 77, 263-293.

Norman, J.M., Kustas, W.P., Humes, K.S., 1996.
Source approach for estimating soil and vegetation energy fluxes
in observations of directional radiometric surface temperature
(vol 77, pg 263, 1995). Agric. For. Meteorol. 80, 297-297.

Propastin, P., Erasmi, S., 2010.
A physically based approach to model LAI from MODIS 250 m data
in a tropical region. Int. J. Appl. Earth Obs. Geoinf. 12, 47-59.

Robertson, B., Beckett, K., Rampersad, C., Putih, R., Ieee, 2009.
QUANTITATIVE GEOMETRIC CALIBRATION & VALIDATION
OF THE RAPIDEYE CONSTELLATION. Ieee, New York.

Sellers, P.J., Dickinson, R.E., Randall, D.A., Betts, A.K., Hall, F.G.,
Berry, J.A., Collatz, G.J., Denning, A.S., Mooney, H.A., Nobre, C.A.,
Sato, N., Field, C.B., Henderson-Sellers, A., 1997.
Modeling the exchanges of energy, water, and carbon between
continents and the atmosphere. Science 275, 502-509.

Sprintsin, M., Karnieli, A., Berliner, P., Rotenberg, E., Yakir, D., Cohen, S.,
2007.
The effect of spatial resolution on the accuracy of leaf area
index estimation for a forest planted in the desert transition zone.
Remote Sens. Environ. 109, 416-428.

Thompson, S.E., Harman, C.J., Konings, A.G., Sivapalan, M., Neal, A.,
Troch, P.A., 2011.
Comparative hydrology across AmeriFlux sites: The variable roles
of climate, vegetation, and groundwater. Water Resour. Res. 47.

Tyc, G., Tulip, J., Schulten, D., Krischke, M., Oxfort, M., 2005.
The RapidEye mission design. Acta Astronaut. 56, 213-219.

Weiss, J.L., Gutzler, D.S., Coonrod, J.E.A., Dahm, C.N., 2004.
Seasonal and inter-annual relationships between vegetation and climate
in central New Mexico, USA. J. Arid. Environ. 57, 507-534.

Wilhelm, W.W., Ruwe, K., Schlemmer, M.R., 2000.
Comparison of three leaf area index meters in a corn canopy. Crop Sci.
40, 1179-1183.

Xie, Y.C., Sha, Z.Y., Yu, M., 2008.
Remote sensing imagery in vegetation mapping: a review.
J. Plant Ecol. 1, 9-23.

Zeng, X.B., Dickinson, R.E., Walker, A., Shaikh, M., DeFries, R.S., Qi, J.G., 2000.
Derivation and evaluation of global 1-km fractional vegetation cover data for land modeling. J. Appl. Meteorol. 39, 826-839.

Zeng, X.B., Rao, P., DeFries, R.S., Hansen, M.C., 2003.
Interannual variability and decadal trend of global fractional vegetation cover from 1982 to 2000. J. Appl. Meteorol. 42, 1525-1530.

Zheng, G., Moskal, L.M., 2009.
Retrieving Leaf Area Index (LAI) Using Remote Sensing: Theories, Methods and Sensors. Sensors 9, 2719-2745.

Large Scale Multi Seasonal Land Cover Mapping in the South Siberian Kulunda Steppe with RapidEye data (Project ID: 501)

Sören Hese, Hans-Jörg Fischer
Friedrich-Schiller-University Jena, Grietgasse 6, 07743 Jena

E-Mail: soeren.hese@uni-jena.de

Large Scale Multi Seasonal Land Cover Mapping in the South Siberian Kulunda Steppe with RapidEye data

Sören Hese, Hans-Jörg Fischer

The Kulunda steppe in the Altai Krai, Russia is one of the most important granaries of the country. It was cultivated during the "Zelina action" back in the 1950s by ploughing the natural grasslands. As a result, the soils of the area have been exposed which led to various types of soil degradation and surface erosion. The aim of the KULUNDA project, funded by the German Federal Ministry of Education and Research (BMBF), is to develop and implement sustainable land use practices that are carbon neutral and can support better policies. The work presented in this paper shows the overall concept and first results from the land use mapping subproject in KULUNDA. We will at a later stage quantify the land use change using multitemporal EO data and develop a soil degradation mapping concept for the Kulunda steppe. Within this subproject RapidEye data provides the spatial high resolution reference dataset for the land use/cover status in 2012 and 2013. The land use/cover change analysis will be done for the 1950s, the 1970s, the late 1990s and 2012. The project will identify different crop types as well as the dominating steppe facies, such as forest steppe, typical and dry steppe. First results show that multi seasonal RapidEye data signatures can differentiate the main crop types on test sites selected from the 2012 ground survey. We also found the selected RapidEye 2012 data acquisition windows to be very critical for the setup and planning of a multi seasonal land use classification concept. Varying harvesting dates and various details of the management practices in the region additionally complicated the land use mapping approach in this work.

1. Introduction

The Kulunda steppe (Figure 1) is a typical example for a conversion region in temperate grasslands. During the time from 1954 to 1963 approximately 420.000 km^2 of steppe area were converted into intensely used farmland. Today the region has received lots of attention as the 'granary of Russia' and this importance will increase. But the large-scale intensive farming of the Kulunda steppe during the last decades proved to be inadequate. The consequence was wide spread soil degradation caused by erosion (Figure 2), decreased top soils and humus content loss, and therefore a decreased concentration of sequestered carbon (Meinel 2002).

Work presented in this paper is part of the KULUNDA project (10.2011-9.2016) „How to prevent the next „global dust bowl"? Ecological and economic strategies for sustainable land management in the Russian steppes: a potential solution to climate change", funded by the Ministry of Education and Research (BMBF) and linked to coordinated projects under the "Sustainable Management" topic of GLUES (Global Assessment of Land use Dynamics, Greenhouse Gas Emissions and Ecosystem Services). The GLUES coordination effort is summarized in e.g. Eppink et al. (2012). KULUNDA is part of the collaborative "Sustainable Land Management" research programme that "aims to improve the understanding of interacting ecological and socio-economic systems, and to help design better land management policies" (Epping et al. 2011).

The overall goals of the KULUNDA project are: „To both improve our understanding and develop methods to quantify the process of water balance, carbon cycle as well as soil and vegetation degradation under the current crop production systems practiced in Kulunda as an example for the Eurasian steppes and to help these soils become a carbon dioxide sink rather than a source thereby, giving the region a positive role in the worldwide concerns of mitigating climate change. KULUNDA aims at guiding the ongoing transformation process towards more sustainable land management practices" (kulunda.geo.uni-halle.de). We expect that KULUNDA will serve as a model for other converted areas of the Eurasian steppe region. The project is a cooperative effort under the lead of the Martin-Luther-University (MLU) Halle (project director: Prof. Dr. M. Frühauf). Subproject groups are organized by work package and subproject structures (Soil Degradation, Soil water and Solute Balance, Organic Carbon, Vegetation, Remote Sensing and Geodatabase, Organic Carbon Modelling, Planning Tools, Agricultural Business Economics, Social and Institutional Variables).

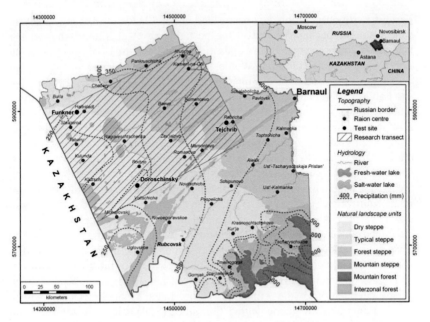

Figure 1: The Kulunda steppe region and project area with the main steppe regions, indicated research transect areas, precipitation data and hydrological information (www.kulunda.eu).

Figure 2: Left: agriculture land use on former steppe land cover in the KULUNDA project area (www.kulunda.eu), right: wind erosion (deflation) in the Kulunda region.

Various Earth observation data based land use and land cover change analysis concepts have been published in the past. Zhang et al. (2009) showed the vegetation cover changes from Landsat MSS/TM data of 1978 to 2005 for the Three Gorges Reservoir Area. Wulder et al. (2008) did a cross sensor change detection on forest landscape comparing Landsat 7 ETM+ with ASTER, SPOT-4 and Landsat 5 TM to develop a rank-order change detection process to minimize multi-temporal and multi-sensor differences in datasets. Coppin et al. (2004) did a review on the most important change detection methods and showed the requirements for multi-temporal datasets. In case of the Soviet and post-Soviet era land use change within the steppe regions, only few remote sensing driven approaches have been published. Hölzel et al. (2002) analyzed land use change in the North Caspian lowland for the post-Soviet transformation period on test areas in the Kalmykien Steppe (west of the Volga delta) with Landsat data from 1989 and 1998 and using a post classification change detection approach with a combined clustering and supervised maximum likelihood classification. Feng and Zhao (2011) used an ecosystem-model driven approach using the CENTURY model in combination with MODIS input data to monitor the grazing intensity and related changes in the Northern steppe of China. Tong et al. 2004 mapped steppe degradation in the Xilin river Basin, Inner Mongolia (China) with a Landsat data derived steppe degradation index (SDI) calculated for 1985 and 1999 and revealed large scale patterns of steppe degradation. Other groups investigated the impact of changing steppe extends for e.g. bird-populations (Kamp et al. 2011). Steppe degradation and desertification monitoring are important recurring topics within the Earth observation science community. However the complex land use/land cover change signature within the Kulunda steppe region hasn't been analyzed with full time series for the major land use change events (including the 1950s – 1970s and late 1990s) before. The use of a multi-seasonal data coverage for more precise land use and land cover classification is not a new concept but with the frequent revisit of the RapidEye constellation the acquisition of multiple coverages over a steppe region with low summer cloud coverage probability is just much more likely successful than with other EO systems (compare also with Conrad et al. 2012).

The aim of the project is to generate land cover change maps, which show the change vector in land use between pre Zelina status (before 1954) and today, using 4 time steps (before 1954, 1970ies, late 1990ies and 2012/13). The 2012/2013 land cover classification will be done using two multi seasonal RapidEye satellite data coverages provided by RESA/DLR through the RESA project 501 "Kulunda land use change mapping". Degradation analysis will take place in 2013 on selected training areas and results (ruleset development) will be transferred to the full KULUNDA project region. The soil degradation mapping for large areas is however a highly experimental component within the project and will be difficult with the reduced spectral signature dimension of spatially higher resolving sensors. We will also use the land use change information to detect potential regions for degradation. Land use/cover will be direct input to the regional carbon modeling group of PIK (Potsdam Institute for Climate Impact Research) within the project. The land degradation mapping product as well as the land use/land cover change map will be provided to the Soil Degradation group and to the Vegetation Analysis group.

2. Project Area and Data

For the development of a land use/cover change product in KULUNDA, large datasets are required to cover the project region (compare with Figure 1 and Figure 3). The steppe is located in the west Siberian plain, Altai Krai in Russia. In the past this area went through conversion processes forming a characteristic biome. Those have been taiga in the colder and semi desert in the warmer periods (Rudaya et al. 2012). Today the area is a transition zone of different climates, resulting in changing natural areas: the forest steppe in the North East, the typical steppe in the central part and the dry steppe in the South West of the Kulunda steppe. The steppe facies reflect a precipitation gradient, which decreases from north-east (600 mm/a) to the south-west (less than 250 mm/a). The soils of the Kulunda steppe mainly developed from quaternary alluvial deposits and postglacial alluvial sediments. Resulting from the prescribed climate, typical steppe soils like Tschernosem and Kastanosem developed. Those soils differentiate by their colour, which is changing with the humus content, resulting from biomass production from black (Tschernosem) in the forest steppe to brown (Kastanosem) in the dry steppe.

2.1 Satellite data

The following datasets in Table 1 were acquired for the project. The 1940s are covered using 26 topographic maps (1945 to 1947), provided by the Russian partner N. Kurepina (IWEB, Barnaul). The topographic maps indicate steppe land cover: 'meadow', 'thicket' and 'tall grass'. Classification of agricultural land use will be more difficult, as land cover is not mapped explicitly.

For the 1970s, Landsat 2 MSS data (8 scenes captured 1975/76, WRS1: Path: 162 to 159; Row: 23 and 24) provided by the USGS in GeoTIF format were acquired. To increase the accuracy of land cover/land use classification, panchromatic Corona Key-Hole KH4b datasets (recorded on panchromatic Kodak Eastman film) were ordered (56 sub-scenes captured in spring 1972). With the high spatial resolution of 1.8 m, this data will be used to increase the spatial resolution of Landsat 2 MSS data using pan fusion techniques (compare 4.1). The coverage of Landsat 2 MSS data is shown in Figure 3B. The late 1990s are covered by Landsat 7 ETM+ data (6 scenes recorded in 1999/2000, WRS2: Path: 150 to 148; Row: 23 and 24) delivered by the USGS in GeoTIF format (compare with Figure 3C). For 2012/2013 RapidEye data was ordered in two acquisition windows in 2012. For better crop type mapping accuracy, two different acquisition windows were suggested by local experts: 1st of June to 15th of July (W1) and 10th of August to 10th of September (W2). RapidEye provided 17 scenes for W1 and 15 scenes for W2 in NITF (National Imagery Transmission Format) format (Figure 5). The available datasets are summarized in Table 1.

Time	Year	Data/Sensor	No. of Scenes	Period
pre Zelina	before 1954	topographic maps	26	1945 to 1947
post Zelina	1970s	Corona KH-4B	56	April to May 1972
		Landsat 2 MSS	8	June and August 1975/76
post Sovjet	1990s	Landsat 7 ETM+	6	August to September 1999/2000
Most recent	2012 & 2013	RapidEye	17	1st June to 15th July
			15	10th August to 10th September

Table 1: Available datasets for the multitemporal satellite data driven land use change mapping in the KULUNDA project.

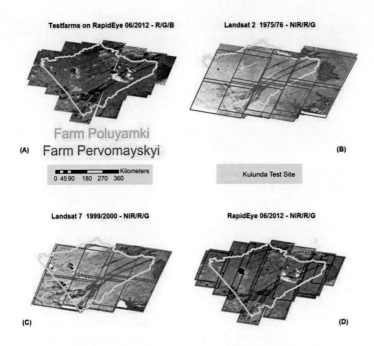

Figure 3: KULUNDA test areas: location of test farms (A), Landsat 2 data mosaic with scene contours (B), Landsat 7 data mosaic with scene contours (C), RapidEye data mosaic from 2012 with scene contours (D).

2.2 In situ field reference data

For calibration and validation of the crop type and land use/land cover classification, a field campaign and ground truthing campaign was performed in June 2012 during the W1 RapidEye data acquisition window. The field campaign was organized in cooperation with local farmers and done together with the other subproject partners. The growth status, crop types as well as the land use types were documented. The plots were also photographed together with a scale measurement and GPS position tracking. During that time 188 field plots were mapped within 3 weeks, 151 of those on and around the test farm in Poluyamki (compare with Figure 3A). In Figure 4 common crops of the area are shown (sunflower (A), different grains (B), peas (C) and buckwheat (D)). The field plots that were not used to create crop and vegetation signatures are used later for the land use/land cover classification validation.

Figure 4: Common crops of the Poluyamki farm area, KULUNDA project area, from June 2012 (compare with map position in Figure 3A), top: field overview, bottom: plants: sunflower (A), grains (B), peas (C) and buckwheat (D).

3. Data Pre-Processing

RapidEye L1B data was provided by RESA/DLR including Rational Polynomial Coefficients (RPC) in NITF format. For georeferencing the included RPC's were used to project the datasets to UTM zone 44 North on WGS84 with a spatial resolution of 6.5 m. Interpolation was performed with a cubic interpolation. Higher order interpolation is always preferred with spatial high resolution data. Slight greylevel changes are accepted. A nearest neighbour interpolation reduces the spatial integrity of the dataset at land cover class transitions with diagonal directions (staircase artefacts). W1 scenes were used as master for the geometric correction and sub-pixel accurate resampling of the W2 mosaic. W1 scenes were also used for georeferencing the 1972 Corona KH4b data to UTM. The Landsat 2 and Landsat 7 data was already provided in UTM zone 44 North. Back-scaling of the multispectral datasets to "At Sensor Radiance" and full processing to scaled reflectance was done using the ATCOR2 atmosphere correction algorithm following Richter (1996). The standard c0/c1 calibration files have been used to calculate "at sensor radiance" (RapidEye L1B data is provided in "at sensor radiance" and only has to be rescaled). No reference spectra were used. Originally it was planned to use an FS3 field spectroradiometer for reference spectra measurements in June 2012 but overall the formal process to use sophisticated equipment in Russia has reached a complexity that led to the decision to not use this instrument within the project in Russia. Landsat ETM+ data was corrected to scaled reflectance using one scene of each time frame as a master and relative correction of neighbouring datasets. The mosaic of time step W1 is shown in Figure 3D and in Figure 5.

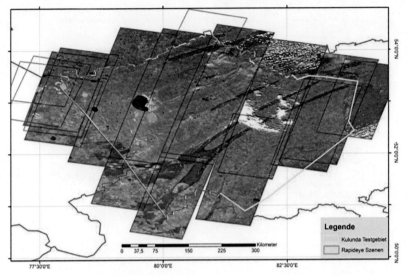

Figure 5: KULUNDA project area and radiometrically processed RapidEye data mosaic from June 2012 (with data coverage gap in the southern steppe region and cloud coverage shown in the central region of the KULUNDA project area).

4. Methods

4.1 Overall change detection concept

The subproject established a post-classification change detection concept. This is a consequence of the project and partner subproject needs. The subprojects will receive land use with spatial explicit distribution for every time step. A direct-multidate analysis (though conceptual more elegant) was therefore not suitable for this analysis. The planned data analysis will compare the classification results of each time step (post classification change detection). The concept is shown in Figure 6. For the pre Zelina, post Zelina and post Soviet times, the classes agricultural areas, steppe, forest and water will be used for the change analysis. A more detailed classification will be done in 2012 and 2013 with RapidEye data. This classification will separate the classes steppe and agriculture in their different facies and crop type. For the change analysis these sub classes will be aggregated (compare with Figure 6).

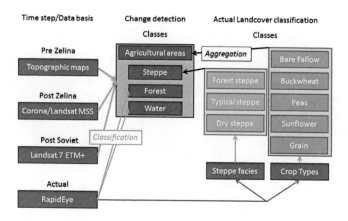

Figure 6: Class hierarchy for the KULUNDA land cover classification and RapidEye based 2012 crop type and steppe facies mapping concept.

For the most recent acquisition window in 2012, a multi-seasonal spectral signature of RapidEye mosaic W1 and W2 was created. The separation of the crop types was done using a bottom-up object orientated image classification concept.

In this paper we provide first results from data analysis of June (W1) and late August (W2) to differentiate the crop types by spectral object means.

4.2 RapidEye spectral crop signature analysis for 2012

The signatures of the dominating cultivated crops within the Poluyamki farm region were derived by choosing homogeneous field plots with single crop types from the test area around the Poluyamki farm. The reflectance distributions for each RapidEye channel in scaled reflectance for the classes buckwheat, grain, peas, sunflower and bare fallow is shown in Figure 7 and Figure 8. Best differentiation of the crop types is indicated in channel 3 and channel 5 for W1 (June dataset) (compare with Figure 8). In August 2012 (W2) best separability is indicated in channel 3, 4 and 5. Overall in August the red edge channel adds clearly to the signature separability. This is mainly due to the different phenology of the crop types and harvesting dates. The analysis of spectral properties of the different steppe facies with representative samples (provided by the Botanical Institute of Martin-Luther-University Halle) will follow in 2013. As those steppe signatures might overlap with the crop signatures shown here in Figure 7 and Figure 8 we will also use shape and object relational image object properties to increase class separability within the steppe classification concept in 2013 (e.g. using within field variability and between field vegetation as indicators for land use types).

Analysis of the phenology indicates that the acquisition date for W1 was too early in 2012 although exactly suggested by local experts. Looking at the second acquisition W2 the crops still show large range values. Some crops have been already harvested. The sunflowers in W2 show outliers that indicate a signature of photosynthetic active plants. Small patches of sunflowers are still photosynthetic active, while the majority already dried out. So the sunflowers are still on the fields, as well as the photosynthetic active buckwheat, while most of the dominating crops and peas are already harvested.

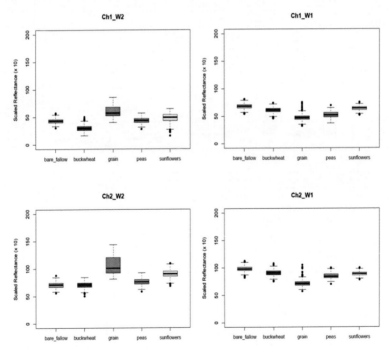

Figure 7: Top: RapidEye channel 1 (blue) spectral signature, bottom: RapidEye channel 2 (green) spectral signature, scaled reflectance (x10) Poluyamki agriculture land use.

We do not know yet if the test area is representative for the Kulunda steppe and if identification of different steppe facies is possible using 2 time steps (planned for 2013). There will also be different harvesting dates and changes due to local precipitation events that will likely complicate the multi seasonal land use mapping. As a result of the 2012 data analyses, the acquisition time frame of RESA KULUNDA 2013 will be shifted to July, to get signatures of the vegetation at the peak of their photosynthetic activity but we will also more closely monitor the actual weather situation within the region in cooperation with the farmers.

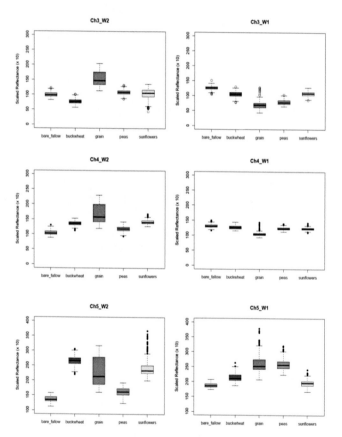

Figure 8: Top: RapidEye channel 3 (red) spectral signature, middle: RapidEye channel 4 (red-egde), bottom: RapidEye channel 5 (NIR), scaled reflectance (x10) test area Poluyamki agriculture land use.

4.3 RapidEye crop type mapping with multi seasonal data (Poluyamki)

For a first land use/land cover classification the ground reference data from 2012 was used to train a Nearest Neighbour classifier with 10 land use/land cover classes on the basis of both the W1 and the W2 data mosaic subsets for a test area around the farm area "Poluyamki" (Figure 9). This non-parametric classification was based on image objects with an object size over-segmenting the smallest field size using a bottom-up region growing segmentation algorithm published initially in Baatz and Schäpe (2000) and later in Benz et al. (2004). The classification concept in this paper was kept simple without use of additional object shape optimisation and/or relational- and class-related features. The overall aim was within this stage of the analysis to primarily investigate the spectral signatures and the potential for the crop type differentiation and to derive fuzzy membership class values for the image objects with the full 10-dimensional spectral RapidEye dataset.

The region has been mapped in summer 2012 with a ground reference campaign. Overall the crop type cultivation and distribution within the Poluyamki farm region is well understood. The input for the final land use change classification will be a more simplified version of this first classification. We do not expect to resolve as many classes in the 70s and 90s as we likely will on the basis of multi seasonal RapidEye data from 2012 (and 2013). But in 2012/2013 we aim to reach full understanding of the separability of as many arable crops in this region as possible. For the land use change mapping the various crop types will be aggregated to form one class "agricultural land use". This will likely be the only differentiation possible in the 1950s and 1970s. As usual we face a very limiting lack of spatial explicit reference data for these periods. For the RapidEye data coverage in 2012/2013 the crop type differentiation will also include the differentiation of wheat, barley and oat (with wheat being - also traditionally - the dominating crop type in this region).

Table 2 shows a validation of the preliminary Poluyamik farm area land use classification. Reference data was mapped during the 2012 field campaign. Overall accuracy for the Poluyamki area so far is only 66.45%. The relatively low value is caused mainly by the bad separability of sunflower and crops. This is also shown by low JM (Jeffries-Matusita) value of 1.42. The low value is likely caused by a similar phenology of crop and peas during the two acquisition windows in 2012.

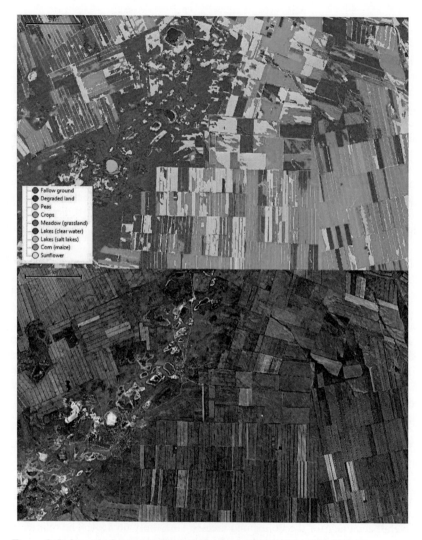

Legend (top left of image):
- Fallow ground
- Degraded land
- Peas
- Crops
- Meadow (grassland)
- Lakes (clear water)
- Lakes (salt lakes)
- Corn (maize)
- Sunflower

Figure 9: Poluyamki farm area (20x30 km subset) in the South of the Kulunda steppe region with agriculture dominated land use.
Top: supervised multi seasonal object-based classification using RapidEye data from June and August 2012,
below: RGB: 5/3/2 from August 2012 (W2 mosaic) with degraded land surface types in the west of the subset.

	Sun-flower	Maize	Crops	Buck-wheat	Fallow	Forest	Mea-dow	Clear water	Salty water	Peas	User Acc.
Sun-flower	51.2	1.3	3.2	2.1	19.2	1.6	21.7	0	0	7.5	**56.8**
Maize	0.6	88.8	0	0	0.5	0.3	0	0	0	0	**98**
Crops	28.6	1.1	23.2	5	4.2	0.7	0.3	0	0	1.4	**54.1**
Buck-wheat	4.3	0.2	0.2	92.7	0	4.1	1.7	0	0	0	**72.7**
Fallow	5.0	7.47	0	0	73.4	0	0.6	0	0	0	**88.7**
Forest	3.8	0	1.9	0	0	93.3	0	0	0	0	**45.7**
Mea-dow	0	1	0	0.1	2.4	0	75.7	0	0	0	**88.2**
Clear water	0	0	0	0	0	0	0	89.3	0	0	**100**
Salty water	0	0	0	0	0	0	0	10.7	100	0.1	**99.1**
Peas	6.3	0.0	71.5	0	0.2	0	0	0	0	90.9	**23**
Prod. Acc.	**51.2**	**88.8**	**23.2**	**92.7**	**73.4**	**93.3**	**75.7**	**89.3**	**100**	**90.9**	

Table 2: Validation results of the Poluyamik farm area - confusion matrix results with user- and producer-accuracies (rounded).

5. Discussion

The planned RapidEye data acquisition windows for the multi seasonal coverages (although discussed with local experts) were placed too early in June for the 2012 acquisition window. We plan to shift the first data acquisition to mid-July and the second data acquisition to mid-August for the 2013 data acquisition. Other complicating factors in this study are related to management practises (e.g. regrowing harvest loss) and mixed crop types. Also harvesting dates are not centrally organized and differ regionally. Soil degradation creates within field variance that increases the range of spectral properties on field parcel base. Most of the fields have a size of 300-400 by 2000-4000 sqm. Field boundaries are usually protected by narrow strips of woodland that are in the range of 5-20 m width. This class is difficult to characterise and shows up constantly as miss-classified crop types. Here the concept clearly needs some class-related and object relational feature descriptions that will be implemented at a later stage. Part of this problem is however also cause by slight geometric registration errors.

We also are facing difficulties to precisely characterise the various transitions from meadow to steppe or to degraded land (caused by grazing). Threshold values for the membership to one of these categories are not always clear and the spectral properties overlap. The degradation types have not yet been parameterised with local reference data. We do expect to include object based texture measures (e.g. Haralik homogeneity) and relational object information (object size and shape in combination with positional information). The overall spectral description will likely not be sufficient to characterize the different degradation types in the region. We will quantify the spectral characteristics of these classes in more detail within a later stage of the project when the steppe classes and test areas are analysed in more detail in 2013.

6. Summary and outlook

Within the first year of the KULUNDA project the subproject 5 "Geodatabase" build the multi temporal Earth observation data basis with Landsat, Corona, and RapidEye Earth observation data ordering, geometric and radiometric preprocessing, atmospheric correction and mosaicking for a full land use/land cover change mapping in the Kulunda steppe region. The ground reference data acquisition was started in summer 2012. A first land use/land cover classification for the first test region has been implemented and the signature separability analysis for the RapidEye data coverage from 2012 is on going. The first spectral separability analysis of RapidEye data in this work showed, that a multi-temporal RapidEye dataset is a valuable basis for land cover mapping in cultivated steppe regions and although validation is not finished yet we expect acceptable accuracies for the field plots with optimised acquisition dates.

The analyses of the combined land cover classifications of four time steps (1950s, 1970s, late 1990s and in 2012/13) will provide a change map for the change introduced by Zelina-Action in the 50s – the conversion of steppe area into arable land that has since undergone severe land degradation. RESA KULUNDA project will apply for another data acquisition in 2013, which will again be accompanied by a field campaign with focus on the degradation classes and steppe classes. Description of degradation types has also been started in winter 2012/13. Results of this work will be used by other KULUNDA sub projects. Land use and land cover information will be used to drive the prognostic vegetation modelling by partner PIK. The land use change and degradation information will be finally used for spatial explicit suggestions for changed management practices. Steppe fazies classification results will be used by the Vegetation sub project of KULUNDA: "Interactions of vegetation with changing land use and climate: baseline data for restoration of habitats and carbon sequestration potential" to calculate distribution and carbon sequestration potential of the non-crop vegetation types but this subproject will also provide spatial explicit reference information. Other links within KULUNDA are towards soil ecology, degradation understanding and defining optimized cultivation systems.

Acknowledgement

We greatly appreciate the thorough review and the constructive comments of our anonymous reviewer, which were instrumental in improving this paper. RapidEye L1B data was provided by the RapidEye Science Archive (RESA) of the German Aerospace Center (DLR) within the RESA project 501. The KULUNDA project is funded by the Ministry of Education and Research (BMBF) and linked to coordinated projects under the "Sustainable Management" topic of GLUES (Global Assessment of Land use Dynamics, Greenhouse Gas Emissions and Ecosystem Services).

References

Baatz, M., A. Schäpe, 2000.
Multiresolution segmentation – an optimization approach
for high quality multi-scale image segmentation, in:
Angewandte Geographische Informationsverarbeitung XII, Beiträge
zum AGIT-Symposium Salzburg 2000 (Strobl, Blaschke, Griesebner
(Hrsg.)), Heidelberg.

Barnes, E.M., T.R. Clarke, S.E. Richards, P.D. Colaizzi, J. Haberland,
M. Kostrzewski, P. Waller, C. Choi, E. Riley, T. Thompson, R.J. Lascano,
H. Li, M.S. Moran, 2000.
Coincident detection of crop water stress, nitrogen status and canopy
density using ground-based multispectral data. Proceedings of the Fifth
International Conference on Precision Agriculture, Bloomington, MN,
USA, 16-19 July 2000.

Benz, U.C., P. Hofmann, G. Willhauck, I. Langenfelder, M. Heynen, 2004.
Multi-resolution, object-oriented fuzzy analysis of remote sensing
data for GIS-ready information, ISPRS Journal of Photogrammetry
and Remote Sensing, 58, 2004, p239-258.

Conrad, C., M. Machwitz, G. Schorcht, F. Löw, S. Fritsch, S. Dech, 2012.
Potentials of RapidEye time series for improved classification
of crop rotations in heterogeneous agricultural landscapes: experiences
from irrigation systems in Central Asia, IEEE Proceedings Vol. 8174,
in Remote Sensing for Agriculture, Ecosystems, and Hydrology XIII,
C. M.U. Neale, A. Maltese, 4.10.2011, DOI: 10.1117/12.898345.

Coppin, P., I. Jonckheere, K. Nackaerts, B. Muys, E. Lambin, 2004.
Digital change detection methods in ecosystem monitoring: a review.
International Journal of Remote Sensing, 10(5), 2004, p1565-1596.

Eppink, F.V., A. Werntze, S. Mäs, A. Popp, R. Seppelt, 2012.
Land Management and Ecosystem Services – how collaborative
research programmes can support better policies, GAIA 21/1 (2012):
p55-63.

Feng, X.M., Y.S. Zhao, 2011.
Grazing intensity monitoring in Northern China steppe: Integrating
CENTURY model and MODIS data, Ecological Indicators 11, 2011,
p175-182.

Hölzel, N., C. Haub, M.P. Ingelfinger, A. Otte, V.N. Pilipenko, 2002.
The return of the steppe – large-scale restoration of degraded land in southern Russia during the post-Soviet era, Journal for Nature Conservation, 10, 2002, p75-85.

Kamp, J., R. Urazaliev, P.F. Donald, N. Hölzel, 2011.
Post-Soviet agricultural change predicts future declines after recent recovery in Eurasian steppe bird populations, Biological Conservation 144, 2011, p2607-2614.

Meinel, T., 2002.
Die geoökologischen Folgewirkungen der Steppenumbrüche in den 50er Jahren in Westsibirien. Ein Beitrag für zukünftige Nutzungskonzepte unter besonderer Berücksichtigung der Winderosion. Dissertation, Universität Halle-Wittenberg, Halle.

Richter, R., 1996.
A spatially adaptive fast atmospheric correction algorithm. International Journal of Remote Sensing, 17(6), 1996, p1201-1214.

Rudaya, N., L. Nazarova, D. Nourgaliev, O. Palagushkina, D. Papin, L. Frolova, 2012.
Mid-late Holocene environmental history of Kulunda, southern West Siberia: vegetation, climate and humans. Quaternary Science Reviews 48, p32-42.

Tong, C., Wu, J., Yong, S., Yang, J., Yong, W., 2004.
A landscape-scale assessment of steppe degradation in the Xilin River Basin Inner Mongolia – China, Journal of Arid Environments 59 (2004), 133-149.

Wulder, M.A., C.R. Butson, J.C. White, 2008.
Cross-sensor change detection over a forested landscape: Options to enable continuity of medium spatial resolution measures. Remote Sensing of Environment 112, 2008, p796-809.

Zhang, J., L. Zhengjun, S. Xiaoxia, 2009.
Changing landscape in the Three Gorges Reservoir Area of Yangtze River from 1977 to 2005: Land use/land cover, vegetation cover changes estimated using multi-source satellite data. International Journal of Applied Earth Observation and Geoinformation 11, 2009, p403-412.

Change Signature Analysis and Rapid Mapping Concepts for Tsunami Flooded Coastal Areas (Project ID: 483)

Sören Hese, Thomas Heyer
Friedrich-Schiller-University Jena, Institute of Geography, Earth Observation, Grietgasse 6, 07743 Jena, phone: +49 (0) 3641 948873,

E-Mail: soeren.hese@uni-jena.de

Change Signature Analysis and Rapid Mapping Concepts for Tsunami Flooded Coastal Areas

Sören Hese, Thomas Heyer

Earth observation based mapping and analysis of natural hazards plays a critical role in various aspects of post disaster activities. Spatial very high resolution Earth observation data provides important information to manage post tsunami activities on devastated land and to monitor recultivation and reconstruction. The automatic and fast use of high resolution Earth observation data for rapid mapping is however complicated by high spectral variability in densely populated urban areas and unpredictable textural and spectral land surface changes. This work presents first results of the RESA project SENDAI to develop an automatic tsunami induced land degradation classification system using Rapideye and TerraSAR-X data of the East coast of Japan captured after the "Great East Japan Earthquake" – the "Tohoku Earthquake". The project analyzes the spectral and textural change signature for various land use types of the Sendai bay area and develops a rapid mapping concept for flooded areas based on mono- and multitemporal data. Additionally vegetation change and potential regreening is investigated within the evacuation zone in various distances to the Fukushima Daiichi nuclear power plant. In this paper results of the multi year spectral and textural land use signature change are provided. First flooded area modeling approaches are explained that are based on mono temporal data. Overall the project also aims to create long-term recover analysis of the flooded land use types with multi annual data coverage between 2010 and 2015.

1. Introduction

The Sendai bay area is located in the North East of Japan and was heavily devastated by a tsunami that followed the M_w 9.0 undersea Tohoku earthquake at 5:46 UTC (UTC+9: 14:46 JST) on Friday, 11 March 2011. The earthquake is also known as the "Great East Japan Earthquake". It was located approx. 70 km East of the Oshika Peninsula of Tohoku (epicenter position). "Tohoku" is the most powerful megathrust (subduction zone type) measured earthquake ever in Japan (Ammon et al. 2011). The Tohoku earthquake created a 5-8 m upthrust that triggered a 6 -12 m high tsunami with maximum modeled coastal tsunami heights of up to 36 m (measured in Miyako – Iwate prefecture) (National Policy Agency Japan 2011). The wave height is very much depending on the coastline shape and the vertical shore profile (PARI 2011). The tsunami reached the coast beginning with 15:12 JST and caused a nuclear level 7 accident at three reactors in the Fukushima I nuclear power plant within the next 48 hours. The disaster also impacted the national economy, electricity supply and tourism.

Various algorithms have been published for tsunami early warning (Beltrami 2011, Eckert et al. 2012, Garay & Diner 2007, Joseph 2011 and Stosius et al. 2011). Some publications directly deal with inundation and tsunami loss simulations (Srivihok et al. 2012) or are modeling vulnerability using building type information (number of floors, building classifications), shoreline distance and elevation (derived from spatial high resolution digital surface models) and fusing the information within a GIS (Eckert et al. 2012). Important work has also been published in the framework of the International Charter Space and Major Disasters by ZKI (Center for Satellite Based Crisis Information of DFD) of the German Aerospace Center (DLR) as part of the SAFER FP7 research programme (GMES Emergency Response Service) or e.g. SERTIT (Universite de Strasbourg). These organizations perform around the clock rapid mapping services during environmental disasters for mapping of flood extend, damaged infrastructure, endangered populations or evacuation areas. Published work of ZKI concentrated on TerraSAR-X flood mapping (Sandro et al. 2009), tsunami early warning and decision support (Steinmetz et al. 2010), and tsunami risk knowledge and assessment (Voigt et al. 2006, Wegscheider et al. 2011 and Strunz et al. 2011). Taubenböck et al. (2008) showed that risk and vulnerability in the tsunami context can be assessed using structural characteristics of urban morphology. This analysis identified the potential of urban structural mapping for the identification of safe areas and the potential number of affected people.

Few studies are working on the spatial/spectral properties of tsunami-induced (post tsunami) land surface changes (Römer et al. 2010, Römer et al. 2011, Yan & Tang 2009, Bovolo & Bruzzone 2007, Leone et al 2004) or rapid mapping techniques of impacted areas. Most of the studies try to improve modeling of future tsunami events by mapping the destruction and linking the degree of destruction to specific building types or urban land use types. The work in this paper uses some of the findings from tsunami flood modeling for better rapid mapping of the changed (post tsunami) land surface. Focus is on robust transferrable approaches with a minimum of needed additional auxiliary data.

This work utilizes multitemporal RapidEye data, TerraSAR-X data to parameterize the spectral and textural change signature that the Tohoku tsunami flooding caused. The project develops rapid mapping approaches, textural and spectral indices to provide means to automatically map changes caused by the tsunami flooding and damage of infrastructure objects (road systems). The overall goal is 1. to analyze the potential of spatial high resolution data for robust automatic zonal mapping of infrastructure damages, flood zone delineation and recovery signature understanding and 2. to analyze the regreening and change information within the evacuated zoning around the Fukushima nuclear power plant (that will be a result of a changed land use in this region). This is done using pre and post tsunami multispectral datasets, TerraSAR-X data and ASTER GDEM V2 terrain height information and street network data. The project determines typical textural and spectral changes that lead to rapid mapping approaches for the identification of destroyed infrastructure. For this task the project derives zonal statistics, textural statistics and image object relational properties from image objects using robust and transferrable classification concepts. Mono- and multi-temporal data analysis for tsunami-induced flood mapping concept development are investigated. Mono-temporal flood extend modeling is preferred as it will be the usual data situation for most Earth observation based rapid mapping approaches and no time consuming and precise relative georeferencing is needed.

The evacuation zone around the Fukushima nuclear power plant will likely show changes in land use due to the absence of on-going human land cultivation and this process will introduce a regreening in this area in the future. SENDAI will monitor the vegetation status in different proximities to the Fukushima power plant and will compare these results to similar other studies. The indirect nuclear power plant core meltdown effects on the region will be mapped with special attention given to the red edge properties of the various vegetation types within this region testing spectral ratios and change ratios for the years 2010-2015.

2. Data and Study Area

RapidEye data was received in 2010, 2011 and 2012 for time periods in August 2010 (pre tsunami), March 2011 (post tsunami), August 2011, March 2012 and August 2012 (Table 1, Figure 1 and Figure 2). More data acquisitions are planned for the March and August time periods in the years 2013, 2014 and 2015. Some areas of the ordered data coverage could not be used due to cloud cover, but overall the data coverage for 2010 and especially for March 2011, August 2011 and August 2012 is excellent for this analysis (Figure 1). RapidEye captured data of the coastal region 20 hours after the tsunami reached the North East coast of Japan (Figure 2).

Stripmap TerraSAR-X data products in HH polarization in Single Look Slant Range Complex (SSC) format (L1B data) were ordered from the DLR EOWEB archive from march 2011 after successfully submitting TerraSAR-X AO proposal COA1415 for TerraSAR-X data (20 products). TerraSAR-X data will be used as an additional dataset for mono-temporal flood modeling tests but these data has not yet been included in this analysis.

As a ground reference layer for the area flooded by the March 2011 tsunami manual digitized map data is used. This data is provided by the "Tsunami Damage Mapping Team" of the Association of Japanese Geographers, http://danso.env.nagoya-u.ac.jp/20110311/map/index_e.html) and is freely available. These topographic maps were manually mosaicked and georeferenced to the RapidEye data coverage for the Sendai bay using 25 ground reference points (Figure 3 shows one of 5 used map coverages). For the land use status in 2011 data from the National Land Digital Information (Grid square data (approx. 100m * 100m) of the Ministry of Land, Infrastructure, Transport and Tourism of Japan is used - no figure provided) and received from the „Tohoku Geographical Association", http://tohokugeo.jp (site accessed in September 2012).

Scene ID	Test site/region	Comments
2010		
2010-08-21T021709_RE2	Sendai bay - used	10% scattered
2010-08-24T021759_RE5	NE coast	
2010-07-28T021343_RE2	NE coast	35 cloudy clustered
2010-07-28T021317_RE2	NE coast	Haze/30% cloudy
2010-07-22T022508_RE5	NE coast	35% cloudy clustered
	NE coast	
2011		
2011-03-14T022000_RE2	Sendai bay, NE coast	20% cloud cover
2011-03-19T022456_RE2	Sendai bay, NE coast -used	30% cloud cover
2011-08-10T022540_RE3	Sendai bay, SE coast	10% scattered
2011-03-12T021626_RE5	SE coast	5% cloud cover
2011-08-05T022005_RE3	NE coast	5-10% scattered
2011-03-12T021602_RE5	SE coast - used	40% cloud cover, snow
2011-08-13T023105_RE1	Sendai bay NE	5%, line drops
2011-08-13T023131_RE1	Fukushima	5%, haze
2011-08-15T022959_RE3	Sendai bay – used	10%
2011-08-16T023044_RE4	Fukushima SE	10% haze
2011-08-27T022447_RE1	NE	5%
2011-08-28T022528_RE2	Sendai bay	20%
2011-08-28T022553_RE2	Fukushima SE	5%
2012		
2012-03-04T022945_RE5	NE	90% Snowy Cloudy
2012-03-14T022159_RE1	SE	40 % Cloudy
2012-03-21T022551_RE3	SE	Ok
2012-04-02T022030_RE1	SE	Ok
2012-04-02T023802_RE5	SE	75 cloudy snowy
2012-04-09T022418_RE3	SE	Ok
2012-04-10T022416_RE4	SE	
2012-04-10T022437_RE4	Fukushima SE	
2012-04-13T023022_RE2	N	
2012-04-15T022851_RE4		95% Snowy Cloudy
2012-04-15T022917_RE4		55 cloudy snowy
2012-07-19T022309_RE4	NW	
2012-08-01T021652_RE3	SW	Ok
2012-08-01T023962_RE2	SW	Ok
2012-08-02T021719_RE4	Fukushima/Sendai	Ok
2012-08-22T021815_RE5	SW	Ok
2012-08-22T021849_RE5		Ok
2012-08-02T021849_RE5	Fukushima/Sendai	

*Table 1:   RESA RapidEye data sets received for the project SENDAI in 2010-2012
(datasets with high cloud coverage were intentionally tasked
(though data acquisition was originally not suggested by RapidEye)
and later ordered from the archive for 2010 -2012 to get one full coverage
for the coastal region).*

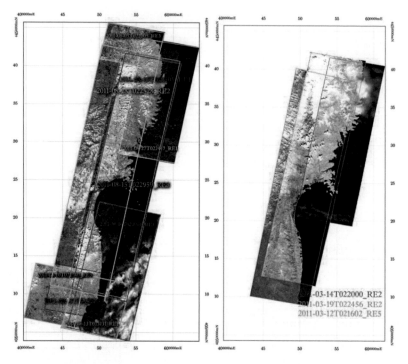

Figure 1: Study sites and RESA RapidEye data coverage for March and August 2011 within the RESA SENDAI project: Sendai bay, Miyagi prefecture, east coast of Japan.

This work uses ASTER GDEM V2 terrain elevation data for the mono temporal flood extend modeling. ASTER GDEM V2 data is an improved version with reduced artifacts (associated with poor stereo data coverage) especially in water covered areas (Tachikawa et al. 2011). ASTER GDEM V2 data was received through the LP DAAC Global Data Explorer covering the east coast of Japan with the data tiles: N36E140, N37E140, N37E141, N38E140, N38E141.

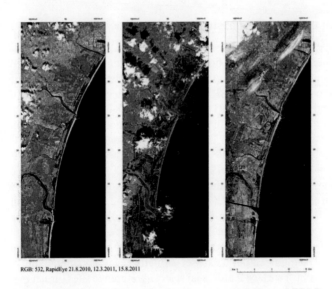

RGB: 532, RapidEye 21.8.2010, 12.3.2011, 15.8.2011

Figure 2: Sendai bay study site, Miyagi prefecture, east coast Japan, RESA RapidEye data coverage from left to right: 21 August 2010, 12 March 2011, 15 August 2011, UTM zone 54, WGS84, 6.5 m, RGB: RapidEye channels: 532.

Figure 3: Topographic map information with indicated tsunami flood extend (Association of Japanese Geographers).

3. Data and Pre-Processing

RapidEye data was provided by DLR (RESA)/RapidEye in NITF format (National Imagery Transmission Format) including RPCs (Rational Polynomial Coefficients). Georeferencing was done using the provided RPC information with ortho-correction using SRTM DTM data in Geotiff format (spatial resolution: 90 m) and reprojection to UTM zone 54 WGS84 with a spatial resolution of 6.5 m with cubic interpolation (spatial intact diagonal image object features are an important prerequisite for successful image segmentation – therefore minor interpolation based grey value changes are accepted). L1B RapidEye data was corrected for atmospheric effects using the ATCOR2 atmosphere correction algorithm (Richter 1996) with a factor back scaling of L1B-data from 16Bit to "At Sensor Radiance" (ATCOR uses: mW cm-2 sr-1 μm-1, RapidEye scale factor 10E-3 is based on W m-2 sr-1 μm-1) and full processing and correction to factor 10 scaled reflectance. Fine-tuning of c0/c1 parameters is done using reference spectra for concrete (Sendai airport from August 2010) and water surfaces. The multi temporal data set is finally tested for comparable reflectance values on robust surface features on selected reference sites (urban highly sealed surface types (homogenous image objects in urban areas) and large inland water areas. The reference sites show similar reflectance values between August 2010, 2011 and 2012. The deviation within the green reflectance values is below 25 DN (2.5% reflectance) and within the NIR reflectance below 43 DN (4.3% reflectance).

4. Methods and Results

Data analysis is structured into two different sub projects within SENDAI. Within sub project I "Sendai bay flood change mapping and modelling" the spectral and spatial change features caused by the tsunami - changing most of the land surface objects within the flooded region - are investigated and results are used to build a rapid mapping model for flooded areas. Sub project II "Land use change within the Fukushima evacuation zone" looks for trends within the vegetation cover and former agricultural land use (mostly paddy rice field land use) that is likely slowly transformed to "natural" vegetation within the next years.

4.1 Subproject "Sendai Bay flood change mapping and modelling"

Reflectance change analysis on agricultural land use:

The multi temporal data from August 2010, March 2011, August 2011 and August 2012 were used to analyse the spectral change signature of flooded areas. Results indicate a very quick restoration of high near infrared reflectance of former vegetated areas. Mean reflectance values in NIR2 however do not reach the "original" values from August 2010 (Figure 4). Within the red edge channel (labelled NIR1 in Figure 4) reflectance change is less pronounced. NIR1 reflectance values in August 2011 are on par with reflectance in August 2010 although with much higher variability. We assume that a consequence of the flooding is a higher variability of the within field reflectance mainly due to topographic variability and random debris agglomerations.

Reflectance ratios with data from 2012 show a comparable reflectance change. Two different NIR ratios are investigated: the NDVI using NIR2 channel (RapidEye channel 5) and a red edge ratio (edgeNDVI). The latter is calculated using the RapidEye red and NIR1 channels and sum normalizing the difference. The NDVI in 2012 showed an ongoing trend for increased variability (Figure 5). Overall the mean NDVI did not reach the same values as in August 2010. This can also be explained with a change and partly a stop of cultivation and land use management in a 500 m distance to the shore. Haralick texture measures using "Homogeneity" and "Correlation" showed lower values in August 2011 and comparable values in August 2012 (Figure 6). The texture measures were calculated object based on agricultural land use. Interpretation is difficult but the stopped cultivation on some fields generated comparable texture measures. The within field spectral variability in 2012 is comparable with the variability in 2011.

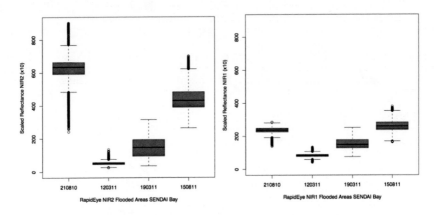

Figure 4: Scaled (x10) RapidEye NIR and RedEdge (NIR1) reflectance on agricultural land use (mainly paddy fields) before and shortly after the „Great Japan Earthquake" Tsunami in 2011 (Sendai Bay/Japan east coast).

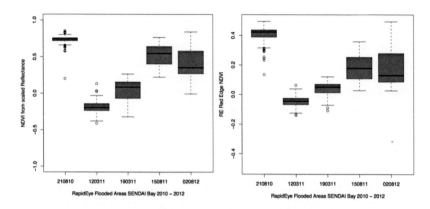

Figure 5: NDVI (left) and Red Edge NDVI (right) based on scaled (x10) RapidEye NIR and RedEdge (NIR1) and red reflectance on agricultural land use (mainly paddy fields) before and shortly after the „Great Japan Earthquake" Tsunami in 2011 (Sendai Bay/Japan East coast). Time frame August 2010 to 2012.

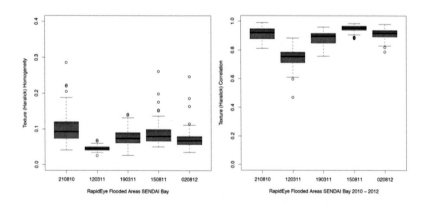

Figure 6: Object based texture measure „Homogeneity" (left) and Correlation (based on Haralick) from RapidEye NIR channel on agricultural land use (mainly paddy fields) before and shortly after the „Great Japan Earthquake" Tsunami in 2011 (Sendai Bay/Japan East coast). Time frame August 2010 to 2012.

While reflectance is an important property for modeling the actual flooded areas it is not sufficient to map those areas in monotemporal data. Textural properties in combination with reflectance are seem critical for a differentiation of the respective modified land cover classes. Analysis of texture metrics "Homogeneity" and the linked measure of "Correlation" indicate however very quick post tsunami changes (Figure 6). Change of textural properties should be taken into account when mapping devastated areas. The direction of change is however very much linked to the original land use type structure or buildup type that is removed by the tsunami, the buildup derived and developed debris clustering/ concentration and coastal geomorphology and draining characteristics of the inundated area. For the Sendai bay area small villages and mostly paddy field structures are dominant (Miyazawa 2011). We will test the textural characteristics in 2013 but there is an indication that textural measures are dominated by the position/shape of water filled sinks within the field boundaries.

A full more complex inundation model will need much more input data than is available for rapid mapping in a post tsunami flood mapping scenario. This work will however integrate some components to increase the mapping accuracy and to step up to "concept transferability" to other coastal regions.

4.2 Tsunami Flood Extend Modeling and Mapping

The project is testing different approaches to post tsunami flood extend modeling using post tsunami RapidEye multispectral data and ASTER GDEM V2 global digital elevation model data. SRTM90 has been evaluated but was not found to be usable for this analysis. The spatial resolution of SRTM90 is not sufficient to delineate small-scale terrain maxima and minima. The overall quality was found to be lacking for this analysis. Especially on the coastal plains some heights were not reasonable. We did not create quantitative analysis but compared to the ASTER GDEM V2 model most of the small scale ridges of some urban areas and infrastructure objects like elevated federal roads were not clearly delineated and buried within the coarse SRTM90 pixels.

So far we tested three different approaches for flood extend modeling. One approach is based on a simple bathtub-model, the second is based on a cost-distance-model with variations using additional cost parameters and a third approach uses an object based growth model with a combined bathtub and water sink region growing.

4.2.1 The Bathtub-Model

A simple method for the generation of hypothetical flood extend is the bathtub approach. Based on land height information, the approach simulates a wave to flow inland until it reaches an elevation equal to the wave starting height. For the assessment of tsunami vulnerability and risk this common approach was used by Eckert et al. (2012), Dall'Osso et al. (2009) and Wood (2009).

In this study the bathtub approach was used for recalculating the tsunami inundation area within a rapid mapping scenario. In addition to the land height information, which was provided by the global digital elevation model *ASTER GDEM V2*, the model is based on a post tsunami multispectral *RapidEye* dataset. The multispectral dataset is used to classify water filled sinks within the inundation area. These sinks mark the minimum expansion of the tsunami wave. For the classification of the filled sinks, a Normalized Difference Water Index is used:

$$NDWI = \frac{NIR - Blue}{NIR + Blue} \tag{1}$$

A fixed NDWI threshold of 0.2 combined with zero height in the digital elevation model is supposed to separate all filled sinks from ocean and other land areas. The next step comprises an iterative bathtub model. The idea behind the approach is to increase the wave starting height until the majority of classified inundation sinks are covered.

At a starting wave height of about one meter the model classifies all areas with a digital elevation equal or less one meter, which are connected to the pre classified ocean. In a next step the percentage of all covered filled sinks within the modeled inundation area is computed. After that the model increases the wave height step by step, classifies inundation area and calculates the covered sinks percentage until (nearly) all sinks are covered.

Figure 7 shows the model result for a test site located in the Sendai plain. At a wave height of about 12 meters nearly all filled sinks (96.2 %) are covered by the modeled inundation area. In comparison to the reference data, the result shows an overestimation of the inundation area. One explanation for the overestimation is that the bathtub model does not consider the slope or surface roughness, also horizontal flow direction changes or infiltration rates are not modeled.

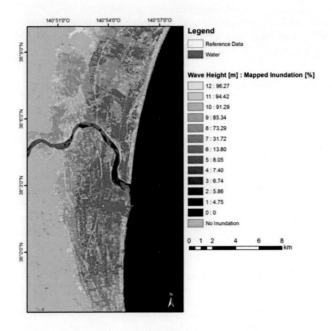

Figure 7: Bathtub model result in comparison with the reference data. For each model iteration the wave height and the corresponding percentage of mapped inundation (water) is shown.

4.2.2 The Cost-Distance-Model

Another approach to simulate the expansion of tsunami waves is the evaluation of the wave travel time. For this purpose rasterized shortest path algorithms are used to identify paths of the least resistance for the tsunami movement. Spaltenberger et al. (2007) introduced the use of cost distances by the evaluation of tsunami travel times based on digital elevation data.

Similar to the Bathtub model approach, the Cost-Distance model is used to model the inundation zone. The model is based on cost distances to find the shortest paths on a surface and determines the tsunami travel time or rather the minimum inundation extent. Therefore the model views pixel centers as nodes and the distance between pixel centers as links. Based on these nodes and links back tracking pathfinder algorithms are used to trace the travel path from destination to source (Xu & Lathrop 1994).

The cost distance approach comprises three steps: (1) calculation of cost surface (2) calculation of least cost paths (3) classification of inundation by iterative increasing of costs.

For an initial model run the cost surface simply consists of digital elevation data.

This primary cost surface could be improved by additional factors to calibrate the model. The additional factors could be slope and aspect or multispectral data based features, which are linked to the surface roughness.

To find least cost paths on the cost surface a rasterized shortest path algorithm provided by ESRI (2010) is used. Within the *Cost Distance function* all 8 adjacent cells for each raster cells are considered to find the least cost path. The cost to travel to one of four directly connected neighbors is computed by:

$$Cost_{horizontal\ or\ vertical} = \frac{Cost\ A + Cost\ B}{2} \tag{2}$$

where Cost A and Cost B represent the values of the cost surface of directly connected neighbors. For a diagonal travel to one of four adjacent cells the cost is computed by:

$$Cost_{diagonal} = \frac{\sqrt{2}\ (Cost\ A + Cost\ B)}{2} \tag{3}$$

where Cost A and Cost B represent the values of the cost surface of diagonal adjacent neighbors. The cost value is than multiplied by the cell size (ESRI 2010). To determine the cumulative cost at each cell location, the cost distance algorithm is based on the widely used Dijkstra shortest path algorithm (Dijkstra 1959).

The final classification approach of the inundation area is very similar to the bathtub model. The first step is the classification of filled sinks by using the NDWI and elevation data. The second step increases water height and calculates percentage of model covered sinks. Instead of increasing wave starting height, the Cost-Distance-Model increases the cost distances or the tsunami travel time until (nearly) all sinks are covered by the model.

Figure 8 shows the model result for the test site located in the Sendai plain. For this result the initial cost surface simply consists of digital elevation data. In comparison to reference data, the model result shows an overestimation of the inundation area.

We will increase the quality of this approach incorporating additional multispectral buildup indicators and special more explicit elevation data derived slope and aspect related cost factors.

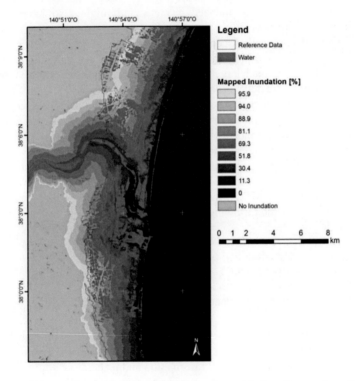

Figure 8: Cost-Distance model result in comparison with the reference data. For each 1 % cost rise (between 0 and 9 % overall costs) the corresponding percentage of mapped inundation (water) is shown.

4.2.3 Object based relational region growing model

As a principle prerequisite it is assumed that the flooding starts from the coastline, while "coastline" includes estuaries and rivers up to a shore-distance of 2000 m – as a first step. We than add criteria to describe A. the terrain height and B. the flooded land surface properties. The overall flood extend modeling is split into the following steps:

I.   For a rapid mapping approach a coastline shape geometry from an external source is preferred as the original coastline geometry is likely covered by tsunami induced changes and might also have been completely removed.

II.   River objects usually function as an amplifier for the destruction power – the tsunami wave is transferred far into the backcountry and land is flooded within much larger distances to the coastline. River formations are therefore treated as coastlines within this concept.

III.   For the flooded area it is expected that the remaining water covered land surface shows a patch-structure with increased shore distance. The region-growing concept therefore has to grow even on patchy and scattered water object structures.

IV.   The flood mapping is done using a region growing concept starting from A the shore/river line and B from the flooded water objects on the basis of ASTER GDTM height information. Area growing inlands is controlled by the following threshold conditions:

    a.   The maximum search distance between water classified objects is reached or

    b.   Overall distance to the shore is exceeded or

    c.   Local maximum terrain height is reached.
       So far slope/aspect differences are not accounted for.

The overall concept follows a bath-type approach suggested by Eckert et al. 2012 but controlled by spectral indicators and classified water objects. The model can be driven without extensive external information and is therefore applicable in other coastal regions. There is however so far no clear information about some critical thresholds (f.e. slope and terrain height thresholds or distance thresholds for various tsunami categories) that are robust and applicable for other tsunami flood events. Calibration of the classification model is difficult as the data basis is weak. Only few strong tsunami events were densely recorded with satellite data in the past and land use/buildup structure and inundation drainage are not directly comparable. Although textural measures are regarded as more robust image analysis features (compared to spectral image properties) - within the tsunami land use change context it is evident that knowledge of original build up structure and density is needed to evaluate the textural information from destruction and debris agglomeration as these are directly linked. An example of a first flood mapping result is available in Figure 9. The object based approach has not been validated but as the region growing is directly linked to the water covered sinks the model does not overestimate the flooded area but it underestimates the region in between detected water filled regions.

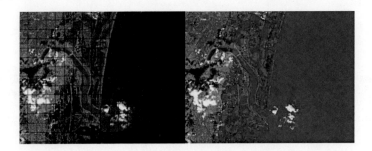

Figure 9: Left: RapidEye RGB data from 12.3.2011 (channel 5/3/2).
Offshore area mapping and region growing on flooded landsurfaces (left),
Sendai bay area subset (16 x 12 km).

4.3 Subproject "Land use change within the Fukushima evacuation zone"

The analysis of the land use and land cover change within the Fukushima 20 km evacuation zone is a long term investigation that will proceed in 2013, 2014 and 2015 - hopefully extended thereafter with RapidEye data or other datasets. A first analysis of 150 samples mainly on paddy rice cultivation land use type

a. within the 20 km evacuation radius and
b. within the main fallout area (elliptically elongated in North-East direction originating from the Daiichi power plant).

Indicated that calibrated and corrected near Infrared reflectance values have decreased leading to reduced NDVI values and reduced red-edge NDVI values in August 2012. Overall spectral variability has increased since 2010 and regrowing of vegetation is not dominant within the tested samples (Figure 10). Overall there is a weak trend towards a reduced vegetation signal. A regreening isn't detectable so far.

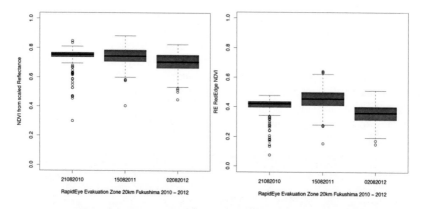

Figure 10: NDVI (left) and Red Edge NDVI (right) based on scaled (x10) RapidEye NIR2 and RedEdge (NIR1) and red reflectance on agricultural land use before (2010) and after the evacuation in march 2011 (Fukushima district/Japan East coast). Data from August 2010, 2011 and 2012. Samples were captured object based within the 20 km evacuation radius (NE Quadrant) on paddy rice field cultivation.

5. Discussion

Mapping of flooded land (and the related changes) without using precisely calibrated multi temporal Earth observation data is difficult to accomplish. Results from this study are indicating low accuracies so far. Terrain height is an important information for modeling the flood expansion. ASTER GDTM data clearly improves the inundation modeling approach but a combination with buildup indicators will likely improve the inundated land classification. The most important aspect – the transferability to other tsunami flooded regions is difficult to validate as test regions do not exist or have different land use and buildup structure. Some surprising signature changes within the Sendai bay in 2012 can be explained with a stop of recultivation – a consequence of the ongoing coastal protection activities.

6. Summary and Outlook

Results in this work show that the spectral land surface properties of the flooded area in the Sendai bay have not reached the original state from 2010. Spectral variability remains much higher due to not completely recovered vegetation of paddy rice field land use and given up agriculture in this region. Mono temporal flood extend mapping of the Tohoku tsunami flood shows that multi temporal data is not necessarily needed when simple rational and context information is used. Overall the flood mapping concept is successful although optimization with additional control parameters is needed to increase the mapping accuracy. So far no tests of transferability have been performed but more detailed validation is in progress.

The project will use additional RapidEye data coverages in 2013 – 2015 to map the recultivation/recovering and changed land use/land cover of the tsunami flooded areas and the evacuated area around Fukushima Daiichi. More spectral features of buildup density for the flood area modeling will be integrated into the spatial modeling concept in order to increase the overall mapping accuracy. The concept will be also extended with TerraSAR-X data (in combination with terrain height). While monotemporal flood mapping is a simple approach from a data calibration and methodological point of view, there are some restrictions within this concept that can be overcome with a multi temporal change detection concept. The direct comparison of the original intact building information or settlement structure derived from Earth observation data with the flooded post tsunami situation allows more detailed and robust change detection (as shown within the spectral and textural image data signature change analysis in sub chapter "Reflectance Change Analysis on Agricultural Land use"). The project will therefore also develop a multi temporal flood mapping approach and discuss both concepts for operational applications.

Within the Fukushima Daiichi evacuation zone reflectance on agricultural land use remains lower in the NIR domain with less pronounced red absorption and in consequence lower NDVI and red edge ratios. The overall trend in this region indicates higher spectral variability, lower vegetation density and stronger patchy appearance of vegetation due to the stopped cultivation in this region. The overall trend has to be validated and explained in 2013 with reference data of regrowing vegetation types and photo coverages of test fields. However - so far we cannot detect a strong regreening in this region.

Acknowledgements

We greatly appreciate the thorough review and the constructive comments of our anonymous reviewers, which were instrumental in improving this paper. RapidEye L1B data was provided by the RapidEye Science Archive (RESA) of the German Aerospace Center (DLR) within the RESA project 483.

References

Ammon, C. J., Lay, T., Kanamori, H., & Cleveland, M., 2011.
A rupture model of the great 2011 Tohoku earthquake. Earth Planets
Space, 1-4, 2011.

Beltrami, G. M., 2011.
Automatic, real-time detection and characterization of tsunamis in
deep-sea level measurements. Ocean Engineering, 38, 1677-1685.

Bovolo, F., & Bruzzone, L., 2007.
A Theoretical Framework for Unsupervised Change Detection
Based on Change Vector Analysis in the Polar Domain. IEEE
Transactions on Geoscience and Remote Sensing, 45, 218-236.

Dall'Osso, F., M. Gonella, G. Gabbianelli, G. Withycombe,
D. Dominey-Howes, 2009.
Assessing the vulnerability of buildings to tsunami in Sydney.
Natural Hazards and Earth System Sciences, 9, 2015-2026.

Dijkstra, E. W., 1959.
A note on two problems in connexion with graphs.
In: Numerische Mathematik, Band 1, 269-271.

Eckert, S., J. Robert, G. Zeug & E. Krausmann, 2012.
Remote sensing-based assessment of tsunami vulnerability and risk
in Alexandria, Egypt. Applied Geography, 32, 714-723.

ESRI, 2010.
ArcGIS Resource Center: Cost Distance (Spatial Analyst).
<http://help.arcgis.com/en/arcgisdesktop/10.0/help/index.html#/Cost_
Distance/009z00000018000000/> (state: 2011) (access: 08-01-2013).

Eckert, S., Jelinek, R., Zeug, G., & Krausmann, E., 2012.
Remote sensing-based assessment of tsunami vulnerability and risk
in Alexandria, Egypt. Applied Geography, 32, 714-723.

Japanese National Police Agency, 2011.
Damage Situation and Police Countermeasures associated with 2011
Tohoku district – off the Pacific Ocean Earthquake". (PDF)
20 April 2011, 18:00 JST, retrieved 15 May 2011.

Joseph, A., 2011.
Tsunamis - Detection, Monitoring, and Early-Warning Technologies.
Academic Press: Burlington/San Diego.

Leone, F., Lavigne, F., Paris, R., Jean-Charles Denain, Vinet, F., 2004.
A spatial analysis of the December 26th, 2004 tsunami-induced
damages: Lessons learned for a better risk assessment integrating
buildings vulnerability, Applied Geography, Volume 31, Issue 1,
January 2011, Pages 363-375 dx.doi.org/10.1016/j.apgeog.2010.07.009.

Michael, J., Garay, D., Diner, J., 2007.
Multi-angle Imaging Spectro Radiometer (MISR) time-lapse imagery
of tsunami waves from the 26 December 2004 Sumatra–Andaman
earthquake *Remote Sensing of Environment*, Volume 107, Issues 1-2,
15 March 2007, Pages 256-263.

Miyazawa, H., 2011.
Land Use and Tsunami Damage in Pacific Coast Region
of Tohoku District, The 2011 East Japan Earthquake Bulletin
of the Tohoku Geographic Association, 25. May, 2011
(http://tohokugeo.jp/disaster/disaster-e.html, accessed in Sept. 2012).

PARI - The Port and Airport Research Institute, 2011.
Urgent survey for 2011 Great East japan Earthquake and tsunami
disaster in ports and coasts - Part I (Tsunami).
<http://www.pari.go.jp/en/files/3653/460607839.pdf>
(last modified: 2011-04-28).

Post, J., Wegscheider, S., Mueck, M., Zosseder, K., Kiefl, R., Steinmetz, T.,
Strunz, G., 2009.
Assessment of human immediate response capability related to tsunami
threats in Indonesia at a sub-national scale, *Nat. Hazards Earth Syst.
Sci.*, 9, 1075-1086, 2009.

Römer, H., Kaiser, G., Sterr, H., & Ludwig, R., 2010.
Using remote sensing to assess tsunami-induced impacts on coastal
forest ecosystems at the Andaman Sea coast of Thailand. *Nat. Hazards
Earth Syst. Sci.*, 10, 729-745.

Römer, H., Jeewarongkakul, J., Kaiser, G., Ludwig, R., & Sterr, H., 2011.
Monitoring post-tsunami vegetation recovery in Phang-Nga province,
Thailand, based on IKONOS imagery and field investigations –
a contribution to the analysis of tsunami vulnerability of coastal
ecosystems. International Journal of Remote Sensing, 33, 1-32.

Sandro, M., Twele, A., Voigt, S., 2009.
Towards operational near real-time flood detection using a split-based automatic thresholding procedure on high resolution TerraSAR-X data. Natural Hazards and Earth System Sciences (NHESS), 9, 303-314. http://www.nat-hazards-earth-syst-sci.net/9/303/2009/nhess-9-303-2009.pdf

Spaltenberger, T., Rosner, H.-J & Hochschild, V., 2007.
GIS-gestützte Modellierung von Tsunamilaufzeiten. - Strobl, J., Blaschke, T. & G. Griesebner (Hrsg.): Angewandte Geoinformatik 2007, Beiträge zum 19. AGIT-Symposium Salzburg, Heidelberg.

Srivihok, R., K. Honda, A. Ruangrassamee, V. Muangsin, P. Naparat, P. Foytong, N. Promdumrong, P. Aphimaeteethomrong, A. Intavee, J.E. Layug, T. Kosin, 2012.
Development of an online tool for tsunami inundation simulation and tsunami loss estimation, Continental Shelf Research, Available online 18 September 2012 (dx.doi.org/10.1016/j.csr.2012.08.021).

Steinmetz, T., Raape, U., Teßmann, S., Strobl, C., Friedemann, M., Kukofka, T., Riedlinger, T., Mikusch, E., and Dech, S., 2010.
Tsunami early warning and decision support, *Nat. Hazards Earth Syst. Sci.,* 10, 1839-1850, doi:10.5194/nhess-10-1839-2010.

Stosius, R., G. Beyerle, A. Hoechner, J. Wickert, Lauterjung, J., 2011.
The impact on tsunami detection from space using GNSS-reflectometry when combining GPS with GLONASS and Galileo, *Advances in Space Research*, Volume 47, Issue 5, 1 March 2011, Pages 843-853.

Strunz, G., Post, J., Zosseder, K., Wegscheider, S., Mück, M., Riedlinger, T., Mehl, H., Dech, S., Birkmann, J., Gebert, N., Harjono, H., Anwar, H., Sumaryono, S., Khomarudin, R. M., and Muhari, A., 2011.
Tsunami risk assessment in Indonesia, *Nat. Hazards Earth Syst. Sci.,* 67-82, 2011.

Taubenböck, H., Post, J., Kiefl, R., Roth, A., Ismail, A., Strunz, G., Dech, S., 2008.
Risk and vulnerability assessment to tsunami hazard using very high resolution satellite data – the case study of Padang, Indonesia, remote sensing – new challenges of high resolution, Bochum 2008, C. Jürgens (ed.).

Tachikawa, T., Kaku M., Iwasaki, A., Gesch, D., Oimoen, M., Zhang, Z., Danielson, J., Krieger, T., Curtis, B., Haase, J., Abrams, M., Crippen, R., Carabajal, C., 2011.
ASTER Global Digital Elevation Model Version 2 – summary of validation results, the ASTER validation team, http://asterweb.jpl.nasa.gov/gdem.asp.

Voigt, S., Kemper, T., Riedlinger T., Kiefl, R., Scholte, K., Mehl, H., 2006.
Satellite Image Analysis for Disaster and Crisis-Management Support. *IEEE Transactions on Geoscience and Remote Sensing,* 45 (6), Seiten 1520-1528. ISSN 0196-2892.

Wegscheider, S., Post, J., Zosseder, K., Mück, M., Strunz, G., Riedlinger, T., Muhari, A., and Anwar, H. Z., 2011.
Generating tsunami risk knowledge at community level as a base for planning and implementation of risk reduction strategies, Natural Hazards and Earth System Sciences, 11, 249-258, 2011.

Wood, N., 2009.
Tsunami exposure estimation with land-cover data: Oregon and the Cascadia subduction zone, *Applied Geography*, 29, 158-170.

Xu, J. & R.G, Lathrop, 1994.
Improving cost-path tracing in a raster data format. *Computers & Geosciences*, 20, 10, 1455-1465.

Yan, Z., & Tang, D., 2009.
Changes in suspended sediments associated with 2004 Indian Ocean tsunami. *Advances in Space Research*, 43, 89-95.

Evaluation of the anisotropy factors on aquatic test sites caused by RapidEye off-nadir data acquisition with the Mobile Goniometric System (MGS) (Project ID: 455_1)

Patrick Wolf, Sebastian Roessler, Thomas Schneider, Arnulf Melzer
Technische Universität München, Limnologische Station,
82393 Iffeldorf, Germany

E-Mail: patrick.wolf@tum.de

Evaluation of the anisotropy factors on aquatic test sites caused by RapidEye off-nadir data acquisition with the Mobile Goniometric System (MGS)

Patrick Wolf, Sebastian Roessler, Thomas Schneider, Arnulf Melzer

Inherent anisotropic properties of natural surfaces affect their reflectance and hence the interpretation of remote sensing data. The Mobile Goniometric System (MGS) was employed to find out the range of variations due to effects attributed to the BRDF of two aquatic surfaces, the terrestrial vegetation of Phragmites australis and a shallow water site with Chara spp. canopy. The paper presents the data acquisition method and briefly describes the fundamental differences in the anisotropic behaviour of the two surface types. The magnitude of the phenomenon was investigated on base of the anisotropic factor (ANIF). While the Phragmites australis canopy showed typical land vegetation characteristics, drastic increases of the remote sensing reflectance at certain viewing geometries at the water test site were observed and attributed to sun glint effects. Our results indicate that for deriving bottom reflectance out of such measurements in addition to the well-known sun glint, water surface and water column effects, the data should be corrected for anisotropy features as well.

1. Introduction

The anisotropic properties of vegetation surfaces, first mentioned by Kimes (1983), affect the classification of remote sensing data (Wardley 1984, Schaaf et al. 2002, Strub et al. 2002) as well as the application of various vegetation indices (Wardley 1984, Kuusk 1991, Dorigo et al. 2005, Coburn et al. 2010). Out of these anisotropic features, bi-directional reflectance distribution functions (BRDF) were described for numerous terrestrial surfaces (Kuusk 1991, Sandmeier et al. 1995, Sandmeier et al. 1999, Solheim et al. 2000, Strub et al. 2002, Biliouris et al. 2003, Peltoniemi et al. 2005, Suomalainen et al. 2009, Feingersh et al. 2010) by collecting data with various goniometer or directional measurement systems like FIGIFIGO (Suomalainen et al. 2009), CLabSpeG (Biliouris et al. 2003), PARABOLA (Deering et al. 1990), EGO facility (Koechler et al. 1994), FIGOS (Sandmeier et al. 1995), MUFSPEM (Manakos et al. 2004) or IGF (Feingersh et al. 2005). However, studies concerning BRDF effects of aquatic vegetation or shallow water sites are rare. Valta-Hulkkonen et al. (2004) and Mobley et al. (2003) investigated the bi-directional effects of

Phragmites australis in CIR aerial photographs and of shallow water bottoms by simulations, respectively. Schneider et al. (2004a) used the anisotropy ratio from directional Chris/Proba data for *Phragmites australis* characterization in the Danube Delta.

In this paper, we present the results of in situ measurements, taken with the Mobile Goniometer System (MGS), first introduced at the Chris/Proba workshop 2004 in Frascati (Schneider et al. 2004b). Data collection took place upon *Phragmites australis* and at a shallow water site with *Chara* spp. canopy. The required constant illumination (Bachmann et al. 2012) was given by a stable high pressure situation in September 2012. This assured that illumination conditions were nearly constant during 30 minutes of one data take. Besides the methodological approach, mainly the differences of the anisotropic factors (ANIF) between terrestrial and aquatic applications are presented. ANIF were calculated out of RAMSES hyperspectral datasets, rescaled to RapidEye. In according to outcomes of Lu et al. (2012), the most drastic effects at the water site were caused by sun glint.

As the RapidEye satellites can record with viewing angles of up to ±20° (RapidEye 2012) and other sensors are equipped with pointing capabilities in the range of +/- 30° or cover large areas, anisotropy effects across the scan line may introduce additional errors. Analogue to land applications, such BRDF measurements may be used in the future to correct remote sensing data of the aquatic environment to the nadir view.

2. Methods

2.1 Bi-directional reflectance distribution function

The bi-directional reflectance distribution function (BRDF) (Nicodemus et al. 1977) describes the anisotropic reflection properties of surfaces as a function of two illumination and two viewing angles. These are the solar zenith angle θ_i, the solar azimuth angle φ_i, the sensor zenith angle θ_r and the sensor azimuth angle φ_r. The BRDF function (Equation 1) is defined by dividing the radiance dL_r [W m^{-2} sr^{-1} nm^{-1}] reflected in one direction (θ_r, φ_r) by the incident irradiance dE_i [W m^{-2} nm^{-1}] from direction (θ_i, φ_i) (Sandmeier/Itten 1999):

$$f_r(\theta_i, \varphi_i; \theta_r, \varphi_r; \lambda) \approx \frac{dL_r(\theta_i, \varphi_i; \theta_r, \varphi_r; \lambda)}{dE_i(\theta_r, \varphi_r; \lambda)} \tag{1}$$

To derive structural information from BRDF data, the anisotropy factors (ANIF) can be calculated with equation 2 (Sandmeier/Deering 1999).

$$ANIF(\theta_i, \varphi_i; \theta_r, \varphi_r; \lambda) = \frac{R(\theta_i, \varphi_i; \theta_r, \varphi_r; \lambda)}{R_0(\theta_i, \varphi_i; \lambda)} \qquad (2)$$

2.2 Test sites

Measurements were carried out upon a population of *Phragmites australis* (common reed) in Iffeldorf (47.8°N, 11.3°E) and at a shallow water site with *Chara* spp. canopy at Lake Starnberg (48.0°N, 11.3°E) in September 2012. Both test sites are located in Upper Bavaria (Southern Germany). Lake Starnberg itself is an oligotrophic finger lake, with an averaged depth of 53.2 meters.

2.3 The Mobile Goniometric System (MGS)

Measurements were carried out with the MGS (Figure 1, a). Instead of the initially used ASD Field Spec FR with a bifurcated cable setup, the RAMSES submersible system of the TriOS Company was used. The advantage of the RAMSES system is a simultaneous acquisition of hemispherical irradiance (E_d) and directional object reflection measurement (L_u). From a nadir height of 10m above the measured surface and a field of view of 7° of the L_u sensor an area of about 1.2m² is covered. The application of the "inscribed-angle" principle for the MGS construction allows keeping changes in the observed area with increasing viewing zenith angle below 10%. Due to little temporal changes of the light field at this time of the year and a fast data acquisition within 30 minutes, nadir (Figure 1, b) and off-nadir (Figure 1, a) hyperspectral measurements were collected at almost constant illumination conditions due to a clear sky situation.

By dividing L_u by E_d, remote sensing reflectances (R_{rs}) were calculated and rescaled to RapidEye spectral resolution afterwards using the spectral response function. While the E_d sensor on the very top of the construction was not moved (Figure 1, c), the recording positions of the L_u sensor at an extension arm (Figure 1, d) varied. Data collection was carried out mainly following the measurement scheme recommended by Schneider et al. (2007). At the azimuth angles of 0°, 30°, 60°, 90°, 135° and 180° relative to the sun azimuth, measurements at 20°, 40° and 60° of zenith were taken (Figure 1, f). Position accuracy is ±3° in both directions from the nominal position (Schneider et al.

2007). The exact measurement position is recorded by an electronic dual axis angle measurement device (Hy-Line Comp.) and used for interpolation when calculating the BRDF "surface" for the respective measurement series. Additional measurements were taken at the sun hotspot and around it in 5° distance in each direction and from nadir position, which results in a total number of 24 view directions measured. At each recording position, the mean and the standard deviation were calculated out of 5 scans. The extension arm can be moved in azimuth and zenith direction by motor and hand, respectively. Additional instruments mounted at the MGS are two Canon G10 digital cameras (Figure 1, e) with a remote control for stereo photographs and a light pointer to control positions at and around the hotspot (Figure 1, d). The power supply was warranted by a 12V DC car battery.

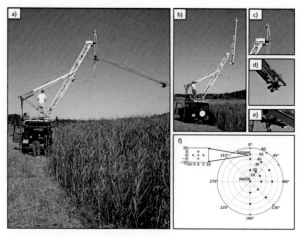

Figure 1: The Mobile Goniometric System (MGS).
a) viewing in the orthogonal plane at 60° zenith angle; b) nadir position;
c) Ed-sensor on the very top; d) Lu-sensor and hotspot control;
e) 2 Canon G10 digital cameras;
f) Measurement strategy of 24 recording positions with a regular raster
of 19 positions (red points) and 5 additional positions in and around
the hotspot (yellow points).

As symmetry of the anisotropic effects with respect to the principle plane was assumed (Suomalainen et al. 2009), the values at the azimuth angles of 30°, 60°, 90° and 135° were mirrored to 330°, 300°, 270° and 225°, respectively. Solely the 5° hot spot measurements were excluded from mirroring. Afterwards, ANIF were calculated at the recording and their mirrored positions by equation 2 (Sandmeier/Deering 1999) and finally interpolated with Delaunay interpolation techniques (Sandmeier 2000) for the complete hemisphere between 0° and 60° of viewing zenith angle. Hence, in nadir position, ANIF is 1. If reflection signals are higher or lower referenced to the nadir measurement, equation 2 will result in values higher than 1 or between 0 and 1, respectively. The particular minimum and maximum values at each band were combined to maximum and minimum reflectance spectra.

3. Results

In case of measurements at the water site, very high reflectance intensities could be recognized at azimuth angles of 135° and 180° (Figure 2, dashed and solid red lines). For example at an azimuth of 180° and a zenith of 40° – opposite to the hotspot – values were up to 100 times higher, depending on the wavelength. To make the values of the anisotropic factor (ANIF) at the water test site comparable to those of the *P. australis* test site, measurements at azimuth angles between 135° and 180° were masked prior to mirroring and interpolating the data.

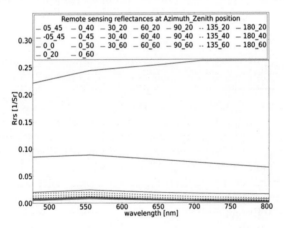

Figure 2: Remote sensing reflectances at the water test site, collected from different directions; most are coloured in green, measurements with high intensities are given in dashed (at azimuth of 135°) or solid (at azimuth of 180°) red.

In case of the *P. australis* (Figure 3), the highest ANIF at every band of the RapidEye sensor can be observed in the particular hotspot (2.5 times higher than nadir). The lowest values can be found at 180° azimuth and 20° zenith angle, with exception of band 803nm, where the minimum is at nadir. According to (Sandmeier et al. 1998, Beisl 2001, Camacho-de Coca et al. 2001) the principle plane exhibits a stronger anisotropy than the orthogonal plane. The maximum and minimum reflectance spectra are plotted in Figure 3 together with the measured nadir spectra, including standard deviations (maximum: red; minimum: blue; nadir: black). It can be seen that the nadir reflectance is close to the minimum reflectance and that for all other view directions and all bands higher intensities are measured (Figure 3, polar plots a) to e)).

At the shallow water site Starnberg (Figure 4), fundamental differences to the *P. australis* site can be observed. Despite the masking between 135° and 225°, there can still be detected high ANIF values (up to 3.5 times higher than at nadir) at the adjacency of 135° and 225° for zenith angles higher than 40°. Comparable increases in the backward plane are only present at 803nm and at zenith angles higher than 50° (Figure 4, polar plot e)). Within all polar plots, there are also regions, where ANIF values are only half of nadir values. According to Figure 3, the maximum (red), minimum (blue) and nadir (black) reflectances are plotted above the polar plots. Similar to *P. australis*, the nadir spectra is closer to the minimum than to the maximum. At both test sites, single standard deviations are very low.

4. Discussion

Goniometric measurements were taken under stable and clear sky conditions. Most of the experimental conditions mentioned by Sandmeier (2000), like a sufficient documentation, additional measurements in hotspot direction or frequently taken reference measurements were fulfilled. Atmospheric corrections were neglected, as the distance between L_u sensor and the objects was only 10m and less. Additionally, the averaged surface area was large enough and the L_u sensor, which collected the reflected light, had a small solid angle (7°) and was mounted in the far field to avoid shadowing caused by the instrument itself (Snyder 1998). Exceptions are given solely for the hot spot and the 5° larger zenith angle in the principal plane. Since the shaded area is small compared to the spot measured from 10m above, the effect is negligible in practice. As reflectance could only be taken at one half of the hemisphere, the data were mirrored at the solar principle plane. However, measurements at both sides of the hot spot were practically identical (at -5° and +5°), such supporting this procedure.

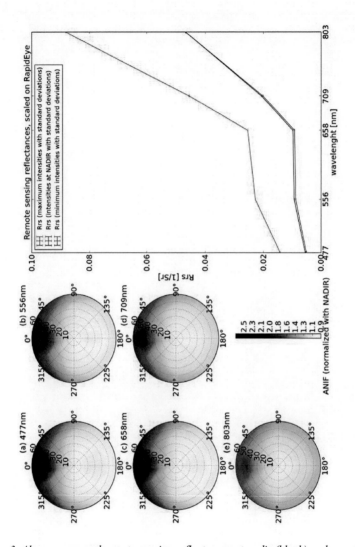

Figure 3: Above: measured remote sensing reflectances at nadir (black) and remote sensing reflectances, combined of the particulate minimum (blue) and maximum (red) intensities at RapidEye bands.
Below: anisotropic factors (ANIF) of Phragmites australis (common reed) at RapidEye bands with azimuths ranging from 0° to 360° and zeniths ranging from 0° to 60° (polar plots a) to e)).

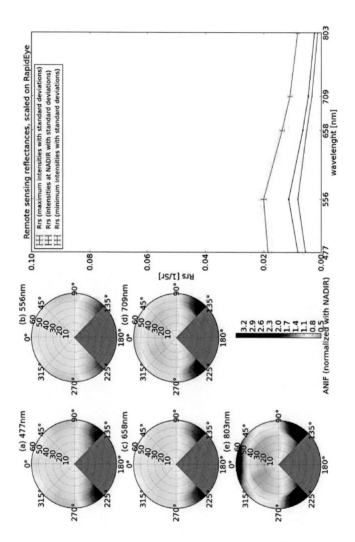

Figure 4: Above: measured remote sensing reflectances at nadir (black) and remote sensing reflectances, combined of the particulate minimum (blue) and maximum (red) intensities at RapidEye bands.
Below: anisotropic factors (ANIF) of the shallow water site at RapidEye bands with azimuths ranging from 0° to 360° and zeniths ranging from 0° to 60° (polar plots a) to e)); region between 135° and 180° was masked, due to high sun glint effects.

At the *P. australis* test site, BRDF effects turned out to be within the expected range as known from other terrestrial surfaces. At all RapidEye bands, the highest differences of the ANIF were measured within the principle plane, the highest values around the hotspot.

The ANIF values from the water test site were obviously controlled by sun glint effects resulting from waves and wavelets on the water surface (Lu et al. 2012). To support classifications of remote sensing data of aquatic surfaces by such kind of goniometric field data, this field data has to be corrected first. Besides sun glint corrections (Lyzenga et al. 2006, Kay et al. 2009), also water surface (Lee et al. 1998) and water column corrections (Albert/Mobley 2003) need to be conducted. In general the findings of Beisl (2001) were confirmed, who recommended that the data take by airborne sensors has to be carried out by flying along the principle plane and scanning perpendicular to it.

With view to scans deviating from the orthogonal plane, BRDF measurements should be used to correct the signal differences. In case of recording for example at a relative azimuth of 45° (to the principle plane), table 1 shows the minimum and maximum values of ANIF (at our test sites), at 550nm and typical pointing capabilities/viewing angles offered by various remote sensing sensors (i.e. RapidEye, Sentinel 2, WolrdView 2, APEX, HyMap, HySpex).

45° azimuth (550nm)	pointing/viewing (°)	5	10	15	20	25	30
water test site	ANIF (min)	0,97	0,95	0,92	0,89	0,88	0,88
	ANIF (max)	1,03	1,06	1,10	1,13	1,20	1,28
P. australis test site	ANIF (min)	1,00	1,00	1,00	1,00	1,00	1,00
	ANIF (max)	1,04	1,09	1,13	1,18	1,24	1,30

Table 1:   Minimum and maximum ANIF at our test sites at a relative azimuth of 45° and 550nm, depending on typical pointing/viewing angles.

Conclusion

The Mobile Goniometric System (MGS) was employed to find out the range of variations due to effects attributed to the BRDF of the measured surfaces. Anisotropic factors (ANIF) of *Phragmites australis* and a shallow water test site with *Chara* spp. canopy were calculated by normalizing the data with the nadir reflectance and compared with respect to their main differences. Opposite to the *P. australis* test site with the expected backward scattering characteristic, the water site measurements of the *Chara* spp. submersed vegetation showed pronounced forward scattering. The wave focussing effect, observed for underwater measurements with the RAMSES set-up at this site was negligible. As main attenuation source in this case the sun glint was identified.

The conclusion is that at view to illumination geometries with sun glint effects superimposing the object signal, a characterisation of lake bottom surfaces by remote sensing methods is not possible. Hence, for interpretation tasks of remote sensing data based on such goniometric measurements, further research in terms of sun glint-, water surface- and water column-corrections has to be carried out.

Finally, after applying the mentioned corrections, the spectral response of terrestrial and aquatic vegetation depends on BRDF effects. By knowing these effects, the possible analyses of off-nadir images – which also offer a shorter revisit time – enhance the monitoring. Especially in case of submerged vegetation a multitemporal monitoring like RapidEye enables is useful, as different phenological changes of different plants improve their spectral differentiation.

Acknowledgements

The authors would like to thank their colleagues at the Limnologische Station of the TUM University and the Bavarian State Ministry of the Environment and Public Health (StMUG) for support and funding.

Literature

Albert, A., Mobley, C. D. (2003).
An analytical model for subsurface irradiance and remote sensing reflectance in deep and shallow case-2 waters. In: Optics Express, 11.

Bachmann, C. M., Gray, D., Abelev, A., Philpot, W., Montes, M. J., Fusina, R., Musser, J., Li, R. R., Vermillion, M., Smith, G., Korwan, D., Snow, C., Miller, W. D., Gardner, J., Sletten, M., Georgiev, G., Truitt, B., Killmon, M., Sellars, J., Woolard, J., Parrish, C., Schwarzschild, A. (2012).
Linking goniometer measurements to hyperspectral and multisensor imagery for retrieval of beach properties and coastal characterization.

Beisl, U. (2001).
Correction of bidirectional effects in imaging spectrometer data. Remote Sensing Laboratories, Zurich.

Biliouris, D., vom Berge, K., Fleck, S., Nackaerts, K., Dutre, P., Muys, B., Willems, Y., Coppin, P., Ieee (2003).
CLabSpeG: a Compact Laboratory Spectro-Goniometer system enabling rapid and complete BRDF assessments of forest elements.

Camacho-de Coca, F., Gilabert, M. A., Meliá, J. (2001).
Bidirectional Reflectance Factor Analysis from Field Radiometry and HyMap data. In: Proceedings of the Final Results Workshop on DAISEX (Digital AIrborne Spectrometer EXperiment), ESA SP-499, ESTEC, 15–16 March 2001, 163-175.

Coburn, Craig A., Van Gaalen, Eric, Peddle, Derek R., Flanagan, Lawrence B. (2010).
Anisotropic reflectance effects on spectral indices for estimating ecophysiological parameters using a portable goniometer system. In: Canadian Journal of Remote Sensing, 36, S355-S364.

Deering, D. W., Eck, T. F., Otterman, J. (1990).
Bidirectional reflectances of selected desert surfaces and their 3-parameter soil characterization. In: Agricultural and Forest Meteorology, 52, 71-93.

Dorigo, W., Richter, R., Müller, A. (2005).
A LUT approach for biophysical parameter retrieval by RT model inversion applied to wide field of view data. Proceedings of 4th EARSeL Workshop on Imaging Spectroscopy. Warsaw.

Feingersh, T., Ben-Dor, E., Filin, S. (2010).
Correction of reflectance anisotropy: a multi-sensor approach.
In: International Journal of Remote Sensing, 31, 49-74.

Feingersh, T., Dorigo, W., Richter, R., Ben-Dor, E. (2005).
A new model-driven correction factor for BRDF effects in HRS data.
In: Proceedings of 4th EARSeL Workshop on Imaging Spectroscopy.

Kay, Susan, Hedley, John D., Lavender, Samantha (2009).
Sun Glint Correction of High and Low Spatial Resolution Images
of Aquatic Scenes: a Review of Methods for Visible and Near-Infrared
Wavelengths. In: Remote Sensing, 1, 697-730.

Kimes, D. S. (1983).
Dynamics of directional reflectance factor distributions for vegetation
canopies. In: Applied Optics, 22, 1364-1372.

Koechler, C., Hosgood, B., Andreoli, G., Schmuck, G., Verdebout, J.,
Pegoraro, A., Hill, J., Mehl, W., Roberts, D.,Smith, M. (1994).
The European otpical facility - technical description and 1st
experiments on spectral unmixing.

Kuusk, A. (1991).
The angular-distribution of reflectance and vegetation indexes in
barley and clover canopiesI. In: Remote Sensing of Environment,
37, 143-151.

Lee, Z. P., Carder, K. L., Mobley, C. D., Steward, R. G., Patch, J. S. (1998).
Hyperspectral remote sensing for shallow waters. I. A semianalytical
model. In: Applied Optics, 37, 6329-6338.

Lu, Yunfeng, Sun, Zhongqiu, Zhao, Yunsheng (2012).
Measurement of water-leaving radiance on smooth water surfaces
at different viewing angles using high-resolution spectroradiometer.
In: Chinese Optics Letters, 10.

Lyzenga, David R., Malinas, Norman R., Tanis, Fred J. (2006).
Multispectral bathymetry using a simple physically based algorithm.
In: Ieee Transactions on Geoscience and Remote Sensing, 44,
2251-2259.

Manakos, I., Schneider, T., Bekakos, M. P. (2004).
A mobile unit for field spectroradiometric measurements. In: Neural,
Parallel & Scientific Computations, 12, 525-44.

Mobley, Curtis D., Zhang, Hao, Voss, Kenneth J. (2003).
Effects of Optically Shallow Bottoms on Upwelling Radiances:
Bidirectional Reflectance Distribution Function Effects.
In: Limnology and Oceanography, 48, 337-345.

Nicodemus, F. E., Richmond, J. C., Hsia, J. J., Ginsberg, I. W., Limperis, T. (1977).
Geometrical considerations and nomenclature for reflectance.
In: Geometrical considerations and nomenclature for reflectance,
52 pp-52 pp.

Peltoniemi, J. I., Kaasalainen, S., Naranen, J., Matikainen, L., Piironen, J. (2005).
Measurement of directional and spectral signatures of light reflectance
by snow. In: Ieee Transactions on Geoscience and Remote Sensing,
43, 2294-2304.

RapidEye (2012).
RapidEye satellite constellation - unrivaled earth observation capacity.
(www.rapideye.com/upload/RE_Constellation.pdf, 09.01.2013).

Sandmeier, S., Muller, C., Hosgood, B., Andreoli, G. (1998).
Sensitivity analysis and quality assessment of laboratory BRDF data.
In: Remote Sensing of Environment, 64, 176-191.

Sandmeier, S., Sandmeier, W., Itten, K. I., Schaepman, M. E.,
Kellenberger, T. W. (1995).
The Swiss field-goniometer system (FIGOS). In: 1995
International Geoscience and Remote Sensing Symposium, IGARSS
'95. Quantitative Remote Sensing for Science and Applications
(Cat. No.95CH35770), 2078-80 vol.3.

Sandmeier, S. R. (2000).
Acquisition of bidirectional reflectance factor data with field
goniometers. In: Remote Sensing of Environment, 73, 257-269.

Sandmeier, S. R., Itten, K. I. (1999).
A field goniometer system (FIGOS) for acquisition of hyperspectral
BRDF data. In: Ieee Transactions on Geoscience and Remote Sensing,
37, 978-986.

Sandmeier, S. R., Middleton, E. M., Deering, D. W., Qin, W. H. (1999).
The potential of hyperspectral bidirectional reflectance distribution function data for grass canopy characterization. In: Journal of Geophysical Research-Atmospheres, 104, 9547-9560.

Sandmeier, St and Deering, D. W. (1999).
Structure Analysis and Classification of Boreal Forests Using Airborne Hyperspectral BRDF Data from ASAS. In: Remote Sensing of Environment, 69, 281-295.

Schaaf, C. B., Gao, F., Strahler, A. H., Lucht, W., Li, X. W., Tsang, T., Strugnell, N. C., Zhang, X. Y., Jin, Y. F., Muller, J. P., Lewis, P., Barnsley, M., Hobson, P., Disney, M., Roberts, G., Dunderdale, M., Doll, C., d'Entremont, R. P., Hu, B. X., Liang, S. L., Privette, J. L., Roy, D. (2002).
First operational BRDF, albedo nadir reflectance products from MODIS. In: Remote Sensing of Environment, 83, 135-148.

Schneider, T., Gege, P., Mott, C. (2004a).
Directional measurements for reed differentiation. Proc. of the 2nd CHRIS/Proba Workshop, ESA/ESRIN. Frascati, Itlay, 28-30 April (ESA SP-578, July 2004).

Schneider, T., Zimmermann, S., Manakos, I. (2004b).
Field goniometer system for accompanying directional measurements. Proc. of the 2nd CHRIS/Proba Workshop, ESA/ESRIN. Frascati, Italy, 28-30 April (ESA SP-578, July 2004).

Schneider, T., Dorigo, W.A., Schneider, W. (2007).
Exploting canopy BRDF; Between theoretical concept and practical implications. In: DROSMON workshop, Vienna, Austria.

Snyder, W. C. (1998).
Reciprocity of the bidirectional reflectance distribution function (BRDF) in measurements and models of structured surfaces. In: Ieee Transactions on Geoscience and Remote Sensing, 36, 685-691.

Solheim, I., Engelsen, O., Hosgood, B., Andreoli, G. (2000).
Measurement and modeling of the spectral and directional reflection properties of lichen and moss canopies. In: Remote Sensing of Environment, 72, 78-94.

Strub, G., Beisl, U., Schaepman, M., Schlaepfer, D., Dickerhof, C., Itten, K. (2002).
Evaluation of diurnal hyperspectral HDRF data acquired with the RSL field goniometer during the DAISEX'99 campaign. In: Isprs Journal of Photogrammetry and Remote Sensing, 57, 184-193.

Suomalainen, J., Hakala, T., Peltoniemi, J., Puttonen, E. (2009).
Polarised Multiangular Reflectance Measurements Using the Finnish Geodetic Institute Field Goniospectrometer. In: Sensors, 9, 3891-3907.

Valta-Hulkkonen, K., Pellikka, P., Peltoniemi, J. (2004).
Assessment of bidirectional effects over aquatic macrophyte vegetation in CIR aerial photographs. In: Photogrammetric Engineering and Remote Sensing, 70, 581-587.

Wardley, N. W. (1984).
Vegetation index variability as a function of viewing geometry. In: International Journal of Remote Sensing, 5, 861-870.

Automated Landslide Detection Using Multi-temporal RapidEye Data
(Project ID: 424)

Robert Behling, Sigrid Roessner, Karl Segl, Hermann Kaufmann
Helmholtz Centre Potsdam GFZ German Research Centre
for Geosciences Section 1.4 – Remote Sensing

E-Mail: behling@gfz-potsdam.de

Automated Landslide Detection Using Multi-temporal RapidEye Data

Robert Behling, Sigrid Roessner, Karl Segl, Hermann Kaufmann

In Southern Kyrgyzstan large landslides represent a wide-spread and regularly occurring natural hazard Due to the large extent of the affected area, automated analysis of multi-temporal satellite data represents the only way for efficient landslide detection. A RapidEye image database could be established for an area of about 12,000 km² containing multiple acquisition dates between 2009 and 2012. The developed automated approach for landslide detection is based on the analysis of temporal trajectories of NDVI values derived from the entire multi-temporal data stack. Specific temporal footprints of vegetation changes enable identification of landslide events. Applying this approach to the whole study area, about 250 landslides could be automatically detected between 2009 and 2012. Subsequent field checks have revealed that the vast majority of events have been correctly identified. Thus, the developed approach is capable of automatically detecting different kinds of mass movements under diverse natural conditions.

1 Introduction

In Southern Kyrgyzstan ongoing tectonic processes and high topographic relief cause natural hazards related to active mountain building affecting the Pamir-Tienshan orogenic system. Besides earthquakes, floods, and avalanches, landslides are one of the major natural hazards in this area and are especially concentrated along the Eastern rim of the Fergana Basin (Figure 1). In this densely populated mountainous region almost every year large landslides endanger human lives and infrastructure. Therefore local authorities responsible for disaster management and risk reduction have a big need for objective and spatially differentiated hazard assessment as a main prerequisite for sensible decision making related to precaution and mitigation. In this context, multi-temporal landslide inventories enabling the analysis of past and recent landslide activity as well as fostering an improved process understanding are of special importance (Fell et al. 2008; van Westen et al. 2008). In Kyrgyzstan, landslide inventories have been carried out since the 1950'ies, whereas approximately 3000 landslides have been reported by the local authorities.

However, regular inventories have been limited to the time period between 1968 and 1992 and focused on areas in the vicinity of populated places. The resulting reports (e.g., Ibatulin 2011) contain verbal descriptions of major events of the last 50 years. However, in most of the cases precise geographic locations of the events are missing. Thus, the existing knowledge on landslide events is incomplete in space and time and leaves the need for a systematic multi-temporal landslide inventory as a basis for objective and comprehensive hazard assessment.

In this context, the Rapid Eye satellite remote sensing data characterized by high temporal and high spatial resolution of 6.5m open up new opportunities for automated landslide detection with the goal of establishing multi-temporal landslide inventories for large areas whereas the possible high temporal frequency of data acquisition allows systematic assessment of landslide occurrence independent from the knowledge about specific triggering events. The presented work is based on the RESA (RapidEye Science Archive) program (grant number 424) enabling customized data acquisition since 2010 for the study area at the Eastern rim of the Fergana Basin. The resulting multi-temporal image database (see section 2) forms the basis for the development of an approach for automated landslide detection based on the analysis of surface cover changes related to landslide activity (see section 3). The results obtained for the study area at the Eastern rim of the Fergana Basin are described in section 4 and further discussed in section 5.

2 Study Area and Database

At the Eastern rim of the Fergana Basin landslides are mainly occurring within the foothills of its surrounding mountain ranges in an elevation range between 700 and 2000 m (Figure 1). The majority of these landslides occur in form of rotational and translational slides in weakly consolidated Quaternary and Tertiary sediments. The lithology of the landslides represents the main factor in determining their type of movement. One type is related to the presence of massive Quaternary loess units of up to 50 m thickness that moves rapidly down the slope with several meters per second. These avalanche-like movements are especially dangerous because of their great destructive power and their sudden occurrence. The other main type is represented by slowly moving (up to several meters per day) landslides occurring in Meso- and Cenozoic sediments with intercalated clays. Independent from their specific type all of these landslides result in degradation and decrease of scarce human living space limited by the high mountain ranges of Kyrgyzstan. The destructtive power of landslides affects transportation and energy infrastructure as well as settlements and often results in evacuation and relocation of people (Roessner et al. 2005).

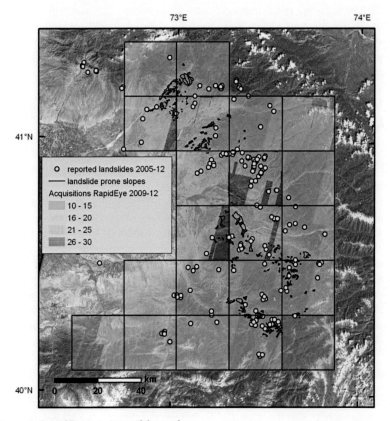

Figure 1: RapidEye coverage of the study area

The RapidEye data which are acquired with in a swath of 70 km enable detailed and efficient analysis of landslide activity for large areas. For this purpose, orthorectified Level-3A data products have been selected in order to minimize pre-processing efforts and to foster an approach which has the potential for global and operational application. The studied region shown in Figure 1 comprises an area of approx. 12.000 km² which is covered by 21

Level-3A RapidEye tiles. The RESA data grant has allowed acquiring data in pre-defined time periods of high process activity with a high temporal repetition rate of up to one acquisition per month since 2010. Together with archive data which have been available for selected parts of the study area since 2009, up to 25 acquisition dates are available for the whole time period from 2009 to 2012. The resulting multi-temporal database consists of approx. 500 Level-3A datasets representing about 20 acquisition dates during the main period of landslide activity between April and September (Figure 1). In areas of highest process activity indicated in Figure 1 by the reported landslides and the landslide prone slopes the temporal coverage is even higher.

3 Automated Landslide Detection

3.1 State of the Art

Existing approaches for automated landslide detection in optical remote sensing data mainly rely on the assumption that slope failures result in disrupted or absent vegetation cover. Their specific realizations represent varying degrees of automation and according to Guzetti et al. 2012 they can be classified by methodological aspects (e.g. pixel-based, object-based) and the number of dates included in the analysis (post-event image analysis, bi-temporal change analysis of pre- and post-event images). The majority of these approaches have been developed for event-based inventories providing information about landslides related to a specific triggering event, such as earthquakes or hydro-meteorological extreme events (e.g., tropical rainstorms). Most of the published studies have been targeted at areas smaller than 100 square kilometers. So far, there have been no attempts made to develop an automated approach for a larger area and for a systematic inventory of landslide events occurring independent from specific and well-known triggering events. Such an approach is needed for the study area at the Eastern rim of the Fergana Basin, since in this region landslide activity is caused by complex interactions between tectonic, geological, geomorphological and hydrometeorological factors leading to regularly reoccurring landslide events (Roessner et al. 2005). Additionally, the limited existing knowledge about past landslide activity in this region requires an automated approach which can extended to a longer-term time series of multi-temporal image data originating from different sensors.

3.2 Overall Approach

The multi-temporal RapidEye database in combination with additional spatial information, such as digital elevation models and geological information forms the basis for the development of an automated approach for landslide identification in order to derive a GIS-based multi-temporal landslide inventory containing the individual landslide events in an object-based form including their qualitative and quantitative characterization. The main part of the approach represents the multi-temporal change detection allowing a separation between changes caused by landslide activity from other land cover changes (e.g. agriculture) and from artifact changes caused by geometric mismatches and radiometric differences between image data with different acquisition properties. In order to minimize such artifacts, adequate pre-processing of the multi-temporal image database is required. Taking into account the high number of approx, 500 datasets, pre-processing has to be carried out in an automated and robust form. Section 3.3 describes the pre-processing methods which have been developed specifically in the frame of the change detection approach which is described in more detail in section 3.4.

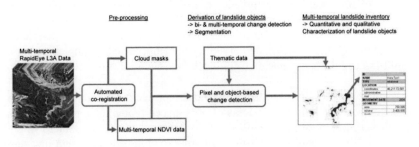

Figure 2: Automated approach for deriving a multi-temporal landslide inventory

3.3 Pre-processing

Before automated change detection can be applied to a multi-temporal image database, pre-processing of the remote sensing images has to be performed. Pre-processing usually includes the three steps of geometric co-registration, radiometric normalization and masking of irrelevant changes in order to gene-rate a comparable dataset and minimize artifact changes (Coppin et al. 2004; Lu et al. 2010).

Although the presented study is based on orthorectified Level-3A RapidEye data products, quality checks have shown that some geometric shifts of up to 50 m exist. In order to compensate for these shifts an image-to-image co-registration method had been developed. It performs an area-based correlation between two images in order to derive optimized shifting parameters for each image datasets without requiring another resampling of the already orthorectified datasets (Behling et al. 2012). In the result, a geometrically adjusted multi-temporal database was created which is characterized by a co-registration accuracy of about one RapidEye pixel amounting to 5 m.

Besides geometric adjustment, the multi-temporal datasets also have to be corrected for radiometric differences caused by different acquisition parameters (e.g. atmospheric conditions, viewing angles, sun angles). Spectral indices, such as the normalized difference vegetation index (NDVI) are commonly used to reduce the effects of such radiometric differences. However, without comprehensive atmospheric corrections or relative radiometric normalization even these indices show a slight variability of their values caused by the above mentioned radiometric differences. In case of the developed NDVI–based change detection approach (see section 3.4), the change of NDVI values caused by the removal or disturbance of vegetation related to slope failures is much higher than the variability of the NDVI values caused by radiometric differences. However, in order to obtain robust indicators for landslide-related surface changes, the remaining variability is compensated by implementing a multi-threshold change detection approach (see section 3.4 for more detail).

The presence of clouds and snow is another problem for automated change detection especially in humid areas of pronounced topographic relief, such as the Eastern rim of the Fergana Basin. They lead to detection of changes which are not related to land cover changes. In order to eliminate them, in a first step the cloud mask product supplied by RapidEye had been used. Analysis of these products has shown that dense clouds and snow cover are well represented. However, in part these products do not contain small and/or thin clouds and they also overestimate the size of the clouds because of a buffer which is applied to the identified cloud pixels. Therefore, a new approach for cloud detection has been developed using the original level 3A data. This approach consists of a double threshold technique based on the radiance values of the blue band and results in three classes of likelihood that a pixel is covered by a cloud. Based on this likelihood dataset, image segmentation is performed. The resulting segments are classified as clouds according to the areal coverage of the likelihood classes within the segments and additional size parameters. In the result this approach enables the detection of dense clouds and snow cover as well as thinner cloud layers and small amounts of snow which is not achieved by the standard RapidEye cloud-mask products.

3.4 Multi-temporal Change Detection for Landslide Identification

The developed multi-temporal change detection approach is based on the analysis of temporal trajectories of the NDVI derived from the pre-processed multi-temporal data stack. These temporal trajectories are obtained for every pixel across the time span of the entire data archive and thus allow analysis of vegetation cover changes over time rather than solely assess the absence of vegetation in a single dataset or the loss of vegetation between two datasets. These specific temporal footprints of vegetation changes (see Figure 3) enable identification of landslide events due to the short-term character of destruction of the vegetation cover caused by landslide events as well as longer-term re-vegetation rates as effects of the disturbance of the surface cover caused by slope failures.

In Figure 3 the derivation of the NDVI temporal trajectories representing the temporal surface cover changes in the analyzed time-period is exemplary illustrated for a landslide complex within the study area. In order to demonstrate typical temporal vegetation changes occurring over a longer time-period, the example is based on a multi-temporal NDVI database comprising image data acquired by the ASTER and RapidEye sensor between the years 2002 and 2012. Figure 3 shows the NDVI trajectory of a landslide which occurred in April 2004. The slope failure caused a severe surface disturbance and a destruction of the vegetation cover which is reflected in the abrupt decrease of the NDVI values between June 2003 and June 2004. After the landslide event the NDVI values remain low because of a slow re-vegetation rate caused by the disturbance and dislocation of soil which makes the landslide body susceptible to erosion and reactivation processes affecting the dislocated masses. This resulting typical shape of the NDVI trajectory is used to distinguish landslides from other temporal vegetation changes which can not be related to landslide processes, such as the other five land cover classes shown in Figure 3. Such a comprehensive assessment and comparison of temporal change patterns represented by the trajectories is not possible by state-of-the-art change detection approaches which are limited to mono or bi-temporal analysis for landslide identification. The trajectories of Figure 3 show that it is difficult to distinguish between harvested fields and landslide-related vegetation change if only 2 or 3 multi-temporal datasets are considered in the analysis. The resulting so-called false-positives can be minimized by analyzing a longer time series of multi-temporal image data.

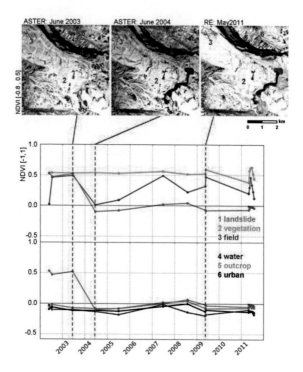

Figure 3: NDVI-based temporal trajectories representing typical vegetation changes related to land cover classes

For this purpose a combined pixel- and object-based approach has been developed which consists of three main steps: 1) bi-temporal change detection, 2) segmentation based on the bi-temporal change result and 3) object-based multi-temporal change detection. The principle of the developed landslide identification approach is described for two subsequent multi-temporal image dataset. Then, this principle is applied to all subsequent image data pairs contained in the entire multi-temporal data stack resulting in objects of surface cover changes related to slope failures for all available time steps. Thus, the developed approach (Figure 4) allows the creation of a dynamic landslide inventory.

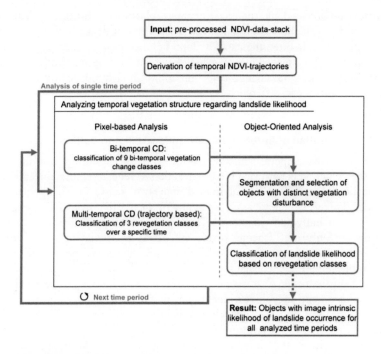

Figure 4: Multi-temporal landslide identification approach based on temporal NDVI trajectories

3.4.1 Multiple Threshold Based Bi-temporal Change Detection

Taking into account that slope failures remove or degrade the so far largely undisturbed vegetation cover, in a first step, the NDVI-based temporal trajectories are analyzed in respect to abrupt vegetation loss between two dates. For this purpose the NDVI is analyzed in any subsequent bi-temporal image pair resulting in the parameters pre and post. Combined with a normalized difference index of the NDVI of the two images, these parameters are used to classify the vegetation change regarding to landslide likelihood. In this context, a strong abrupt vegetation loss resulting in bare soil represents the ideal case in form of a high likelihood for landslide occurrence (index very high and post < 0). However, most of the natural processes do not create such distinct surface conditions. In contrast, they are rather fuzzy in their spatial and temporal dispersion as well as in their process intensity. Therefore, the classification of landslide likelihood is performed on a scale of 9 classes (see Figure 6c). This way, less pronounced surface cover changes related to landslides can also be recognized, e.g. if the vegetation cover is already less dense before landslide occurrence. This is often the case, if slope failures occur as secondary movements in already displaced masses which have not fully been re-vegetated yet. This multiple threshold change detection approach also reduces the susceptibility for radiometric differences contained in the NDVI values (see section 3.3).

3.4.2 Segmentation of Bi-temporal Landslide Likelihood Datasets

Based on this bi-temporal landslide likelihood dataset resulting from the first step, segmentation is performed in order to derive vegetation loss objects. This segmentation procedure is subdivided into two steps. First, all spatially connected pixels which are assigned to any of the existing landslide likelihood classes form individual segments. These segments represent objects which contain not only ideal change pixels but pixels belonging to any of the 9 classes. In a second step, a selection of these objects is performed by analyzing the proportion of the consisting landslide likelihood classes in a specific segment. In the result of this selection, objects with a strong vegetation disturbance are kept and objects containing a (too) high percentage of pixels characterized by non-ideal vegetation changes are eliminated. Thus, this approach ensures the derivation of landslides as single objects even if they represent partly not the optimal case of strong vegetation disturbance such as landslides occurring in a sparsely vegetated older landslide body or landslides whose runout zones cover an already harvested field.

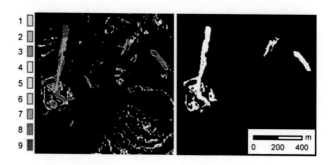

Figure 5: Segmentation based on bi-temporal change
(left: subset of figure 6c; right: segmentation result)

250

3.4.3 Object-oriented Multi-temporal Change Detection

After the described multiple thresholding and subsequent object selection, a lot of the initially identified objects remain as false-positives since they are characterized bi-temporal vegetation changes similar to the ones typical for landslides. In this context, the main problems are fields that are vegetated in the pre-event image and harvested in the post-event image, exemplarily shown in the south western part of the subset in Figure 6. In order to eliminate these false positives, in the third step the typically long-lasting re-vegetation process of landslides is considered. Based on the NDVI temporal trajectories four different classes of re-vegetation rates are distinguished in a specific time period after the bi-temporal event using a pixel-based classification approach. The considered time period can be adapted to the specific natural conditions influencing the re-vegetation rates. Based on the classification of re-vegetation, the landslide segments derived from bi-temporal analysis are further characterized according to their landslide likelihood. Figure 6d shows that fields are mainly characterized by higher re-vegetation rates (classes 0 or 1) than landslides (classes 2 or 3). This object-oriented classification based on the proportions of the re-vegetation classes leads to the final result of an image-intrinsic likelihood that this object represents a landslide.

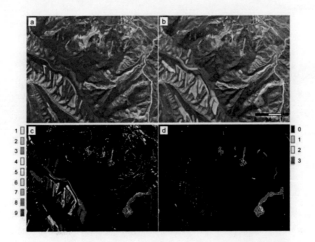

Figure 6: Analyzed vegetation changes between RapidEye data from 2009-05-26 (a) 2012-06-04 (b). c: Bi-temporal change (9 classes of vegetation loss: 1 low to 9 high); d: Multi-temporal change shown for all bi-temporal derived objects depicted as white polygons (4 re-vegetation classes: 0 very fast to 3 very slow)

4 Results

Results of the developed approach are exemplarily shown in Figure 7 for a 4 x 5 km subset of the study area which is also represented by Figure 6. Figure 7 depicts landslides as vectorized objects which have occurred in 2010 and 2012 overlaid on a perspective view of a recent RapidEye dataset. It can be seen that landslides of different sizes, shapes and in different stages of development (fresh failures, reactivation, relocation) can be automatically detected.

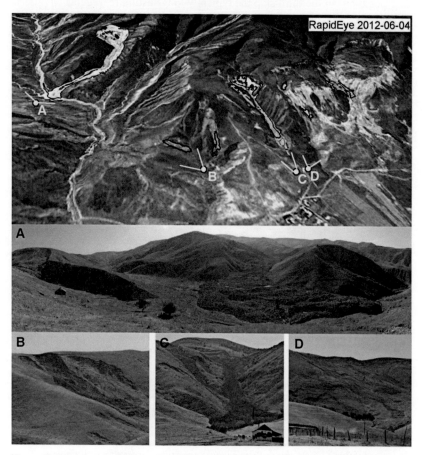

Figure 7: Mapping results in a 4 x 5 km subset of the study area. Detected landslide polygons depicted in a perspective view (black: 2010, red: 2012) and visited in a field survey in September 2012

Figure 7a shows a recent failure that happened in 2010 which is approx. 1.3 km long and up to 400 m wide and results in an accumulation zone of about 20 m thickness at the toe of the landslide. At the location of this landslide the RapidEye image of 2009 shows a closed vegetation cover and no clearly visible signs of an active landslide body can be detected. Besides these relatively fresh failures the approach also allows the detection of reactivated landslides and relocation of landslide material within recent landslide bodies covered by sparse vegetation. In contrast to the fresh failures, the resulting vegetation disturbance is less distinct but still identifiable by the developed multi-temporal change detection approach. Figure 7b for example shows an enlargement of a landslide that has already existed in 2009. In the 2010 (black polygon) and 2012 (red polygon) images two reactivations of this already existing landslide had been detected resulting in an enlargement of the crown area of the landslide and displacement of material further down the slope. Figure 7 also contains some small polygons in the right part representing relocation of material caused by erosion processes within an active landslide complex. Figure 7c displays an example occurred within weakly consolidated sedimentary rocks whereas all other examples have occurred within loess. These results show that the developed approach based on multi-temporal RapidEye data is suitable for mapping recent landslide activity under varying natural conditions of land cover, lithology and landslide activity.

In a next step this approach has been applied to the entire multi-temporal RapidEye image database comprising the whole study area for the years from 2009 to 2012. For every analyzed time period a shapefile has been created containing the image-intrinsic likelihood of a landslide occurring within this period. A visual evaluation of the derived objects resulted in the selection of about 250 objects most likely representing landslide events. The size of these objects ranges between 500 and 250,000 square meters and the total area affected by these landslide amounts to 5.5 million square meters. About half of these events happened between 2009 and 2010. For the same period of time (2009-2012) the Ministry of Emergency Situations of Kyrgyzstan has only reported 40 events.

The obtained results have been verified during a four-week field survey which took place in September 2012. During this survey about 100 of the 250 detected landslides have been visited and in almost all of these cases the field checks confirmed recent surface changes related to landslides. Exceptions were primarily caused by the extraction of construction material (e.g., clay and gravel) at the bottom of hillslopes representing artificial mass movements. This field survey has revealed that the developed approach is capable of automatically detecting different kinds of landslides caused by a variety of slope processes, such as rotational and translational landslides and debris flows under diverse natural conditions. Thus, it could be shown that the approach can be used for reliable landslide detection at a regional scale.

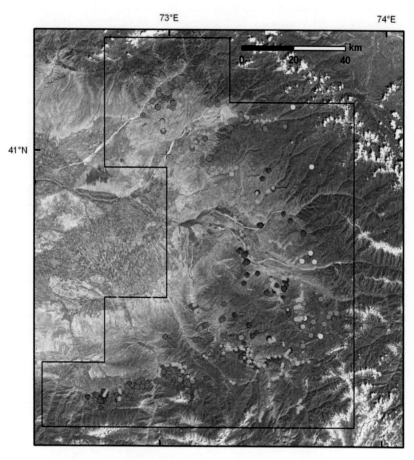

Figure 8: Automatically detected landslides between 2009 and 2012
(different colored circles: landslide of different movement date; stars:
GPS points of the field survey in September 2012)

5 Discussion and Outlook

The developed approach using multi-temporal RapidEye data allows automated detection of landslides in an object-based form enabling the systematic derivation of a multi-temporal landslide inventory for large areas required for objective hazard and risk assessment. Although compared to previous years process activity had been rather low during the analyzed time period between 2009 and 2012 and no specific triggering event has been known, a total of about 250 landslides could be automatically detected. This shows constant ongoing high process activity occurring independently from distinct triggering events. This situation emphasizes the need for multi-temporal landslide inventories in regions dominated by complex slope failures, such as the Eastern rim of the Fergana Basin.

In this context, the high temporal and spatial resolution of the RapidEye data is of key importance for a detailed analysis of the current state of landslide activity. Additionally, the high temporal repetition rate enables a rather precise temporal determination of landslides in the frame of a multi-temporal landslide inventory. The high spatial resolution allows detecting smaller events which may be an indicator for subsequent larger and more destructive slope failures. This way, the RapidEye data support identification of possible precursors for upcoming hazardous events which can support early warning.

Despite the high rate of correctly detected slope failures, visual evaluation of the obtained results has revealed the existence of some false positives. They are mostly caused by remaining geometric mismatches between the multi-temporal image data due to non-systematic geometric errors resulting from the original orthorectification process that can not be corrected using the shift-based co-registration procedure. False positives are also caused by temporal vegetation changes between other land cover classes which are similar to landslides-related ones. However, they represent a small minority.

In a next step the developed approach will be applied to a longer time-series containing multi-temporal image data acquired by a variety of optical sensors starting from 1986 whereas annual coverage is available from 1996. Future work will also investigate the potential of including additional spatial data, such as DEM information in the analytical process in order to further improve the reliability of automated detection of landslides. The resulting automated detection system will be a useful tool for deriving spatially differentiated quantitative information about process activity at a regional scale.

Acknowledgements

This work was funded by the German Federal Ministry of Research and Technology (BMBF) within the framework of PROGRESS (Potsdam Research Cluster for Georisk Analysis, Environmental Change and Sustainability). We also thank the German Aerospace Agency (DLR) for providing RapidEye data by the RESA (RapidEye Science Archive) program.

References

Behling, R., S. Roessner S., Segl K., Rogass, C., Wetzel H. U., Kaufmann H. 2012.
Automatische geometrische Koregistrierung multitemporaler Satellitendaten zur Inventarisierung von Hangrutschungen. In: Borg, Daedelow, und Johnson. (Eds.), Vom Algorithmus zum Produkt - 4. RESA Workshop: 35-50.

Coppin, P. Jonckheere, I. Nackaerts, K., Muys, B. & Lambin, E., 2004.
Digital change detection methods in ecosystem monitoring: a review. International Journal of Remote Sensing, 25(9): 1565-1596.

Fell, R., Corominas, J, Bonnard, C, Cascini, L., Leroi; E. & Savage, W., 2008.
Guidelines for landslide susceptibility, hazard and risk zoning for land use planning. Engineering Geology, 102(3-4): 85-98.

Guzzetti, F., Mondini A. C., Cardinali M., Fiorucci F., Santangelo M., Chang K. 2012.
Landslide inventory maps: New tools for an old problem. Earth-Science Reviews 112 (1–2): 42–66.

Ibatulin, C. V. 2011.
Monitoring of landslides in Kyrgyzstan. Ministry of Emergency Situations of the Kyrgyz Republic, Bishkek: 145 pp. (in Russian).

Lu, D., Moran E., Hetrick S. & Li G. 2010.
Land-Use and Land-Cover Change Detection. Advances in Environmental Remote Sensing: Sensors, Algorithms, and Applications, 7: 273.

Roessner, S., Wetzel, H.-U., Kaufmann, H. & Sarnagoev, A. 2005.
Potential of satellite remote sensing and GIS for landslide hazard assessment in Southern Kyrgyzstan (Central Asia). Natural Hazards, 35(3): 395–416.

van Westen, C.J., Castellanos, E. & Kuriakose, S.L., 2008.
Spatial data for landslide susceptibility, hazard, and vulnerability assessment: An overview. Engineering Geology, 102(3-4), S.112-131.

Water Body and Tree Line Change Mapping
(Project ID: 473)

Marcel Urban, Natalya Rakityanskaya, Sören Hese

Friedrich-Schiller-University Jena, Earth Observation Group, Grietgasse 6, 07743 Jena, phone: +49 (0) 3641 948873 / +49 (0) 3641 948887

Siberian Federal University, 79 Svobodny Prospect, Krasnoyarsk 660041, Russia

E-Mail: marcel.urban@uni-jena.de, soeren.hese@uni-jena.de

Water Body and Tree Line Change Mapping

Marcel Urban, Natalya Rakityanskaya, Sören Hese

The goal of this project (RESA ID 473) is to map 1. water body changes, 2. vegetation structure and tree line changes on selected test sites covering the taiga-tundra transition zone of Russia and 3. Arctic river delta changes (with focus on the Lena delta, Mackenzie delta region and the Laptev region). Recent scientific studies have emphasized these regions to be highly affected by the global climate change by identifying modifications in surface water dynamics and changes in land cover and vegetation structure.

1. Motivation

The arctic environment is subject to significant changes (Grace 2002; Moritz et al. 2002; Nelson 2003). Temperature conditions have never been as high as during the last century in the arctic regions compared with the last 300 years (Moritz et al. 2002). An increase in temperature provokes an intensification of vegetation activity, which causes surface structure changes and modification in phenological dynamics (Hinzman et al. 2004; Myneni et al. 1997). Moreover, changes in snow cover and sea ice extent are found to have also a critical impact to the environmental and ecological dynamics in the arctic regions (Post et al. 2012). Emissions of greenhouse gases, such as methane and carbon dioxide caused by melting permafrost soils and changes in vegetation structures, are of high importance for the global climate system (ACIA 2004; Anisimov and Reneva 2006; Kaplan and New 2006; Nelson 2003; Smith et al. 2009).

Recent studies have identified changes in vegetation structure for Siberia (D. Blok et al. 2010), Alaska (K. Tape, Sturm, and Racine 2006) and the pan-Arctic Circle (Myers-Smith et al. 2011). Intensification of vegetation activity and the modification of the vegetation structure will influence the energy budged, storage capacity, permafrost dynamics and the climate system in the arctic region and on a global scale.

The main goal of this project is to (1) monitor changes of lakes in a resolution relevant for small scale and detailed thermokarst water body changes, (2) map vegetation and land cover information (e.g. migration of tree species into tundra regions and shrub encroachment to the north) with a spatial and spectral resolution needed for permafrost degradation specific vegetation types. Additionally (3) this project will investigate river delta changes in the Lena delta, the Mackenzie delta and the Laptev coastal region in cooperation with AWI Potsdam using historical Key-Hole datasets.

2. Data & Methodology

The time windows for the acquisition of RapidEye data are the summer month (June – September) for the years 2011, 2012 and 2013. It is planned to receive a full coverage for each site and for each year. Table 1 summarizes the used RapidEye and Landsat MSS imagery for this study.

Region	Data	ID	Date
Taymir	RESA	2012-07-22T061155 RE5	2012-07-22
		2012-09-01T063247 RE2	2012-09-01
	Landsat MSS	LM11590081973207AAA05	1973-07-26
		LM11590091973207AAA05	1973-07-26
Yamal	RESA	2011-06-23T074359 RE1	2011-06-23
		2011-06-23T072420 RE2	2011-06-23
		2011-06-24T072237 RE3	2011-06-24
		2011-09-11T074055 RE5	2011-09-11
	Landsat MSS	LM11740131973222AAA05	1973-08-10
		LM1170013 01319730824	1973-08-24
		LM11700141973236AAA05	1973-08-24

Table 1: RESA RapidEye data and Landsat MSS imagery utilized for this study.

The analysis of vegetation structure changes was done by comparing historical Landsat MSS imagery from 1973 and RapidEye data from 2011/2012. The workflow is shown in Figure 1. We used an object oriented segmentation and classification approach. The identification of samples for the supervised classification procedure was done using high resolution Google Earth imagery. After the export of the classification results, a regular grid (5km by 5km) was defined and percentage cover information for each land cover class was derived. This zonal approach allows retaining each spatial resolution.

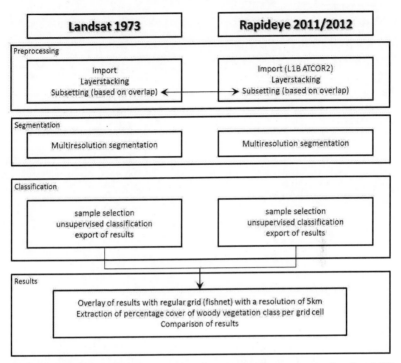

Figure 1: Workflow of vegetation structure change identifications using Landsat MSS and RapidEye imagery.

The RapidEye imagery was provided by DLR/RapidEye in NITF format (National Imagery Transmission Format) with RPCs (Rational Polynomial Coefficients). Coppin and Bauer (1996) defined two mandatory pre-processing steps to enhance the comparability of two time steps - an accurate image registration and radiometric calibration of the compared satellite imagery.

The Landsat MSS images are processed with the Level 1 product generation system (LPGS), where the raw data is terrain corrected (L1T) and geometric corrected using cubic convolution as resampling method. The Landsat MSS data has a spatial resolution of 60m.

The RapidEye data is corrected for atmospheric effects using ATCOR2 (Richter 1996). Reprojection to UMT WGS84 with a spatial resolution of 5 m was done using the provided RPC information.

3. Study Area

The observation of vegetation structure (tree line) is done for two selected study regions situated at the Yamal and Taymir Peninsula in Russia.

The Yamal region is characterized by large reservoirs of oil and gas deposits. The oil and gas exploration activities in this region have partly contaminated the landscape (through oil spills and drilling mud contaminations).

The Taymyr peninsula covers an area of approx. 400.000 km² at the arctic coastline of the republic of Krasnoyarsk in Siberia. This region is characterized by continental climate conditions, underlying continuous permafrost and thermokarst. It is formed by the rivers Yenisei and Ob which discharge into the Arctic ocean.

4. Results

Vegetation structure changes have been analyzed for the Taymir Peninsula and the Yamal region in northern Eurasia.

Figure 2 shows the changes of woody vegetation cover between 1973 and 2012. The tree line reference from Walker et al. (2005) is shown in blue. The results show percent woody vegetation cover of > 60% for the regions south of the tree line reference. Unfortunately, one of the Landsat MSS scenes was partly covered by clouds and ice. Observing the transition area of the tree line, a decrease of woody vegetation cover percentage to the north becomes visible. North of the tree line reference only single patches of woody vegetation are detected. Comparing both time steps, an increase of woody vegetation cover between 1973 and 2012 is mapped. Especially, the fluvial terrace of the river Ketha is showing higher woody vegetation cover percentage in the RapidEye scenes. Moreover, northernmost parts seem to show an increase in woody vegetation cover.

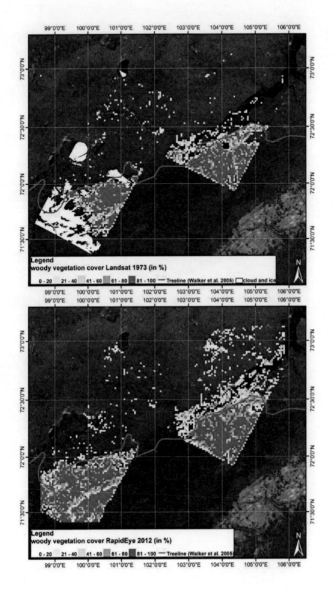

Figure 2: Percent woody vegetation - changes between 1973 (Landsat MSS – on top) and 2012 (RapidEye – on bottom). The tree line is shown in blue based on Walker et al. (2005).

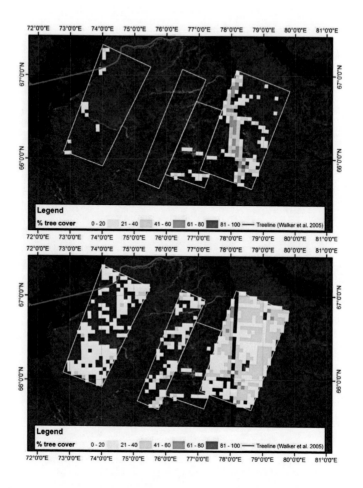

Figure 3: Percent woody vegetation - changes between 1973 (Landsat MSS – on top) and 2011 (RapidEye – on bottom). The tree line is shown in blue based on Walker et al. (2005).

The results of the vegetation structure analysis for the Yamal region are shown in Figure 3. In contrast to the Taymir test site, only trees have been classified for this study site. The results are showing an intensification of tree cover in the classes 20 – 40 % and 40 – 60 % between 1973 in 2011. The eastern part of the study area shows the most significant changes in tree cover.

The presented work shows preliminary results only, since this study was done only for two time steps and without validation of the vegetation structure and tree cover changes. Nevertheless, modification in vegetation structure and changes in dynamics from additional land surface parameters (LST, Snow Cover, etc.) over the last decades have already been identified within these regions, which were provoked by changes in the global climate system (Grace 2002; Moritz et al. 2002; Nelson 2003, Hinzman et al. 2004; Myneni et al. 1997). Hence, the results are giving a first impression of the modification of the land surface within these regions of northern Eurasia measured by historical and recent high resolution Earth observation data.

Literature

ACIA (Arctic Climate Impact Assessment), 2004.
Impacts of a warming arctic. Cambridge University Press.

Anisimov, O. A. & S. S Reneva, 2006.
Permafrost and changing climate: the Russian perspective. - Ambio 35, 4. 169-175.

Blok, D., M. Heijmans, G. Schaepman-Strub, V. Kononov, T. C. Maximov, F. Berendse. 2010.
Shrub expansion may reduce summer permafrost thaw in Siberian tundra. - Global Change Biology 16, 4. 1296-1305.

Coppin, P. R. & M. E. Bauer. 1996.
Digital change detection in forest ecosystems with remote sensing imagery. - Remote Sensing Reviews 13, 3-4. 207-234.

Grace, J. 2002.
Impacts of Climate Change on the Tree Line. - Annals of Botany 90, 4. 537-544.

Hinzman, L. D., D. A. Stow, A. Hope, D. McGuire, D. Verbyla, J. Gamon, F. Huemmrich, S. Houston, C. Racine, M. Sturm, K. Tape, K. Yoshikawa, C. Tweedie, B. Noyle, C. Silapaswan, D. Douglas, B. Griffith, G. Jia, H. Epstein, D. Walker, S. Daeschner, A. Petersen, L. Zhou, R. Myneni. 2004.
Remote sensing of vegetation and land-cover change in Arctic Tundra Ecosystems. - Remote Sensing of Environment 89. 281-308.

Kaplan, J. O. & M. New. 2006.
Arctic climate change with a 2 °C global warming: Timing, climate patterns and vegetation change. - Climatic Change 79, 3-4. 213-241.

Moritz, R. E, C. M. Bitz & E. J. Steig. 2002.
Dynamics of recent climate change in the Arctic. - Science 297, 5586. 1497-1502.

Myers-Smith, I. H, B. C. Forbes, M. Wilmking, M. Hallinger, T. Lantz, D. Blok, K. D. Tape, M. Macias-Fauria, U. Sass-Klaassen, E. Lévesque, S. Boudreau, P. Ropars, L. Hermanutz, A. Trant, L. Siegwart Collier, S. Weijers, J. Rozema, S. Rayback, N. M. Schmidt, G. Schaepman-Strub, S. Wipf, C. Rixen, C. B Ménard, S. Venn, S. Goetz, L. Andreu-Hayles, S. Elmendorf, V. Ravolainen, J. Welker, P. Grogan, H. E. Epstein, D. S Hik. 2011.
Shrub expansion in tundra ecosystems: dynamics, impacts and research priorities. - Environmental Research Letters 6, 4. 1-15.

Myneni, R. B., C. D. Keeling, C. J. Tucker, G. Asrar & R. R. Nemani. 1997.
Increased plant growth in the northern high latitudes from 1981 to
1991. - Nature 386, 698-702.

Nelson, F. E. 2003.
(Un)frozen in time. - Science 299, 5613. 1673-1675.

Post, E., T. R Christensen, B. Elberling, A. D. Fox & O. Gilg. 2012.
Ecological Dynamics Across the Arctic Associated with Recent
Climate Change. - Science 325. 1355-1358.

Richter, R. 1996.
A spatially adaptive fast atmospheric correction algorithm. -
International Journal of Remote Sensing 17, 6. 1201-1214.

Smith, S., F. E. Nelson, V. E. Romanovsky, J. Brown, G. D. Clow,
R. G. Barry, T. Zhang, H. H. Christiansen, M. Monteduro & R. Sessa. 2009.
ECV T7 Permafrost. Permafrost and seasonally frozen ground. -
http://www.fao.org/gtos/doc/ECVs/T07/T07.pdf.

Tape, K., M. Sturm & C. Racine. 2006.
The evidence for shrub expansion in Northern Alaska and the
Pan-Arctic. - Global Change Biology 12. 686-702.

Walker, A. D., M. K. Raynolds, F. J. A. Daniels, E. Einarsson, A. Elvebakk,
W. A. Gould, A. E. Katenin, S. S. Kholod, C. J. Markon, J. Carl,
E. S. Melnikov, N. G. Moskalenko, S. S. Talbot, and B. A. Yurtsev. 2005.
The Circumpolar Arctic vegetation map. - Journal of Vegetation
Science 16. 267-282.

Walker, D. A., M. K. Raynolds, F. Daniëls, E. Einarsson, A. Elvebakk,
W. Gould, A. E. Katenin, S. S. Kholod, C. J. Markon, E. S. Melnikov,
N. G. Moskalenko, S. S. Talbot & B. Yurtsev. 2005.
The Circumpolar Arctic vegetation map. - Journal of Vegetation
Science 16, 3. 267-282.

Uncertainties of LAI estimation from satellite images due to atmospheric correction (Project ID: 502)

Theresa Mannschatz[1,2], Peter Dietrich[1]

[1] Helmholtz Centre for Environmental Research,
 Department Monitoring and Exploration Technologies,
 Permoserstr. 15, Leipzig
[2] University of Technology Dresden, Institute of Soil Science and Site Ecology,
 Pienner Str. 19, Tharandt

E-Mail: Theresa.Mannschatz@ufz.de

Uncertainties of LAI estimation from satellite images due to atmospheric correction

Theresa Mannschatz, Peter Dietrich

Water and energy balance models that explicitly consider vegetation are Soil-Vegetation-Atmosphere-Transfer (SVAT) models. Vegetation development is very dynamic, but often kept constant by the user over longer periods in hydrological and SVAT modeling. The leaf area index (LAI) is an indicator for plant development that strongly influences several relevant hydrological processes. Generally, a temporal measurement or monitoring of LAI is challenging or impossible in remote areas. A promising tool to overcome this problem is high-temporal resolution remote sensing imaging, with image capture taking place continuously over land surfaces all year round. First of all, this allows a more dynamic SVAT parameterization in remote areas and secondly, makes it possible to model on large scales. LAI is often estimated from vegetation indices calculated from band ratios. This paper shows that atmospheric correction influences LAI retrieval from satellite image, which can lead to higher uncertainties in water balance modeling.

1. Motivation

Knowledge of the water balance is, for instance, essential in land management, especially in case of large land use changes (such as converting grassland to forest plantations). Since water balance processes are complex, Soil-Vegetation-Atmosphere-Transfer (SVAT) models are applied to account for the role vegetation plays in affecting the water balance and energy fluxes. These models additionally help us to get a better understanding of hydrological processes by simulating different land use and climate change scenarios. Vegetation affects the water and energy balance through transpiration, water uptake, interception and water storage within the plant. Additionally, vegetation development is highly dependent upon seasonal variations (water availability, temperature). In contrast, the plant development stages over the year are often assumed by the user to be stable for longer periods for hydrological and SVAT modeling (Arora, 2002). Furthermore, information concerning certain plant specific parameters is often taken from literature. Nevertheless, evapotranspiration is a dynamic process, depending on stomata conductance, size, arrangement and amount of leafs that contribute to make vegetation a dynamic model component. An indicator than can be used for evapotranspiration prediction is known as leaf area index (LAI[1]). Evapotranspiration is also affected by temporal development and absolute LAI values (Metselaar et al., 2006). Generally, the measurement or even monitoring of LAI is challenging. The increasing availability of high-temporal resolution remote sensing is a promising tool to monitor e.g. LAI development over the course of the year. First of all, this allows a more dynamic SVAT parameterization in remote areas and secondly, makes it possible to model on large scales (Yao et al., 2008).

One approach retrieving LAI data is based on empirical relationships between vegetation indices (VI) and LAI field measurements (Zheng and Moskal, 2009). The most common vegetation indices are calculated through spectral band ratios from satellite images. Nevertheless, the estimation of LAI from VI time series requires true reflectance values of the land surface, which helps ensure comparability between the different satellite scenes. For this purpose, atmospheric correction is applied to satellite images to remove any atmospheric influences (Hadjimitsis et al., 2010). This paper shows the effects of diverse parameterization of atmospheric correction models on VI retrieval and any impacts this has upon LAI estimation. For this purpose, we will: (i) present a short overview of LAI importance for SVAT modeling, (ii) describe the study area and for investigation used satellite data, (iii) apply different atmospheric correction schemes on several satellite scenes, and (iv) compare retrieved LAI values from each image for all locations to understand their variability due to processing scheme used. Finally, the issue of scene comparability is evaluated through analysis of the overlapping area of two scenes, which were imaged on same date and were subject to similar atmospheric correction.

2. LAI influence on SVAT modeling

These uncertainties in LAI retrieval may influence the water balance model results. Most SVAT models use the Penman-Monteith equation to predict evapotranspiration that is often conducted dependent on LAI (Horn and Schulz, 2010). Similarly, aerodynamic surface resistance and interception capacity are a function of LAI (Jansson and Karlberg, 2013). The magnitude

---

[1] LAI is the ratio of total one-sided area of photosynthetic tissue and unit ground surface area (Zheng and Moskal, 2009).

of LAI influence on modeled water balance components is linked to the sensitivity of the applied SVAT model. For instance, LAI, provided by MODIS time-series, ranging from 2.5 to 5 (North America, temperate to continental humid climate) results in yearly cumulative evapotranspiration values of around 400 mm to 600 mm, respectively (Horn and Schulz, 2010). At a native, humid, Eucalyptus dominated forest, it was found that the ecosystem changes from a net carbon source to a net strong carbon sink when LAI changed from 0.5 to 3.5 (Van Gorsel et al., 2011). In SimSphere SVAT model, LAI contributes with 3.4% to percentage variance of daily average net radiation (Petropoulos et al., 2009). SVAT model DaisyGIS (Abrahamsen, P. & Hansen, 2000) demonstrates high sensitivities of nitrate leaches due to LAI changes, resulting in a nitrate leaching increase of up to 262% when the LAI was reduced by 15% (Veihe et al., 2005). In summary, LAI influences several components of a SVAT model and thus has a large impact on water balance estimation.

3. Study Site

The study site is located in Northeastern Brazil in the state of Bahia (Figure 1). It is a bamboo (Bambusa Vulgaris) plantation of approximately 5 km² that is operated by Penha Papeis e Embalagens. This plantation has been in operation and existence since the mid-1970th, approximately. Plants are planted in rows with an approximate separation of 3 m to 6 m. Generally, bamboo is harvested after 3 years and continues growing rapidly from the stump after harvest. The plantation area is divided into fields that are harvested at different times. Due to this fact, bamboo plants at different growth development stages (0-3 years) are present here. The climate after Köppen is designated as being an Af (equatorial fully humid) climate and characterized with the precipitation value of the driest month: $P_{min} > 60$ mm (Kottek et al., 2006). According to the Brazilian Soil Classification system, the plantation is located on clayey Vertisols (Embrapa, 2006).

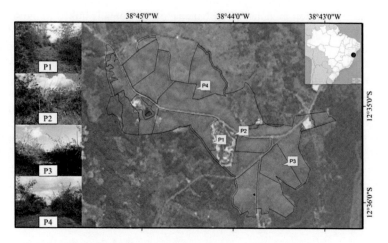

*Figure 1: Location of study site (Northeastern Brazil, bamboo plantation)
with P1-P4 representing particular locations for detailed image analysis.
Plant height is approximately 1.5-4 m (UTM, WGS84, Map: ASTER image
from 17.06.2010 (LP DAAC, 2011), overview map: d-maps.com).*

4. RapidEye Images

The RapidEye satellite delivers images with 5 spectral bands: blue, green, red,
red edge and near infrared (NIR) (Rapideye, 2007). Frequent coverage of the
land surface is especially important in humid tropical regions where generally
high cloudiness occurs. For this reason, it was realistic to obtain one image
per month that covers most of the study site. To get a better understanding of
plant development, time-series of longer periods than one year are desirable,
in order to catch similar development stages twice. Since, temporal development of LAI plays a very important role in the modeling process, time-series
are important for e.g. to understand the eventual seasonality of LAI e.g. due to
dry and rainy seasons. The study site is covered by two tiles, a northern and
southern scene with an overlapping area of about 5.1 km² (Figure 2). The
results presented in this paper, are based on 5 images from 2012. Three scenes
(16.01.2012; 28.01.2012; 04.03.2012) show the northern part and two scenes
(28.01.2012; 09.03.2012) cover the southern part of the study site.

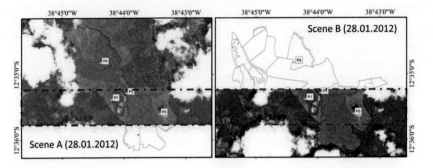

Figure 2: RapidEye images (product 3A, resampled resolution 5m) from 28.01.2012 that displays the overlapping (red dashed line).

5. Methods

In principle, the image values of a certain location, of atmospherically corrected images from the same date should return identical vegetation index (VI) values for the analyzed locations. This assumption should still be true for all accurately executed atmospheric correction schemes, since VI are based on spectral band ratios.

Image processing consists of (i) cloud removal, (ii) application of different atmospheric correction schemes and (iii) pixel as well as image comparison. From the selected scenes (named in section 4), clouds were removed based on cloud mask cover data. Cloud mask was delivered with matching image by RapidEye. The cloud mask was then manually revised and adjusted using ArcMap 10 software. Adjusted cloud mask was then merged with the remote sensing image to eliminate data values (no data) for the cloudy areas. The necessity of cloud removal prior to atmospheric correction was tested on several images before and then visually verified, based on a scatterplot of red versus NIR band data. Images containing clouds that were subject to atmospheric correction showed, on one hand, pixel artifacts in several image areas and, on the other hand, discontinuities in the red versus NIR plot.

Atmospheric correction was carried out using ATCOR 2 (flat terrain) and ATCOR 3 (hilly terrain) models in ERDAS IMAGINE 2010 to remove atmospheric effects in order to enable time-series scene comparison. The correction procedures require several atmospheric and satellite-dependent parameters, namely solar zenith, solar azimuth, sensor tilt, satellite azimuth and the land surface elevation (ERDAS and Geosystems, 2011). The parameters are extracted from the metafile of satellite images or are calculated using ATCOR. The topographic information was obtained from a digital elevation model (SRTMv4 DEM) with a spatial resolution of 90 m (Jarvis et al., 2008). Atmospheric correction is then controlled by selecting appropriate visibility level, type of aerosols, 'target box of concern' for spectral analysis and adjacency effect. For further parameter description the reader is referred to the ATCOR manual (ERDAS and Geosystems, 2011). Additionally, a haze reduction was conducted for selected scenes (ERDAS and Geosystems, 2011). Spectral adjustment of the images was verified for each scene for same invariant ground control points (e.g. street, mature bamboo forest). To compare the effect of image processing on resultant pixel values of the corrected images, several modifications, mainly to visibility (7 km to 40 km) and spectral adjustments, were tested within one scene (Table 1). Simultaneously, the ATCOR model estimates two empirical LAI values for each corrected image, based, on $SAVI^2$ (LAI_{SAVI}) and $NDVI^3$ (LAI_{NDVI}) (Eq. 1, (ERDAS and Geosystems, 2011)).

(Eq. 1) $$LAI = -\frac{1}{a2} \times \ln\left(\frac{a0 - VI}{a1}\right)$$; with VI = SAVI or NDVI, and plant specific parameters $a_0 = 0.82$, $a_1 = 0.78$, $a_2 = 0.60$ (for cotton). This allows investigation of the effect of atmospheric correction on resultant LAI (ERDAS and Geosystems, 2011, Richter, 2003).

SAVI is defined as (Equation 2) [(NIR - red) / (NIR + red + L)] x (1+L), with adjustment factor L, which is derived from a scatterplot of NIR and red band data (Huete, 1988). Nevertheless, for $SAVI^2$ derivation, the ATCOR models assume fixed values for adjustment factor L. Subsequently, four locations (P1-P4) were selected that represent vegetation and exist on most images. For those locations, the reflectance of spectral bands 1, 2 and 3, as well as the corresponding LAI values were extracted (Figure 1). The image data of P1 to P4 from each scene were then compared for each atmospheric correction scheme. This analytical procedure ensures a first overview of the influence of atmospheric correction on reflectance and thus resultant LAI.

---

[2] SAVI = [((NIR-Red)*1.5) / (NIR+Red+0.5)] (Soil-Adjusted Vegetation Index) (ERDAS and Geosystems, 2011)
[3] NDVI= (NIR-Red) / (NIR+Red) (Normalized-Difference Vegetation Index) (Huete, 1988)

In order to verify the location value variability of two different scenes obtained from same date, two scenes (Scene B, C (28.01.2012)) were selected that completely cover the study site. Subsequently, both images were similar atmospherically processed (processing scheme 13 and 20 (Table 1) and their corresponding overlapping pixels were compared. Theoretically, the image values of a certain location, of equal atmospherically corrected images from the same date should return identical image values for the analyzed locations. If these overlapping values differ, their retrieved LAI estimates would be different as well. In this case, the question arises of, how best to combine these images in order to obtain true results that accurately represent nature.

6. Results and Discussion

The main objective is to qualitatively investigate the influence of atmospheric correction on vegetation indices (VI) and correspondingly estimated LAI values. In the following section, the results for Scene A (obtained 16.01.2012), Scene B (28.01.2012, north) and Scene C (28.01.2012, south) are presented as example results for all other analyzed satellite scenes. The mean ± standard deviation (SD) of LAI of all studied scenes is summarized in Table 2.

Scene	Processing scheme	Scale Factor	Target box (px)	Visibility (km)	Adjacency Effect (m)	ATCOR	Haze removal	Atmosphere
16.01.2012 (north) Scene A	1	100	5	35	300	ATCOR2	no	maritime, tropical
	2	100	5	25	300	ATCOR2	no	maritime, tropical
	3	100	5	40	300	ATCOR2	yes	maritime, tropical
	4	100	5	40	300	ATCOR2	no	maritime, tropical
	5	100	5	25	300	ATCOR3	yes	maritime, tropical
	6	100	5	25	300	ATCOR3	no	maritime, tropical
	7	100	5	24	300	ATCOR3	yes	maritime, tropical
28.01.2012 (north) Scene B	8	100	5	7	500	ATCOR2	yes	maritime, tropical
	9	100	5	35	300	ATCOR2	no	maritime, tropical
	10	100	5	35	300	ATCOR2	yes	maritime, tropical
	11	100	5	13	300	ATCOR2	yes	maritime, tropical
	12	100	5	13	300	ATCOR3	yes	maritime, tropical
	13*	100	5	20	300	ATCOR3	no	maritime, tropical
28.01.2012 (south) Scene C	14	100	5	35	300	ATCOR2	no	maritime, tropical
	15	100	5	25	300	ATCOR2	yes	maritime, tropical
	16	100	5	13	300	ATCOR2	no	maritime, tropical
	17	100	5	35	300	ATCOR2	no	maritime, tropical
	18	100	5	25	300	ATCOR3	no	maritime, tropical
	19	100	5	25	300	ATCOR3	yes	maritime, tropical
	20*	100	5	20	300	ATCOR3	no	maritime, tropical

* processing schemes used for north and south scene comparison of 28.01.2012 (section 5.2)

Table 1: Parameterization schemes of ATCOR models for atmospheric corrections of north and south scene from 28.01.2012 (parameters omitted for other scenes).

6.1 Pixel Comparison

At each location, NDVI seems to produce significantly higher absolute LAI values than SAVI (Figure 3). This might be explained by the choice of L factor (L=0.5) in the ATCOR model. (Huete, 1988) suggests that a L value of around 0.25 should be used for areas with dense vegetation.

VI is derived from a spectral band ratio, whose results are expected to be independent from the magnitude of reflectance values (band 3, band 5, equation 1). In the case, that both bands are similarly modified in magnitude by atmospheric correction scheme, it can be assumed that the then calculated VI values of a certain location (P1-P4) of the same scene should be equal for each of the applied processing. However, the comparison of LAI values for P1-P4 of the Scene A (north) an Scene B (north) obtained on 16.01.2012 and 28.01.2012, respectively, show that the difference between reflectance values (%) of band 1 to 3 and the calculated LAI values for each processing procedure does not show a straightforward constant offset. Measures that help illustrate this issue better are the overall mean and SD of all location values (P1-P4) (Figure 4). LAI_{SAVI} curves for the different processed images show a roughly similar shape and are closer together than LAI_{NDVI} curves that do not reveal a simple correctable offset. This is particularly illustrated by the overall mean and SD (P1-P4) of LAI_{NDVI}. LAI_{NDVI} shows a good consistency at P2, which is due to the tendency of NDVI to reach early saturation at LAI = 7.3 (P2 in Figure 3). Generally, NDVI is reported to saturate related to vegetation type when LAI reaches 2-5 (Haboudane, 2004). This may indicate that SAVI is not as strongly affected by atmospheric correction as NDVI. Nevertheless, this hypothesis cannot clearly be affirmed through the results (mean and SD) of all analyzed scenes (Table 2). For instance, the mean SD of all analyzed scenes at each location P1-P4, ranges from ±0.08 to ±1.5 for LAI_{NDVI} and from ±0.07 to ±1.0 for LAI_{SAVI}, respectively. In detail, at P1 to P4, the min and max of SD for Scene A (16.01.12) varies from ±0.00 to ±1.22 for LAI_{NDVI} and from ±0.09 to ±0.49 for LAI_{SAVI}. Scene B (28.01.12) showed min and max SD ranging from ±0.13 to ±1.79 for LAI_{NDVI} and from ±0.10 to ±2.05 for LAI_{SAVI} (Table 2).

6.2 Scene Comparison

After describing the LAI variability along several parameterizations of ATCOR model, the second approach aims to investigate, if overlapping satellite images from the same time interval provide the same LAI when they experience similar atmospheric correction. For this purpose, the LAI_{SAVI} and LAI_{NDVI} of an overlapping area of about 0.6 km² (Scene B (north) and Scene C (south) from 28.01.2012) were compared. The overall distribution of LAI$_{SAVI}$ and LAI$_{NDVI}$ displays a similar pattern. However, the mean LAI ranges from 2.3 (Scene B) to 2.5 (Scene C) and is equal to 4.2 (Scene B and Scene C) for LAI$_{SAVI}$ and LAI$_{NDVI}$, respectively (Figure 5). Band 3 and band 5 are used to calculate the VI.

Subsequently, one scene was subtracted from the other in order to obtain the absolute difference between both images. The mean absolute difference of band 3 and band 5 is equal to reflectance = 1.1% (max = 8.9%) and reflectance = 4.1% (max = 17.4%). Consequently, this leads to different LAI values being estimated for each scene. This difference is most likely related to the fixed L factor in equation 1. Thus, calculation of VI from the corrected images can yield results with significant variations, even when the same atmospheric correction scheme is applied.

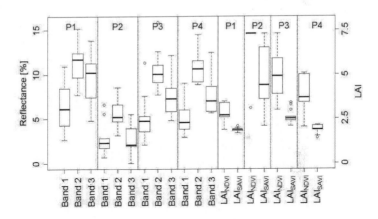

Figure 3: Graph shows for each location (P1-P4) reflectance (Band 1, 2, 3) and LAI based on NDVI and SAVI, respectively. Plot is based on data of Scene A (16.01.2012) and B (28.01.2012), with LAI assumed to be similar.

Besides of difference in magnitude between LAI$_{SAVI}$ and LAI$_{NDVI}$, the mean absolute difference between both satellite images ranges from 0.22 for LAI$_{SAVI}$ and 0.27 for LAI$_{NDVI}$. These LAI differences seem to be acceptable, but explicitly for densely vegetated areas, the absolute difference reaches 2.7 for LAI$_{SAVI}$ and up to 4.7 for LAI$_{NDVI}$ (Figure 5). NDVI is saturated for both satellite images where LAI$_{NDVI}$ exceeds 7.3, leading to a LAI difference of zero.

Scene	Processing	P1	P2	P3	P4
			LAI$_{NDVI}$ (mean ± SD)		
16.01.12; North; Scene A	Total	3.1 ± 0.60	7.3 ± 0.00	5.0 ± 1.22	4.5 ± 0.75
	ATCOR2	2.8 ± 0.67	7.3 ± 0.00	4.5 ± 0.90	4.1 ± 0.79
	ATCOR3	3.5 ± 0.00	7.3 ± 0.00	5.7 ± 1.39	5.0 ± 0.04
28.01.12; North; Scene B	Total	2.6 ± 0.13	6.6 ± 1.71	5.4 ± 1.79	3.2 ± 0.63
	ATCOR2	2.7 ± 0.10	6.3 ± 2.10	5.0 ± 1.96	3.1 ± 0.73
	ATCOR3	2.5 ± 0.14	7.3 ± 0.00	6.1 ± 1.70	3.5 ± 0.33
28.01.12; South, Scene C	Total	2.6 ± 0.11	7.3 ± 0.00	3.7 ± 0.45	/ ± /
	ATCOR2	2.6 ± 0.13	7.3 ± 0.00	3.6 ± 0.53	/ ± /
	ATCOR3	2.7 ± 0.07	7.3 ± 0.00	3.8 ± 0.28	/ ± /
04.03.12; North	Total	2.7 ± 0.50	7.1 ± 0.42	4.1 ± 1.44	3.3 ± 0.52
	ATCOR2	2.5 ± 0.34	7.0 ± 0.47	3.4 ± 0.78	3.2 ± 0.53
	ATCOR3	3.3 ± 0.59	7.3 ± 0.00	5.7 ± 1.11	3.5 ± 0.40
09.03.12; South	Total	3.1 ± 1.00	/ ± /	4.9 ± 1.82	/ ± /
	ATCOR2	2.9 ± 1.10	/ ± /	3.6 ± 1.60	/ ± /
	ATCOR3	3.2 ± 1.11	/ ± /	6.2 ± 0.79	/ ± /
			LAI$_{SAVI}$ (mean ± SD)		
16.01.12; North; Scene A	Total	1.8 ± 0.09	3.9 ± 0.49	2.4 ± 0.19	2.1 ± 0.13
	ATCOR2	1.8 ± 0.06	3.6 ± 0.47	2.3 ± 0.17	2.0 ± 0.11
	ATCOR3	1.9 ± 0.00	4.2 ± 0.29	2.5 ± 0.06	2.2 ± 0.00
28.01.12; North; Scene B	Total	2.0 ± 0.10	5.8 ± 2.05	2.9 ± 0.41	1.8 ± 0.23
	ATCOR2	1.9 ± 0.10	5.4 ± 2.49	2.9 ± 0.50	1.8 ± 0.26
	ATCOR3	2.0 ± 0.14	6.7 ± 0.28	2.8 ± 0.28	1.7 ± 0.24
28.01.12; South, Scene C	Total	1.9 ± 0.04	5.7 ± 1.28	2.5 ± 0.18	/ ± /
	ATCOR2	1.9 ± 0.05	5.4 ± 1.25	2.5 ± 0.22	/ ± /
	ATCOR3	1.9 ± 0.00	6.1 ± 1.70	2.4 ± 0.00	/ ± /
04.03.12; North	Total	1.6 ± 0.14	4.1 ± 1.31	2.2 ± 0.29	1.8 ± 0.13
	ATCOR2	1.6 ± 0.08	3.9 ± 1.37	2.1 ± 0.23	1.8 ± 0.13
	ATCOR3	1.8 ± 0.60	4.4 ± 1.73	2.5 ± 0.22	1.9 ± 0.13
09.03.12; South	Total	2.4 ± 0.45	/ ± /	2.6 ± 0.62	/ ± /
	ATCOR2	2.2 ± 0.60	/ ± /	2.2 ± 0.66	/ ± /
	ATCOR3	2.6 ± 0.23	/ ± /	3.0 ± 0.22	/ ± /

Table 2: Mean and standard deviation (SD) of LAI$_{NDVI}$ and LAI$_{SAVI}$ for each location P1, P2, P3, P4 related to atmospheric correction processing scheme. Total gives the overall mean ± SD of ATCOR2 and ATCOR3. Gaps (/) are due to cloud coverage.

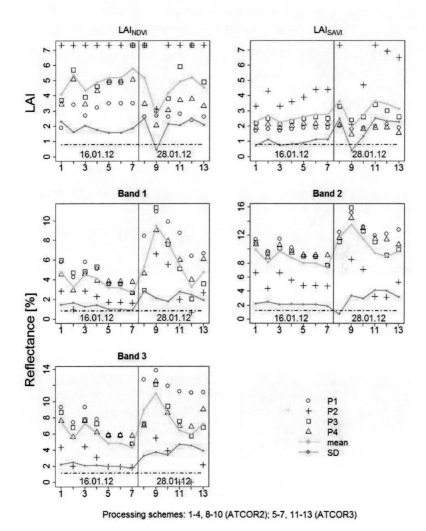

Figure 4: Comparison of LAI_NDVI, LAI_SAVI and reflectance (Band 1, Band 2, Band 3). Graphs show the values for locations P1-P4 for each atmospheric correction scheme (1-13, Table 1) of RapidEye Scene A (16.01.2012) and Scene B (28.01.2012, north). Mean and standard deviation (SD) of reflectance, and LAI is calculated for each atmospheric correction scheme over P1-P4. LAI values are desired to be similar over all processing schemes at each specific location.

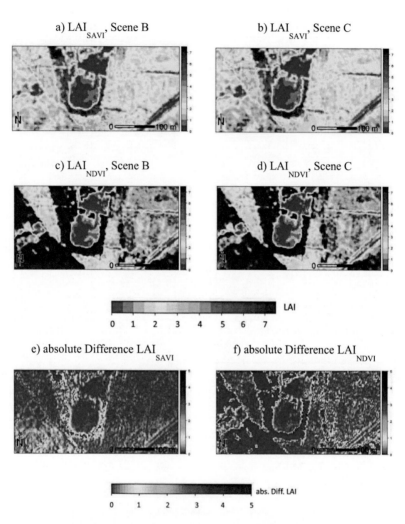

Figure 5: a), b) LAI based on SAVI and c), d) based on NDVI for Scene B (north) and
Scene C (south) from 28.01.2012; Absolute difference (Scene B – Scene C)
of e) LAI based on SAVI and f) LAI based on NDVI. In figures c) and d)
LAI_{NDVI} reaches saturation at LAI about 7.3 (dark red areas). This leads
in figure f) to areas with absolute differences of zero (dark green areas).

6. Summary and Outlook

We (i) showed that reliable LAI estimates are essential for SVAT modeling, since small LAI uncertainties result in high prediction uncertainties in modeling. The results (ii) highlight that differences in retrieved LAI of one scene can be caused solely by selected atmospheric correction scheme. Atmospheric correction procedure unevenly changes spectral information of each pixel in adjustment of the assumed atmosphere influence (ERDAS and Geosystems, 2011). This leads to differences in band ratio and thus influences the VI calculation and LAI derivation. This is not a trivial relationship being difficult to correct. It is therefore challenging to decide which atmospheric correction model parameterization results in trustful LAI estimates. In the case of an empirical derivation of LAI from field measurements, the findings suggest that each atmospherically corrected image requires ground truthing.

In summary, for the in detailed studied scenes, LAI differences related to atmospheric correction attained SD values between 0.1 to 0.5 and 0.0 to 1.2 for LAI_{SAVI} and LAI_{NDVI}, respectively. The comparison of two images from a similar time, area and atmospheric correction, still reveal mean absolute differences ranging from 0.22 for LAI_{SAVI} and 0.27 for LAI_{NDVI}. Generally, if LAI variability subject to atmospheric correction conforms more to the rule than the exception, then parameterization of a SVAT model based on remote sensing data would in turn highly affect water balance modeling. In order to rank LAI variability in this context, it is helpful to consider that typical LAI for vegetation ranges generally from 3 to 19 (Asner et al., 2003). We found that LAI_{NDVI} saturated at 7.3. For that reason, it was impossible to detect further LAI_{NDVI} variability above 7.3. The usage of more robust VI for LAI estimations (such as SAVI) is promising, since it produced for most scenes the smallest LAI differences within the range of atmospheric correction schemes. Furthermore, SAVI does not tend to saturate at early LAI.

In this context, this paper gives insights into the difficulties of LAI estimation from remote sensing images and should be seen as an overview study. Further research on this issue is required in order to provide practical guidelines for image correction that ensure consistent LAI derivations are achieved.

Acknowledgements

The research was funded by scholarship program IPSWAT, an initiative of (BMBF). Furthermore, this work was kindly supported by Helmholtz Impulse and Networking Fund through Helmholtz Interdisciplinary Graduate School for Environmental Research (HIGRADE) (Bissinger & Kolditz 2008). We sincerely thank DLR for providing data from the RapidEye Science Archive. We thank Dr. Erik Borg for the project support. Special thanks to native English speaker Christopher Higgins for proof reading this text.

References

Abrahamsen, P. & Hansen, S., 2000.
Daisy: an open soil- crop-atmosphere system model. Environmental.
Modelling & Software 15, 313–330.

Arora, V.K., 2002.
Modelling vegetation as a dynamic component in soil-vegetation-
atmosphere-transfer schemes and hydrological models. Reviews
of Geophysics 40, 1006–1032.

Asner, G.P., Scurlock, J.M.O., Hicke, J.A., 2003.
Global synthesis of leaf area index observations : implications for
ecological and remote sensing studies. Global Ecology & Biogeography
12, 191–205.

Embrapa, 2006.
Sistema Brasileiro de classificação de solos, 2nd ed. Embrapa-SPI -
Centro Nacional de Pesquisa de Solos, Brasília.

ERDAS, Geosystems, 2011.
ATCOR for ERDAS IMAGINE 2011-Haze Reduction, Atmospheric
and Topographic Correction - User Manual ATCOR 2 and ATCOR 3,
Imagine. ERDAS - GeoSystems.

Haboudane, D., 2004.
Hyperspectral vegetation indices and novel algorithms for predicting
green LAI of crop canopies: Modeling and validation in the context
of precision agriculture. Remote Sensing of Environment 90, 337–352.

Hadjimitsis, D.G., Papadavid, G., Agapiou, A., Themistocleous, K.,
Hadjimitsis, M.G., Retalis, A., 2010.
Atmospheric correction for satellite remotely sensed data intended for
agricultural applications: Impact on vegetation indices. Earth 89–95.

Horn, J., Schulz, K., 2010.
Post-processing analysis of MODIS leaf area index subsets. Journal
of Applied Remote Sensing 4, 043557.

Huete, A.R., 1988.
A Soil-Adjusted Vegetation Index (SAVI). Remote Sensing
of Environment 25, 295–300.

Jansson, P.-E., Karlberg, L., 2013.
CoupModel manual - Coupled heat and mass transfer model for soil- plant-atmosphere systems [WWW Document]. Manual. URL http://www2.lwr.kth.se/CoupModel/NetHelp/

Jarvis, A., Reuter, H.I., Nelson, A., Guevara, E., 2008.
Hole-filled seamless SRTM data V4. International Centre for Tropical Agriculture (CIAT), USGS/NASA.

Kottek, M., Grieser, J., Beck, C., Rudolf, B., Rubel, F., 2006.
World Map of Köppen-Geiger Climate Classification - (updated with CRU TS 2.1 temperature and VASClimO v1.1 precipitation data 1951 to 2000). Meteorologische Zeitschrift 15, 259–263.

LP DAAC, 2011.
ASTER L1B; NASA Land Processes Distributed Active Archive Center (LP DAAC), USGS/Earth Resources Observation and Science (EROS) Center.

Metselaar, K., Van Dam, J.C., Feddes, R.A., 2006.
Screening and understanding the importance of soil hydrology related factors in a SVAT scheme - Reports in the Framework of the KvR project CS3. Wageningen Institute for Environment and Climate Research.

Petropoulos, G., Wooster, M.J., Carlson, T.N., Kennedy, M.C., Scholze, M., 2009.
A global Bayesian sensitivity analysis of the 1d SimSphere soil-vegetation-atmospheric transfer (SVAT) model using Gaussian model emulation. Ecological Modelling 220, 2427–2440.

Rapideye, 2007.
RapidEye [TM] Image Product Specification.

Richter, R., 2003.
Value Adding Products derived from the ATCOR Models, Report DLR-IB 654-03/03. DLR, Wessling, Germany.

Van Gorsel, E., Kljun, N., Leuning, R., Berni, J.A.J., Cabello-Leblic, A., Held, A., Haverd, V., Hopkinson, C., Chasmer, L., Youngentob, K., 2011.
Use of High Resolution Lidar and Hyperspectral Data to Evaluate the Sensitivity of Net Ecosystem Exchange to Stand Structural and Plant Chemical Properties. In: 34th International Symposium on Remote Sensing of Environment. Sydney, Australia, pp. 1–4.

Veihe, A., Jensen, N.H., Boegh, E., Frederiksen, P., Pedersen, M.W., 2005.
Sensitivity of DaisyGIS to LAI: Implications for land use based
modelling of nitrate leaching 106, 75–86.

Yao, Y., Liu, Q., Li, X., 2008.
LAI retrieval and uncertainty evaluations for typical row-planted crops
at different growth stages. Remote Sensing of Environment 112,
94-106.

Zheng, G., Moskal, L.M., 2009.
Retrieving Leaf Area Index (LAI) Using Remote Sensing: Theories,
Methods and Sensors. Sensors 9, 2719–2745.

DeMarine-Environment –
Suitability of RapidEye Data for Monitoring of the Wadden Sea (Project ID: 290)

Kerstin Stelzer[1], Martin Gade[2], Winny Adolph[3], Jörn Kohlus[4]

[1] Brockmann Consult GmbH
[2] Universität Hamburg, Institut für Meereskunde
[3] Nationalparkverwaltung Niedersächsisches Wattenmeer
[4] Nationalparkverwaltung Schleswig-Holsteinisches Wattenmeer

E-Mail: kerstin.stelzer@brockmann-consult.com

DeMarine-Environment –
Suitability of RapidEye Data for Monitoring of the Wadden Sea

Kerstin Stelzer, Martin Gade, Winny Adolph, Jörn Kohlus

Monitoring of the intertidal flat area along the North Sea coast, i.e. the Wadden Sea, underlies a number of reporting duties and requirements from European and national directives. Some of these can be met by applying remote sensing techniques, especially when combining different sensors and ground data within a synergistic classification scheme. The work presented here has been conducted within the DeMarine Umwelt (Environment) project, which is a joint-research project supporting and developing marine GMES services in Germany, and is currently supported by DeMarine-2, in sub-project SAMOWatt. The projects are co-funded by the Federal Ministry of Economics and Technology via DLR, RapidEye data were obtained via the RESA archive.

1. Remote Sensing of Intertidal Flats

Optical sensors are used for classification of sediment properties of intertidal flats, and good results have been achieved by the classification of different sediment types, vegetation, and mussel beds. The quality of the classification has been validated by comparison with ground data. In combination with other data sources such as synthetic aperture radar (SAR), additional information could be obtained that improve the classification results. RapidEye data were one of the optical data sources for developing and testing products for the monitoring authorities. The spatial resolution of RapidEye data fulfills the requirements of the coastal authorities especially in comparison to Landsat or SPOT-4 data. However, the spectral resolution is lacking the SWIR band which is critical for our classification method of intertidal flats, because it provides best information about the status of the water coverage. Even during low tide, large areas of the flats might be covered by a layer of a few centimeters of water, which influences the spectral signal significantly and which can be corrected by using the information from the SWIR band. In this respect, SPOT-4, -5 and Landsat data are better suited for our application.

2. Classification Scheme

Combination of optical data, SAR data and ground information has been performed within a synergistic classification scheme that uses features extracted from the respective data sources. From optical data this comprises abundances derived by spectral unmixing, band ratios and band gains. From the SAR data, and here mainly from TerraSAR-X data, statistical measures derived from multi-temporal data sets have been used. The features of the different data sources are combined in a knowledge-based decision tree, which separates the pixels into the different surface classes. Typical surface classes in intertidal flat areas that can be differentiated by remote sensing techniques are different sediment types (sand, mud), macro algae or sea grass coverage and mussel beds.

3. Products and Services

Our main goal is to develop and to provide products to national park and coastal management authorities that can be directly used within monitoring programs as well as to gain a better understanding of the environment. Products developed within the DeMarine projects are classifications of the intertidal flat surfaces, but also temporally integrated products such as probability maps for water coverage, mussel beds or sediment types. Within DeMarine-2's sub-project SAMOWatt our goal is to retrieve improved classification as well as products focusing on change detection, mobility of patterns and time series. A concept for integration of the novel products into the monitoring work, including a costs estimate for a respective service, is envisaged for the end of the DeMarine 2 project in 2015.

4. Team

The team consists of remote sensing experts (optical and SAR) and the users themselves. This ensures an optimal link between requirements, product definition and development. The products shall eventually become part of the operational monitoring and provide best suited information.

Bi-temporal land cover classification for the hydrological understanding of a large dryland river in the Brazilian Semiarid (Project ID: 387)

Alexandre C. Costa[1], Saskia Foerster[2], Axel Bronstert[3], José C. de Araújo[4], Helba A. de Q. Palácio[5]

[1] Research Institute for Meteorology and Water Resources of the State of Ceará, Av. Rui Barbosa 1246, CEP 60.115-221, Fortaleza – CE, Brazil.

[2] German Research Centre for Geosciences, Department of Geodesy and Remote Sensing, Telegrafenberg, 14473 Potsdam, Germany.

[3] University of Potsdam, Institute of Earth and Environmental Sciences, Karl-Liebknecht-Str. 24/25, D-14476 Potsdam, Germany.

[4] Federal University of Ceará, Department of Agricultural Engineering, Bloco 804 - Campus do Pici, CEP 60 455-970, Fortaleza - CE, Brazil.

[5] Federal Institute of Education, Sciences and Technology, Rodovia Iguatu\Várzea Alegre Km 05, CEP 63.500-000, Iguatu – CE, Brazil.

Bi-temporal land cover classification for the hydrological understanding of a large dryland river in the Brazilian Semiarid

Alexandre C. Costa, Saskia Foerster, Axel Bronstert,
José C. de Araújo, Helba A. de Q. Palácio

Abstract

Hydrological data analysis, remote sensing and modelling have been used to characterize the hydrology of a large reach of the Jaguaribe River, the largest intermittent river in Brazil, located in the northeastern semiarid region. However, some processes of the river's hydrological system such as groundwater pumping along the river and runoff generated from tributaries into the river reach have not been fully understood yet and, consequently, previous assumptions on these processes have to be analysed in detailed studies. Both processes rely highly on the land cover characteristics along the river. Therefore, the objective of this work is to classify the land cover to support research activities on meso-scale hydrology along a large river reach in the Brazilian Semiarid. We defined a region with about 200 km² along 30 km of this reach, where channel transmission losses and groundwater pumping occur predominately and monitored tributaries flow into the river. Bands 2 (Green), 3 (Red) and 5 (NIR) of two satellite images of the RapidEye system in 2010 were stacked, in order to perform a supervised multi-temporal classification. A total of 67 ground-truth data were used for training and 73 for validation of the classification result. The Global Efficiency and the Kappa Coefficient were used as performance criteria for the land cover classification. The free software Spring developed by the Brazilian National Institute for Space Research was used to classify the chosen stack based on the Bhattacharya algorithm. We defined eight land cover classes of interest: Agriculture, Bare soil and Urban area, Dense tree Caatinga (the Brazilian dry forest is called Caatinga), Open Tree Caatinga, Degraded Caatinga, Pasture and Grassland, Moist Vegetation and Water. The land cover classification reached a Global Efficiency of 84% and a Kappa Coefficient of 0.80, which qualifies it as a very good result. The dominant classes in the region were Agriculture, Pasture/Grassland and Degraded Caatinga. They covered together almost 70% of the whole area. Also, they were well spread over the region, while Degraded Caatinga occurred more frequently in middle/high lands. Bare Soil/Urban Area, Dense Tree Caatinga and Moist Vegetation played a minor role. The sum of their areas was not greater than 20% of the whole area. Moreover, they could be mainly found in concentrated parts of the landscape. The class Open Tree Caatinga can be neglected for meso-scale studies of water fluxes. The non-classified area reached almost 8% of the region, which was formed basically by clouds and their shadows. Based on the classification result, the influence of groundwater pumping on the channel transmission losses of the dryland river can be now estimated from the agriculture fields. Further field work will be carried out in order to characterize these fields regarding to dominant cultures (banana, maize and beans) and applied techniques, including irrigation and draining. Moreover, the parameterization of a hydrological model regarding to the landscape cover properties (e.g. LAI and albedo) can be performed based on the developed land cover classification. The runoff, which has been monitored since 2012, generated from a medium-sized tributary of the large dryland river, will then be simulated using a hydrological model, as long as reliable streamflow data are available.

Estimation of the Seasonal Leaf Area Index in an Alluvial Forest Using RapidEye-Based Vegetation Indices (Project ID: 469)

Adina Tillack[1], Anne Clasen[1,2], Michael Förster[1], Birgit Kleinschmit[1]

[1] Geoinformation in Environmental Planning Lab,
  Technical University of Berlin, 10623 Berlin, Germany
[2] Helmholtz Centre Potsdam, GFZ German Research Centre for Geosciences,
  14473 Potsdam, Germany

E-Mail:
adina.tillack@googlemail.com, anne.clasen@tu-berlin.de,
michael.foerster@tu-berlin.de, birgit.kleinschmit@tu-berlin.de

Estimation of the Seasonal Leaf Area Index in an Alluvial Forest Using RapidEye-Based Vegetation Indices

Adina Tillack, Anne Clasen, Michael Förster, Birgit Kleinschmit

Extended Abstract

In preparation of the German hyperspectral EnMAP satellite mission, the project ForestHype deals with the estimation of forest biophysical, biochemical and structural attributes with novel algorithms of imaging spectroscopy. The Technical University of Berlin focuses on the analysis of biodiversity-monitoring in alluvial forests. Within this project not only high spectral resolution, but also high temporal resolution imagery is important. Therefore, RapidEye data was applied to exploit the phenological information of this type of data within forest applications.

There is an immediate need for strategies to monitor the spatial-temporal dynamics of forest biotopes, because of missing methods and data. One key indicator for physical and biological processes related to vegetation dynamics is the leaf area index (LAI), valuable to monitor the biomass of forests. It is defined after Watson (1947) as the total one-sided area of photosynthetic tissue per unit soil surface area, showing a high seasonal variability based on the phenological development of trees.

Within this study the LAI was estimated during the entire vegetation period in 2011, every 2 to 3 weeks from April to November. This was done through field measurements and satellite-derived spectral vegetation indices (SVIs) in two alluvial forest sites located in the northeastern part of Germany. Measurements were carried out in black alder (Alnus glutinosa) stands, a typical species at waterlogged soils. The main aim of this study was the validation of seasonal relationships between field-measured LAI, using a LI-COR 2200 plant canopy analyser (PCA), and four satellite-derived spectral vegetation indices (SVIs) of 10 RapidEye images (Day of the Year (DOY): 99, 110, 116, 125, 142, 157, 197, 267, 290, 312): the normalized difference vegetation index (NDVI) , the red edge NDVI (NDVI-RE) , the modified red edge simple ratio (mSR-RE) , and the curvature. These indices were compared by 4 phenological phases (leaf flushing until crown closure, leaf growth under crown closure, decreasing leaf chlorophyll content, and leaf senescence), and over the entire vegetation period, using the coefficient of determination (R^2).

The results suggest that the seasonal variations of LAI and SVI based on the alluvial forest phenology of Alnus glutinosa. Strong to weak relationships between field-measured LAI and satellite-derived NDVI, NDVI-RE, mSR-RE, and curvature were obtained. In the four phenological phases, different SVIs dominated:

NDVI-RE in the period of leaf flushing until crown closure ($R^2 = 0.62$):

$$LAI = -2 + 8.9 \cdot NDVI\text{-}RE \tag{1},$$

mSR-RE in the period of leaf growth under crown closure ($R^2 = 0.422$):

$$LAI = -1.2 + 1.1 \cdot mSR\text{-}RE \tag{2},$$

NDVI-RE in the period of decreasing leaf chlorophyll content ($R^2 = 0.182$):

$$LAI = 0.29 + 7.2 \cdot NDVI\text{-}RE \tag{3},$$

NDVI in the period of leaf senescence ($R^2 = 0.829$):

$$LAI = -2 + 7.3 \cdot NDVI \tag{4}.$$

Therefore, the implementation of the RapidEye red edge channel improved the LAI-SVI relationships, particularly during periods with few variations in the LAI. The analysis of the entire vegetation period revealed that the NDVI had the coefficient of determination ($R^2 = 0.942$) because it was the most stable index due to moderate LAI values (average max. LAI = 4.63).

The satellite-based vegetation indices used in this study provided reliable estimates and described the temporal changes and spatial variability in the LAI well. The results indicate that multi-temporal estimations of LAI are important because of the changing phenology and different environmental influences throughout the year.

Literatur

Conrad, C., Fritsch, S., Lex, S., Löw, F., Rücker, G., Schorcht, G., Sultanov, M., et al., 2012.
  Potenziale des "Red Edge" Kanals von RapidEye zur Unterscheidung und zum Monitoring landwirtschaftlicher Anbaufrüchte am Beispiel des usbekischen Bewässerungssystems Khorezm. In E. Borg, H. Daedelow, & R. Johnson (Eds.), RapidEye Science Archive (RESA) - Vom Algorithmus zum Produkt, 4. RESA Workshop (pp. 203–217). Berlin: GITO mbH Verlag Berlin.

Datt, B., 1999.
  A New Reflectance Index for Remote Sensing of Chlorophyll Content in Higher Plants: Tests using Eucalyptus Leaves. Journal of Plant Physiology, 154, 30–36.

Gitelson, A., & Merzlyak, M. N., 1994.
  Spectral Reflectance Changes Associated with Autumn Senescence Features and Relation to Chlorophyll Estimation. Journal of Plant Physiology, 143, 286–292.

Rouse, J. W., Haas, R. H., Schell, J. A., & Deering, D. W., 1973.
  Monitoring vegetation systems in the Great Plains with ERTS. In S. C. Freden & M. A. Becker (Eds.), Third ERTS Symposium (Vol. 1, pp. 309–317). NASA SP-351.

Sims, D. A., & Gamon, J. A., 2002.
  Relationships between leaf pigment content and spectral reflectance across a wide range of species, leaf structures and developmental stages. Remote Sensing of Environment, 81, 337–354.

Tucker, C. J., 1979.
  Red and Photographic Infrared Linear Combinations for Monitoring Vegetation. Remote Sensing of Environment, 8, 127–150.

Watson, D. J., 1947.
  Comparative physiological studies on the growth of field crops. Annals of Applied Biology, XI(41), 41–76.

Remote Sensing Estimation of Wood Biomass within Brandenburg forests in the Euroregion POMERANIA, using Rapid Eye Data (Project ID: 491)

Stefan Kärgel[1], Simon Klinner[1], Albert Janzen[2]

[1] Landeskompetenzzentrum Forst Eberswalde (LFE)
[2] Hochschule für nachhaltige Entwicklung Eberswalde (FH)

E-Mail: Stefan.Kaergel@lfe-e.brandenburg.de

Remote Sensing Estimation of Wood Biomass within Brandenburg forests in the Euroregion POMERANIA, using Rapid Eye Data

Stefan Kärgel, Simon Klinner, Albert Janzen

The goal of this project (RESA ID 491) is to estimate overall wood biomass stocks in the study area as well as other relevant forestry parameters, for example the tree species composition of forests. In order to achieve this, remote sensing data shall be connected to terrestrial datasets.

1. Motivation

Above-ground woody biomass is central information for many stakeholders like forestal or agricultural companies, environmental institutions and decision-makers. Within the framework of "Foreseen POMERANIA", a german-polish EU INTERREG IV A project[1], started in 2011, remote sensing data from Euroregion POMERANIA shall be used to derive such information and provide it in a public accessible biomass information system. Among MERIS, MODIS, Landsat, GLAS and Worldview 2 satellite data, RapidEye is used in the project. These remote sensing techniques are allowing reasonable analyses of large areas.

2. Study Area and Data

The study area is situated in north-east Brandenburg (Germany) and comprises the two administrative districts "Barnim" and "Uckermark". The whole Brandenburg part of Euroregion POMERANIA covers approximately 4500 km². As initial data, RapidEye scenes from 2nd May 2009 are used. The scenes are provided in the preprocessed data format "3A" and are completely cloud-free. In addition to the RapidEye data, forest inventory data was used as terrestrial reference. It is based on a 4 x 4 km grid and provides information about the timber stock and the tree species. The data belongs to the "IS08" and the "Zwischeninventur des Waldes im Land Brandenburg" from 2008 (Müller 2010). As validation data for all classification maps, an extract of the "Daten-speicher Wald 2", a forest management database (Redmann & Regenstein 2010) with forest inventory data for every stand was used.

---

[1] Website of the EU Project: http://www.up.poznan.pl/pomerania/d/, (14.01.2013)

3. Results

By linking up forest inventory data and RapidEye data, several classification maps for timber stocks and tree species are produced. The applied classification method is the traditional pixel-based Maximum-Likelihood Method.

1. Categorical timber stock map with four timber stock classes and three tree classes for one scene (625 km²), surrounding area of lake "Werbellinsee" in the administrative district Barnim (Figure 1/left)

2. Categorical timber stock map with four timber stock classes and three tree classes for sixteen scenes, comprising the administrative districts Barnim and Uckermark

3. Tree species map with five tree classes for sixteen scenes, comprising the administrative districts Barnim and Uckermark (Figure 1/right)

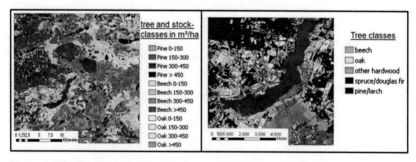

Figure 1: left: Categorical timber stock map for one scene / right:
map extract of the tree species map with five tree classes for sixteen scenes

The first result (Figure 1/left) is a categorical timber stock map with four timber stock classes and three tree classes for the dominating species pine, beech and oak, based on a 625 km² RapidEye scene (scene-nr. 3363511). The overall accuracy of the map amounts to 75,4 %. In the next approach, a larger area should be considered. Therefore sixteen RapidEye scenes, covering nearly the whole Brandenburg part of POMERANIA, were mosaiked and classified for the maps two and three. Again, IS08 forest inventory data was used for groundtruthing. Map two is characterized by the same classes as map one, but its overall accuracy is reduced to 54,3 %. This reduction can be explained by the recalculation of grey values due to mosaiking.

Map three (Figure 2/right) should distinguish as many tree species as possible with sufficient accuracy. Because of partly very similar spectral signatures of tree species like spruce - douglas fir and pine – larch (Immitzer et al. 2012), aggregations had to be made. Finally, five tree species classes could be distinguished clearly. The overall accuracy of this classification amounts to 81,3 %.

4. Outlook

Based on a comparison of different terrestrial and remote sensing methods for wood biomass estimation, recommendations on their practical applications are made. The results of this project, especially maps are provided through web-based Geoservices to stakeholders and practice.

Acknowledgements

We would like to thank the RapidEye AG and the RapidEye Science Archive (RESA) of DLR for the provision of the remote sensing data.

References

Immitzer, M., Atzberger C., Koukal T., 2012.
Eignung von WorldView-2 Satellitenbilder für die Baumarten-klassifizierung unter besonderer Berücksichtigung der vier neuen Spektralkanäle. Journal for Photogrammetry,In: Remote Sensing and Geoinformation Science. Heft 5/2012, 573-588.

Müller, J., 2010.
Wie nachhaltig wird gewirtschaftet? – Ergebnisse der Großraum-inventur 2008 auf den BWI-Punkten im Land Brandenburg.
In: Ministerium für Infrastruktur und Landwirtschaft (Mil) des Landes Brandenburg, Landeskompetenzzentrum Forst Eberswalde (LFE) (2010) (Eds.): Wissenstransfer in die Praxis, Beiträge zum 5. Winterkolloqium am 25. Februar 2010 in Eberswalde, Eberswalder Forstliche Schriftenreihe Band 44, p. 8-13.

Redmann, M., Regenstein, M., 2010.
Datenspeicher Wald, Version 2. AFZ-DerWald, 13/2010, 10-12.

Using MaxEnt for partially supervised classification of agricultural land cover
(Project ID: 490)

Benjamin Mack, Björn Waske
University of Bonn, Institute of Geodesy and Geoinformation

E-Mail: bmack@uni-bonn.de

Using MaxEnt for partially supervised classification of agricultural land cover

Benjamin Mack, Björn Waske

Extended Abstract

Remote sensing data is abundantly used to map land cover over large areas. Usually, supervised classification algorithms are applied to derive the land cover information from the image data. To work well, these algorithms demand for representative and exhaustive training data. Such reference data is often expensive to acquire (in terms of time, costs, and/or expert knowledge). In many situations the end-user of a land cover map is interested in one (or very few) specific class(es) only. Here, partially supervised classification (PSC) can be an efficient alternative, because for these methods training data is required only for the class of interest (i.e. the positive class), and not for all the other classes (i.e. the negative class). Thus, the effort needed to collect the training data can be decreased considerably. This advantage comes along with the limitation that the classifier must be trained with less a-priori information. Consequently the classifier training is usually more challenging.

MaxEnt (Philips et al. 2006) is promising PSC which has been shown to perform good in urban (Li and Guo 2010) and forest applications (Saatchi et al. 2008). It is a machine learning method based on the maximum entropy principle. Additionally to the positive training data MaxEnt uses unlabeled data to improve the predictive performance. The output of the MaxEnt model is a continuous variables which is proportional to class conditional probabilities. To derive a binary land cover map a threshold must be applied. Different threshold techniques exist which can be grouped in 'subjective' and 'objective' approaches. Contrary to the first group, methods from latter category do not need any user input.

The two main objectives of the study presented here are the following:

- Evaluation of MaxEnt for PSC of agricultural land cover with multi-temporal RapidEye data.

- Evaluation of a threshold technique based on a probabilistic approach which does not need any user input and result in optimal classification accuracy.

The study site is located in a rural area in Luxembourg. The proposed method is independently tested for different agricultural crops. The results achieved with MaxEnt are compared to the results achieved with a fully supervised Support Vector Machine (SVM).

The accuracy assessment shows that MaxEnt is a powerful PSC method. Given the adequate threshold can be found, accuracies are comparable to those of the fully supervised SVM. In general, the proposed automatic threshold technique is more reliable than 'subjective' threshold techniques.

Acknowledgements

The study is realized in the framework of the EnMAP-BMP project funded by: German Aeropspace Center (DLR) and Federal Ministry of Economics and Technology (BMWi), (DLR/BMWi: FKZ 50EE 1011).

RapidEye data are provided from the RapidEye Science Archive (RESA) by DLR under the proposal id490.

Ground truth data was made available by RPG-AGRICOLE 2011 (c) Ministre de l'Agriculture, de la Viticulture et du Developpement rural, Grand Duchy of Luxembourg.

References

Li, W., Guo, Q. (2010).
A maximum entropy approach to one-class classification of remote sensing imagery. In: International Journal of Remote Sensing 31 (8), 2227-2235.

Phillips, S. J., Anderson, R. P., Schapire, R. E. (2006).
Maximum entropy modeling of species geographic distributions. In: Ecological Modelling 190 (3-4), 231-259.

Saatchi, S., Buermann, W., ter Steege, H., Mori, S., Smith, T. B. (2008).
Modeling distribution of Amazonian tree species and diversity using remote sensing measurements. In: Remote Sensing of Environment 112 (5), 2000-2017.

Contextual and Infrastructure linked Spectral Oilspill Mapping in West Siberia (Project ID: 472)

Sören Hese, Rene Michaelis
Friedrich-Schiller-University Jena, Institute of Geography, Earth Observation, Grietgasse 6, 07743 Jena, phone: +49 (0) 3641 948873

E-Mail: soeren.hese@uni-jena.de

Contextual and Infrastructure linked Spectral Oilspill Mapping in West Siberia

Sören Hese, Rene Michaelis

The OILSPILL project investigates oil contamination mapping techniques for the main exploration areas in West Siberia based on Rapideye data and multi-temporal Landsat data. For this region the project will for the first time create and publish a contamination map and statistics for different contamination stages in West Siberia. Validation will be done with known reference test sites from the OSCAR project from 2007.

1. Motivation and Study Area

Research on the application of Earth observation data and image processing methods for oil spill detection concentrated in the past on marine pollution scenarios. Terrestrial oil spill pollution monitoring with remote sensing did not receive very much attention. This is due to the regional and small scale character of terrestrial oil spill contaminations often also complicated by mixed spectral signatures of recovering vegetation, dead vegetation and contaminated soils and sands. With increasing demand on the global markets for crude oil it can be expected that the environmental impact for areas with intensive terrestrial production of oil and gas will continue to be a major environmental issue in the future. Earth observation can deliver precise information about the state and change of the ecosystem in these regions. The presented proposal of the OILSPILL project (Oil Spill Contamination mapping in Russia) concentrates on high spatial resolution data to detect small scale contaminations and later to precisely date the oil spill events with multi-temporal Landsat data.

The west Siberian region has compared with the Russian average lower health rates often related to the environmental quality of living with a potential (suspected) relationship with a "higher than average" (IWACO 2001) level of diseases. The number of indigenous people of West Siberia based on traditional family structured hunting, rein-deer herding, fishing and nomadic lifestyle (Khants, Mansis, Nenets) has been severely reduced since the 1950s (IWACO 2001). The Khanty-Mansiyskiy area in West Siberia is one of the most important territories for the Russian oil and gas production with 58% of the total Russian oil production (status in 2001) and being on the 3rd place with its national gas production (IWACO 2001). The Russian Federation belongs to the top 5 energy producers with European countries being the major importers. The Samotlor oil field is the second largest ever found but the production has gone down from close to 3.5 million barrels per day (mb/d) in the late 80s to 0.3 mb/d (referring to information from BP from 2003). As only few new super-giant oil fields have been discovered in the last decades there clearly is a trend towards more intensive exploration of the remaining fields probably leading to more soil and vegetation contaminations in some areas.

It is the goal of this project to generate oil contamination related EO based information on 2 arctic test sites with the central oil exploration area in western Siberia (Surgut region and Jamal region in West Siberia) as part of the OIL-SPILL project. The complexity of the spectral change signature of oil contaminated soils and sands complicates the classification of crude oil contaminated areas on land. For this project an object based approach partly knowledge driven using red edge information of degraded vegetation in contaminated areas will be used as already tested and validated by Hese and Schmullius (2009). This project will produce an oil contamination map for the main exploration areas in West Siberia (Table 1) based on Rapideye data and multitemporal Landsat data.

Study Areas in West Siberia	
1.	West Siberia, Surgut region
2.	West Siberia, Jamal region

Table 1: Two different study areas in Russia are used in the RESA OILSPILL project.

2. Data

RapidEye data from summer 2011 and 2012 was ordered through the RESA project for a time window opening 15.6.2011 and closing 30.9.2011 and respectively in 2012 with one full area coverage each year. Received coverage is illustrated in more detail in status report 3 from January 2013 (final data acquisition status). Overall we received 25 Level 1B data takes in June/July 2011, 24 data takes in September 2011 and 16 data takes in August 2012. The data acquisition time window has been the snow free period from July to September with 1 full data coverage in a 6-8 week data acquisition window.

The dataset will be also the basis for historical analysis of this region (contamination development) and will provide the baseline for future mapping of increased exploration in this region. RESA OILSPILL will cover the region only once and use Landsat TM5/ETM+ to create a multitemporal dataset. The northern parts of the Jamal region were snow covered during the data acquisition time and will not be used in this study.

3. First Results & Outlook

The project finished a first classification concept development on the former OSCAR project test areas (Hese & Schmullius 2009) and analysed a set of red edge ratios for the differentiation of contaminated surface types. We used 100 representative 2x2 Pixel objects for every class and mapped the statistical distribution of the respective ratio (Difference Vegetation Index (DVI), Enhanced Vegetation Index (EVI) (Matsushita et al. 2007:2639), Soil Adjusted Vegetation Index (SAVI) (Huete 1988), Normalized Difference Vegetation Index (NDVI) (Matsushita et al. 2007:2639) and the Normalised Difference Red Edge Index (NDRE) (Eitel 2011:3642) based on red edge and red (NDRE_rot) and red edge and NIR (NDRE_NIR). Additionally we developed a „rededge-curve" feature (N/diff_re) by using the red, red edge and NIR information. A lineare function was calculated and the difference (diff_re) of the measured red edge grey value and the linear function at the position of the red edge is derived.

Max JM	oil cont	bare soil	tundra	tundra_vital	industrie	infrastructure	water
oil cont		NIR|1.306	DVI|1.413	NIR.diff|1.410	Rot|1.412	Blau|1.370	Mean.NIR|1.386
bare soil			Max.diff.|1.408	NIR.diff|1.412	Rot|1.399	SAVI|1.346	Mean.NIR|1.414
tundra				EVI|1.345	SAVI|1.414	SAVI|1.414	DVI|1.414
tundra_vital					NIR_diff|1.414	NDVI|1.414	Max.diff.|1.414
industrial						EVI|0.542	NIR|1.414
Infrastructure							Brightness|1.396

Table 2: Best separability based on Jeffries Matusita and respective distance values for the used ratios.

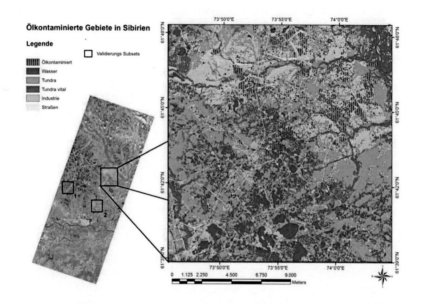

Figure 1: Oil contaminated area classification in West Siberia
(north of the city Surgut, Ob river) object based using ratio thresholding
and distance to infrastructure buffers.

The first classification concept based on ratios was derived for the primary test site using two topologically connected image object scales and an infrastructure buffer (figure 1). Results will be validated and the concept will be transferred to the other two test sites and finally to the larger data mosaic in 2013 with zonal spectral time series analysis of Landsat ETM+ data under verified contaminated areas from 2013.

Literature

Eitel J.U.H., Vierling, L.A., Litvak, M.E., Long, D.S., Schulthess, U., Ager, A.A., Krofcheck, D.J. & Stoscheck, L., 2011.
Broadband, red-edge information from satellites improves early stress detection in a New Mexico conifer woodland. Remote Sensing of Environment 115, 3640-3646.

HESE, S., SCHMULLIUS, C., 2009.
High spatial resolution image object classification for terrestrial oil spill contamination mapping in West Siberia. Int. J. Appl. Earth Observ. Geoinform. (2009), doi:10.1016/j.jag.2008.12.002.

Huete, A.R. (1988).
A Soil-Adjusted Vegetation Index (SAVI). Remote Sensing of Environment 25, 295 - 309.

IWACO Report, 2001.
In: Lodewijkx, M., Ingram, V., Willemse, R. (Eds.), West Siberia - Oil Industry Environmental and Social Profile. Final Report, June 2001.

Matsushita, B., Yang, W., Chen, J., Onda, Y. & Qiu G., (2007).
Sensitivity of the Enhanced Vegetation Index (EVI) and Normalized Difference Vegetation Index (NDVI) to Topographic Effects: A Case Study in High-Density Cypress Forest. Sensors, 7, 2636-2651.

Superpixel segmentation for object-based land use / land cover classification of RapidEye data (Project ID: 498)

Jan Stefanski, Benjamin Mack, Björn Waske
University of Bonn, Institute of Geodesy and Geoinformation

E-Mail: j.stefanski@uni-bonn.de

Superpixel segmentation for object-based land use / land cover classification of RapidEye data

Jan Stefanski, Benjamin Mack, Björn Waske

Extended Abstract

Over the last decade, object-based image analysis has been emerged to an important technique to solve diverse remote sensing tasks. The generation of adequate segments is a prerequisite for object-based image analysis. Usually, the generation of an ideal segmentation level is costly and user-depended.

In this study a relatively new segmentation algorithm - the Superpixel Contour (SPc) algorithm (Mester et al, 2011) - is presented in combination with an strategy to optimize segmentation results. Therefore, the SPc is used to generate a set of different levels of segmentation, using various combinations of parameters in a user-defined range. Finally, the best parameter combination is assessed by the cross-validation-like out-of-bag (OOB) error provided by the Random Forest (RF) classifier (Breiman, 2001).

The performance of the proposed strategy is discussed in detail in context of land cover classification of a multitemporal RapidEye data set from a study site in Luxembourg. The rural study area is characterized by agricultural land use, forests and urban regions, with grassland, corn and winter wheat being the main crops. The classification aims on identifying the following 8 agricultural land cover classes: grassland, potatoes, corn, spring barley, winter barley, winter rape, winter triticale and winter wheat. In addition, the proposed strategy is transferred to a RapidEye data set acquired over Northwestern Ukraine, close to the border to Poland. The region experienced drastic changes in political and socio- economic structures. Large farmland areas become abandoned or land parcellation has taken place. The specific objective was the differentiation between land use intensities, such as large farmland and kitchen gardens or subsistence agriculture.

Experimental results of this study lead to three main findings:

- Multitemporal RapidEye data is adequate to classify specific agricultural crops and land use classes

- Superpixel Contour is capable to generate adequate segments when optimized by the proposed strategy concerning classification accuracy and visual examination

- Superpixel Contour performs similar to the benchmark eCognition's Multiresolution segmentation (Baatz and Schäpe, 2000) in terms of accuracy and visual inspection

Furthermore, results prove that the unbiased OOB error rate is suitable to determine the optimal segmentation with regard to the classification accuracy.

Therefore, no additional test data is required. In addition, RF is well suited for classification, because it is simple to handle, can handle diverse remote sensing data and performs well, even with small training sample sets.

Overall, the proposed strategy is operational and easy to handle and thus economizes the findings of ideal segmentation parameters for the Superpixel Contour algorithm.

Acknowledgements

This study was partly funded by the German Research Foundation (DFG) through a Research Grant (WA 2728/2-1).

RapidEye data are provided from the RapidEye Science Archive (RESA) by DLR under the proposal id490. and proposal id498.

Ground truth data was made available by RPG-AGRICOLE 2011 (c) Ministre de lAgriculture, de la Viticulture et du Developpement rural, Grand Duchy of Luxembourg.

Literature

Mester, R., Conrad, C. and Guevara, A.,2011.
"Multichannel segmentation using contour relaxation: fast super-pixels and temporal propagation". Proceedings of the 17th Scandinavian conference on Image analysis, ser. SCIA'11. Berlin, Heidelberg: Springer-Verlag, 2011, pp. 250–261.

Breiman, L., 2001.
"Random Forests". Machine Learning, vol. 45, pp. 5–32, 2001.

Baatz, M. and Schäpe, A., 2000.
"Multiresolution segmentation: An optimization approach for high quality multi-scale image segmentation". Angewandte Geographische Informationsverarbeitung, pp. 12–23, 2000.

Index of authors